THE BEATLES
IRISH CONCERTS

Colm Keane has published 17 books including the number one bestsellers *Padre Pio: The Irish Connection* and *Nervous Breakdown*. He is a graduate of Trinity College, Dublin, and Georgetown University, Washington DC. As a broadcaster, he won a Jacob's Award and a Glaxo Fellowship for European Science Writers. Among his recent publications are *Hurling's Top 20*, *Gaelic Football's Top 20* and *Ireland's Soccer Top 20*.

THE BEATLES
IRISH CONCERTS

COLM KEANE

CAPEL
ISLAND

First published in Ireland in 2008
by
CAPEL ISLAND PRESS
36 Raheen Park, Bray,
County Wicklow, Ireland

ISBN 978-0-9559133-0-3

Printed by ColourBooks Ltd, Dublin

Typesetting and cover design by Typeform Ltd

For Seán

CONTENTS

INTRODUCTION

Strolling through Dublin at the beginning of November 1963, columnist Tom Power of the *Sunday Independent* witnessed an extraordinary spectacle. Walking towards him was the living manifestation of a Beatle. He wore a collarless jacket, with a waistcoat and jeans. He also sported a mop top haircut with a long fringe and hair down over the collar. "It couldn't be – not until next Thursday – but it was right here in Dublin, a real live Beatle loping easily up South Great George's Street," Power wrote later in his 'Night Out' column.

The style was generations removed from the dark, drab suits young people wore up to then, with the hair cut short at the back and sides. The manner and attitude was new too. It stirred fears in Ireland of a foreign 'invasion', of cultural decadence, of social decay, of a breakdown in law and order. It drove adults to distraction, reminding them of screaming girls, hysteria, madness and mayhem. Parents worried about the collapse of sexual morality. Schools forced pupils to cut their hair. Newspapers editorialised about how the youth of the country ought to be brought to their senses.

"Naturally, I wondered how this refugee from the Mersey got in," Power wrote, conscious that the Beatles were performing in Dublin the following Thursday. "'Scuse me,' said I in my best Liverpudlian, 'but aren't you a Beatle?' 'Yes,' he

1

said, looking doubtfully at my un-hep clothes. His name, he said, was 16-year-old Brendan Bennett from Cabra West and he worked in a Dublin meat factory for £4 a week.

"Most distinguished was his 'Beatle' hairdo which he had styled for 7/6 on the Navan Road, and his four rings, two per hand, like Ringo Starr. It was the 'suit' that fascinated me. It was completely collarless with four front buttons all covered in the dark brown with gold fleck material of the jacket. The pockets were set at an angle and the sleek lines were unbroken by anything so old fashioned as flaps.

"Inside he wore a matching waistcoat – and that was his suit for which he said he paid a Henry Street tailoring firm the noble sum of 17 guineas! Beatle suits apparently come minus trousers; one just has to finish off the dandy outfit with JEANS! I'm sure the Dublin tailors would love a rash of Beatles – look at all the trouble it would save them making trousers!"

That week – the first week of November 1963 – a sense of fear and apprehension, a dark foreboding, an atmosphere of impending doom settled over the city of Dublin. Newspaper editors gravely went about their business, sanctioning stories and columns predicting slaughter ahead. The Garda Síochána and the RUC, staff at the Adelphi cinema in Dublin and the ABC Ritz cinema in Belfast, the Dublin and Belfast Corporations, and the authorities at Dublin and Aldergrove airports were all anticipating trouble. As we now know with hindsight, they were right to be worried – after all, the Beatles were coming to town!

What concerned them was the frenzied, feverish – some called it 'insane' or 'deranged' – phenomenon called 'Beatlemania'. Like all mass hysteria, it had started small and spread fast. Someone, somewhere, must have uttered the first scream. Somebody, in some venue, must have been the first to hyper-ventilate and pass out. Hurricane-like, it picked up speed as it travelled along, consuming people in its path while sweeping them away in a sea of emotion.

Girls screamed, cried hysterically, pulled their hair out, ripped off clothes, complained that their heads were bursting apart, fainted and suffered convulsions – and not one of them could explain why. Detached, mature, restrained girls went to Beatles' concerts promising they wouldn't scream yet within seconds were behaving as if demented. Boys were 'rowdy' and 'boisterous'. They also rioted.

A deluge of objects greeted the Beatles onstage. Fans threw pens, jelly babies, autograph books, toys and boxes of chocolates along with personal notes and love letters. George was struck on the ear by a coin. Paul was almost blinded by a safety-pin. The group were forced to escape from venues through underground tunnels or over the roofs of houses. Beatlemania was, by November 1963, a bright idea gone mad, a strange fascination gone berserk, an obsession gone off the rails.

Way back in May, when things were considerably calmer and quieter, the first hints emerged of a pending Beatles' visit to Ireland. The promotion company involved was the John Smith Entertainment Bureau of Reigate, Surrey. Its owner, John Smith, was a former Irish soldier who had been born in County Kildare. He later drifted into the promotion business in the south of England, where he organised a handful of concerts for the Beatles. He also handled Irish tours for a range of stars. Among those Smith brought over were Marty Wilde, the Tornados, Acker Bilk, Kenny Ball and Karl Denver.

Smith's plans for an Irish Beatles' tour in early summer included Cork, where he had spent two happy years as an army recruit. The economics made sense. With two back-to-back shows in Dublin and another two in Belfast, a total of 9,000 paying customers would attend the performances. With the Savoy in Cork added on, the extra 4,500 bodies would improve unit costs and profit margins substantially. But it wasn't to be. Smith's plan fizzled out and the Beatles never played Cork.

Patrons of the Savoy missed out on a group that, at the time, were sitting on top of the British charts with their single 'From

Me To You'. Their earlier hit 'Love Me Do' had peaked at number seventeen the previous December and 'Please Please Me' had gone to number one in most charts during the early spring. The group had also toured as support to stars like Helen Shapiro and Roy Orbison – and submerged them all. Although not unique for an act at the time, it was by any standards a promising run of success.

The question that occupied Beatles' manager Brian Epstein was what to do next. His master plan for the year ahead was simple. A single would be released every three months and an LP every six months. The media would be bombarded with news of the Beatles. Above all, the group would tour, tour and tour again, reaping the financial rewards appropriate to successful pop artistes. Plans were already in place for exhaustive summer appearances in holiday resorts such as Blackpool, Margate, Great Yarmouth and Brighton. Appearances were also arranged for major British cities including Manchester, Liverpool and London. But, looking ahead, a big money-spinning tour was needed for the autumn and the lead-up to Christmas.

That June, two Englishmen set their minds to devising the details of the pre-Christmas tour. One was the group's manager Brian Epstein, who was still running his stable of stars from his North End Music Stores (NEMS) headquarters in Liverpool. The other was legendary concert promoter Arthur Howes, who had given the Beatles their first big break supporting Helen Shapiro. "Arthur Howes was a small little man with a Las Vegas-type dynamic personality," says former musician and promoter Paul Russell, who knew him. "Nothing would faze him. He talked out of the side of his mouth, smoked two cigarettes at a time and was a nervous wreck. But he was on the button every time. Arthur Howes was not a money person, he was a power freak. He was in with Brian Epstein very big."

Initially based in Peterborough, Howes had moved to London where his company Arthur Howes Promotions had established itself as the leading British promoter of pop acts. His staff booked theatres, arranged accommodation and organised transport. They also had responsibility for the financial management of gargantuan tours traversing the landscape of Britain. Among the acts he promoted were Louis Armstrong, Del Shannon, Chuck Berry, Neil Sedaka, Paul Anka, Bobby Rydell, the Everly Brothers, Adam Faith, Gene Vincent, Ella Fitzgerald, Count Basie and Cliff and the Shadows.

"Arthur Howes seemed to get all the top shows to promote," remarks Jeff Williams of the Kestrels, who performed on many of Howes' tours including two with the Beatles. "He was the promoter of all these pop shows that went around with all these big pop artistes. They would all work for Arthur Howes. If you saw the guy, he was so insignificant. You would have thought that the big agents at that time, like the Grades and the Delfonts, would have been behind the whole thing. But they weren't. Arthur Howes was always a mystery to me. Although there were some dodgy promoters at that time, he was an honourable man. His shows were very well-organised. They always had a road manager and they always used the best coaches, including when we went to Dublin and Belfast. He was a genuine guy."

Howes and Epstein came up with an intensive, six-week, virtually non-stop series of concerts scheduled to start at the beginning of November and end in mid-December. The plan was to maximise revenue and minimise costs by staging two shows per night in a wide range of locations in England with a short excursion to Ireland. The bulk of the venues were ABC cinemas, Odeon cinemas, Gaumont cinemas and a small number of local theatres. The schedule included the ABC cinema in Belfast, which had only recently changed its name from the Ritz. Unfortunately, Dublin didn't make it onto the list.

In July, an impresario with strong Irish connections got wind of the forthcoming tour. His name was Peter Walsh. An accomplished manager and promoter, he had recently returned to England from Ireland where he promoted music acts. Of all the big impresarios at the time, Walsh never lost sight of the hunger in Ireland for chart-topping pop stars. To exploit the market, his agency Starlite Artistes maintained an office at 2 Lower Hatch Street in Dublin. Walsh was convinced that with his background and know-how, and his office in Ireland, he could handle a Beatles' visit to Dublin.

Walsh, who was born near Manchester, had cut his teeth on management and promotion during a five-year spell in Ireland in the 1950s. Initially he handled céilí bands and dance orchestras. Soon he was importing jazz outfits. The story is told how he first encountered cannabis being smoked by a band contracted to play at the Olympia Ballroom in Waterford. Noticing their guest-house bedroom was clouded with strange-smelling smoke, he asked them, 'Jesus, what sort of cigarettes are they?' It took many years before he discovered the answer. By then Walsh was in London expanding his music empire.

Walsh's agency boasted a stable of stars that included Brian Poole and the Tremeloes, the Brook Brothers and the Kestrels. He had also co-promoted a package tour from May into June 1963 which featured the Beatles as support to bill-topper Roy Orbison. Beatles' manager Brian Epstein was thrilled with his group's inclusion in the tour. He was even more pleased when Walsh agreed to feature another of his acts on the bill – the as-yet-unknown Gerry and the Pacemakers. As it transpired, between the time the tour was arranged and the time it took place, both the Beatles and the Pacemakers had number one hits. Orbison plunged down the bill, to be replaced by the Beatles as bill-toppers and the Pacemakers as main support. The tour was a raging success. A bond was forged between Epstein and Walsh.

"I can see how they would have gelled," Brian Poole says of the two music moguls. "Brian Epstein and Peter Walsh were the same type of people – gentlemen. The Beatles, us and Gerry were young lads who were boisterous, street lads really, although all of us came from good families. We were the typical musicians of those days. But Epstein and Walsh were different. I'll give you an image of both of them – either black homburg or camelhair coats. That was what those gentlemen wore. They spoke with quite upper-class accents appropriate to the areas they came from. They drove lovely cars. But, of course, the money came from us."

Through Epstein, Walsh learned of the planned autumn tour and the visit to Belfast. Spotting that the date prior to Belfast – 7 November – was free, he made his pitch. "Peter Walsh suggested to Arthur Howes, 'I will fill that date,'" Paul Russell, Walsh's colleague who ran the Starlite Artistes office in Dublin, remembers. "It wasn't that Dublin was a great venue. The Adelphi wasn't the best. But Howes had a spare date. It was the only one he had free. We weren't ready for it but Peter Walsh persuaded Howes to include it.

"I think Arthur Howes was in awe of Peter Walsh and that's why he agreed to the Dublin date. Peter was very impulsive and dynamic. He was a very hyper person, very up, with language all over the place. He had hernias and he was always sick. He was always saying, 'Jesus Christ, what is going on? I'm going to join the priesthood!' His famous phrase was 'Jesus wept!' He used to wear the mohair suits but he was portly and nothing really fitted him. He was a tremendous, dynamic twister. He could twist anything around and that's why he got that date."

The three prime movers and shakers – Epstein, Howes and Walsh – concluded the deal in central London, where they had offices located within less than half a mile of each other. Arthur Howes held court in Greek Street in Soho, while Peter Walsh's Starlite Artistes was housed about a seven or eight minute walk away in Henrietta Street, Covent Garden. Brian Epstein's NEMS had established a press office right between the two, in Monmouth Street. Although Epstein had yet to fully relocate from Liverpool, where the headquarters of NEMS was still based, he spent an increasing amount of time in the capital. It was there, in London, that the details of the tour, including the visits to Dublin and Belfast, were devised and fine-tuned.

News of the pending arrival of the Beatles filtered through to Paul Russell in Dublin "roughly around July," he recalls. "Effectively, Peter Walsh was saying, 'Over to you, Paul.' There was a lot of work to do." Issues like security, the suitability of facilities and tour logistics needed handling by the Starlite Artistes office at 2 Lower Hatch Street. Press and publicity needed handling too. There was also the delicate issue of a growing hostility to British bands 'polluting' the Irish political and musical landscape. "A lot of people resented this intrusion," Russell explains. "The Sixties was leading up to a lot of anti-British stuff. Even though the BBC was prevalent in those days, anything non-Irish, especially of this calibre, would be resented. We heard a terrible lot of rumours that they were going to blow up the place. The undercurrent was there."

No one was better qualified to ease things along in Dublin than Paul Russell. He knew the Beatles, having spent three weeks by their side during the Roy Orbison tour of the UK from May into June 1963. "I had toured even before that with Roy Orbison in Ireland," Russell recollects. "I had put him up in my home in Dublin. I don't think he spoke to me five times. He was a very private person and he was very conscious of being an albino. In the morning I would find the bathroom sink covered in black with the dye for the hair and the eyebrows. He was like a blind man with the glasses, but the minute he sang he was electric.

"Roy Orbison asked for me to go on his tour of the UK. I was like a keeper to him. As a result, I got to know the Beatles on a nightly basis. I spent a lot of time on the tour in the dressing-room with them. Derek Taylor, who was the PR man of all times, would tell them about presentation on the stage – never turn your back on the audience, no giddiness, don't upstage one another, don't be silly and don't waste time on the microphone saying anything, just get in there and keep moving with the guitars. Everything was programmed into how they should look on the stage.

"Brian Epstein, who was very naïve but a great visionary, would come into the dressing-rooms and line them up for inspection. He would inspect the Beatle boots, the hairstyle, the hairspray, everything. He'd stop the giddy stuff that was going on and line them up. If they had cufflinks, he'd check if they were on right. He would then go to the back of the theatre and he would watch everything. He was a perfectionist. Believe me, he missed nothing.

"Paul McCartney was very paranoiac – 'How will I look?' 'How will it sound?' 'How is this?' 'How is that?' He was the technician of the group. He was the one who was 'show business'. Lennon would stand in the corner objecting to everything. He was arrogance personified. 'It's only a gig, mate,' he would say. He was on top of the world. He was not so much obnoxious but a spanner in the works. I saw McCartney blessing himself several times and to me he was the epitome of the Beatles. He was always so conscious that 'this must go right, otherwise we are finished.' He would always say to me, 'Thanks, mate,' as they would go out on the stage."

Paul Russell also knew the Kestrels and the Brook Brothers, two of Peter Walsh's charges who were billed as support acts on the autumn tour. More importantly, back in 1963 Russell had clout. He was the 'man of the moment' in Dublin. Tall and dapper, he epitomised the well-dressed, ambitious, quick-thinking mover and shaker about town. He had 'swagger'. Everything was going for him. As presenter of *The Showband Show* on Telefís Éireann, he was recognisable throughout Ireland. As drummer and vocalist with the Viscounts showband, he was looked upon as a star. As representative for Starlite Artistes, he was one of the principal importers of pop acts to the country. Almost everybody in Ireland back in the '60s knew of Paul Russell.

"I knew Paul for a few years," says broadcaster Ken Stewart.

"I used to write articles for the *Evening Press* about performers coming in on tour with Starlite Artistes. I remember on one occasion going out to Dublin Airport with Paul in this huge American convertible to collect Dusty Springfield. We brought her back in. I met virtually all the artistes who came over at the time. Paul was a very genial person, very hard-working. He had a great sense of humour and was a risk-taker in a sense too. He seemed to love what he was doing with Starlite Artistes, *The Showband Show* and his own group as well, the Viscounts. He was a very likeable, colourful guy, a showman. He knew the Beatles and most likely knew Brian Epstein at the time. At one stage he gave me a programme of the tour they did with Roy Orbison, signed by all four Beatles. It was logical that Paul would be involved when they came over to Ireland."

Russell's love of the limelight was inherited from his father, the legendary Kerry footballer who had played for his county during its 'golden age' in the 1920s and early 1930s. Winner of six All-Ireland medals, Paul Russell senior had chalked up critical scores in vital championship matches as Kerry achieved a coveted four-in-a-row from 1929 – 32. However, a steady job like his father had in the Guards was of no interest to Russell. Instead he immersed himself in music, listened to Radio Luxembourg, memorised hit tunes, bought records and devoured the music press. He also acquired a set of drums, leading to his involvement with the Viscounts, which he formed in 1959.

"The Viscounts were regarded as the 'in' thing at the time," according to Brian Tuite, drummer and subsequent manager with rival band the Stellas. "We were in awe of them. Whatever show was on, the Viscounts were on it. Even in the way they dressed the Viscounts were a step above everybody else. These lads pissed champagne. Paul was the golden boy. He was the original 'mister cool' around town. He became an item with Grace Emmanuel, who was a well-known model in Dublin. She was beautiful, a stunner, an absolute cracker and had just arrived on the scene. She was Portuguese, a chocolate colour, with a great figure. They became the fashionable thing."

Young, ambitious entrepreneurs like Paul Russell symbolised, and helped generate, the emerging prosperity in Ireland in the 1960s. Many turned their backs on secure jobs with pensions, opting instead for riskier forms of employment. Gay Byrne departed the world of insurance for broadcasting. Terry Wogan followed suit, quitting his job with the bank for Radio Éireann. Russell turned his back on his job as a car salesman to find fame and fortune as a drummer, broadcaster and promoter.

The country they worked in was changing too. Employment was booming and cash was plentiful. Emigration was falling. Dublin's Liberty Hall was under construction. So was Hawkins House, rising from the ashes of the old Theatre Royal. The landmark O'Connell Bridge House was also being built. Car ownership was expanding. The first stretch of the Naas dual carriageway had opened. US President John Fitzgerald Kennedy, who was over for a visit in summer 1963, remarked on the progress being made.

The music scene was thriving. Dancehalls sprung up sporting exotic names like the Crystal, Olympic, Cloudland, Majestic, Majorca, Orchid and Arcadia. The top showbands pulled in crowds of 2,000 – 3,000 for Sunday night dances. Foreign acts flooded into the country on tour. Bucket-loads of cash could be made. Performing 45-minute sets, Roy Orbison, on one night alone, played Belfast at half past six, Lurgan at eight, Belfast again at ten and Omagh at midnight. Part-time promoter Jim Aiken chucked in his teaching job having earned more from one night as a promoter than from a full year as a teacher.

Radio programmes sponsored by Chivers, Birds, Jacobs, Ranks and Maxwell House, among others, began to spin the occasional pop disc. There also was *Hospitals Requests*. Cafés with jukeboxes were flourishing. A new pop magazine, *Spotlight*, went on sale. Savings were used to buy record players. Although slow to respond, Radio Éireann featured programmes like *The Seventeen Club* with Gay Byrne and *Ireland's Top Ten* with a range of presenters. Telefís Éireann launched *Pickin' The Pops* with Gay Byrne and *The Showband Show* with Paul Russell. Commenting on the new teen revolution in broadcasting, one reviewer said, "The kids have all but seen the artistes in person."

In the circumstances, the Beatles seemed destined to travel to Ireland. In truth, however, their arrival was a much closer-run thing. By the time of their visit in November '63 the group were bordering on mega-stardom. That wasn't the case when the dates were arranged four months before, in the heart of the summer. During the intervening months, the Beatles had risen from Cavern Club luminaries to national stars and were bordering on legendary status. So rapid was the rise that had the autumn tour venues been organised closer to the time of the trip, the group might never have played in Dublin and Belfast.

Spotlight magazine, in production since the spring of 1963, scooped the news of the forthcoming visit. Columnist 'Steve', during a trip to London in late summer, met up with Beatles' manager Brian Epstein while interviewing another of his acts, the Big Three. "The boss man said negotiations were going on at present for the Beatles to tour Ireland in October," 'Steve' reported. The news, although slightly inaccurate regarding the date of the shows, was published in the September edition of the pop magazine.

The tour was formally announced – with banner headlines – in early October. A full-page advertisement, splashed across the front cover of the *New Musical Express*, gave details of the acts and the venues. "Arthur Howes Presents....The Exciting!... Dynamic!... Fabulous!... The Beatles," the headline proclaimed. The cover also featured photos and details of the support groups – the Brook Brothers, Peter Jay and the Jaywalkers, the Vernons Girls, the Kestrels and compère Frank Berry. The advertisement listed 7 November and 8 November as the dates for the visit to Ireland. The venues were identified as the

Adelphi cinema in Dublin and the ABC Ritz cinema in Belfast – both part of the UK-based circuit, Associated British Cinemas (ABC).

Massive press coverage, and what can only be called 'hype', followed the announcement. The instigator was Paul Russell, whose initials appropriately reduced to 'PR'. Columnists like 'Paul Jones' in the *Evening Press*, 'Tempo' in the *Evening Herald* and the pages of *Spotlight* magazine presented details of the imminent shows. Telefís Éireann's news division was promised access to the Beatles on arrival. *The Showband Show*, which Paul Russell presented on TV, was lined up for an interview with the group. Then, on Friday 11 October the evening papers featured ads stating that tickets would be on sale the following afternoon and evening. With the Adelphi box office open from 1 – 7 pm, ticket prices were listed at 6/6, 8/6 and 10/6.

The excitement was palpable. Even today, Brendan Bennett – that dedicated follower of fashion from Cabra West who was spotted by the *Sunday Independent* sashaying around Dublin – remembers the buzz. With a ticket costing 8/6 already in his pocket, he laid out his Beatle suit, polished his Beatle boots, counted out his Beatle rings and washed his Beatle haircut in preparation for the greatest night of his life. Now in his 60s, he recalls how together with two friends – also suitably dressed in Beatles gear – he travelled by bus from Cabra West all the way to Clerys in the centre of Dublin. The three of them, he says, were a sight to be seen. Luckily there weren't four of them or hysteria might have erupted on the No. 22 bus!

DUBLIN AIRPORT

Shortly after noon on Thursday, 7 November 1963 Aer Lingus flight EI 155 from London broke through the heavy cloud cover, landed smoothly and taxied to the main terminal building at Dublin Airport. A few minutes later the captain shut down the engines. Dressed in a fashionable three-quarter length coat, Paul McCartney, aged 21, was the first to emerge through the rear passenger door of the plane. Collar up, full of smiles, he skipped down the steps from the Viscount to the tarmac below.

John Lennon, aged 23, exited next, bracing himself against the exceptional November chill. His coat was draped over his arm. A travel-bag hung from his shoulder. Ringo Starr, the oldest of the Beatles at 23 years and 4 months, followed behind him, hands pressed into pockets, his collar also turned up. Last to disembark was George Harrison, aged 20 and the youngest of the group, adjusting his shoulder-bag as he hurried down the steps from the plane.

Overlooking the scene, a crowd of young teenagers stood screaming on the first-floor viewing balcony of the old airport building. Behind them, at the back of the balcony, were the ground-to-ceiling windows of the airport restaurant. Underneath, on the floor below, were the baggage carousels. Out on the apron were the baggage trolleys and the Beatles' plane. The four Beatles were so close, one teenager said, that you felt you could touch them.

Girls accounted for the bulk of those present. Three of them, asked by a reporter for their names, refused saying they were "on the bounce" from school. A few of the boys wore odd haircuts with fringes down to their eyes. Hair covered their ears and necks. Many cheered when the Beatles emerged from the plane. Others, who were star-struck, stared in awe.

"The weather wasn't great," says Rita Hempenstall, who was aged 15 and one of the fans watching the Beatles from the first-floor observation deck. "It was a cold day and rainy. I remember I was looking at them through railings. They looked fabulous. I was really excited, especially when they looked up and waved. I was there with my friend. She had called to me and asked would I like to go see the Beatles coming in. I was ironing at the time and I just dropped everything and went.

"We didn't have tickets for the concert so we decided to head out to the airport by bus. My favourite at the time was John Lennon. I was just hoping he'd look in our direction. He was my number one. I had a little thing for him. Paul was my second favourite. I had all the records and I never stopped playing them. It was great to see them. I never felt like that about any other group ever again. It was the Beatles and that was it."

Higher up, on the second floor of the old airport building, was a smaller balcony crammed with ground staff. "That was known as the meteorology balcony," former security officer Paddy Cowley recalls. "The weathermen had antennae and little boxes there, where they'd collect information. The staff would be allowed to go out onto it. There were dozens of them there – the catering staff, office staff and staff from other buildings who got special passes to get in. The minute the aircraft touched down, staff left their offices for a few minutes and went onto the balcony. They had a perfect view."

Down on the apron, Paul Russell, co-ordinator of the Beatles' Dublin visit, led the official welcoming party. "It was like meeting old friends," remarks Russell, who knew the Beatles from the earlier Roy Orbison tour of the UK. "Paul McCartney came down the steps and came straight to me. I had this great thing about him. He was gracious and gentlemanly. There was something about him. He gave me a hug. I remember I said to him, 'It is my pleasure to welcome you to Dublin.' He said, 'Paul, it's my pleasure to see you again, mate.' I will never forget that. Ringo said, "Allo, mate.' But John or George and I never exchanged words. They just stood there like sheep.

"I had a black overcoat on. I had the Beatle boots and the close Perry Como haircut, as they called it. They would always say to me, 'Paul, you look like an Irish priest. Why don't you grow your hair long?' I'd say, 'I'm lucky it's not falling out like you guys.' They loved that. Then I turned around and saw the crowd on the balcony, the screaming and waving. The people were hysterical. Every stewardess within the airport was down there, looking and gawking. I had never seen anything like this before. Everyone knew that Beatle hysteria had arrived."

Alongside Russell was Telefís Éireann news reporter Frank Hall who, despite the bad weather, wore a sports jacket and slacks. His hand-held microphone was attached by cable to a camera crew. He listened as Russell told the Beatles they looked well and jokingly promised them a tour of the Guinness brewery. Russell then introduced the Beatles to Hall. Press photographers and reporters stood around, recording the event. Beside them were curious airport baggage handlers, security officers and technical staff, watching with interest.

"I was on security duty down on the apron," says Paddy Cowley. "I was about 100 feet away from the Beatles, which was the same distance I was away from JFK just a few months before. We were called 'wardens' at the time and we were all over the place, trying to control anyone getting into the 'air side', onto the ramp or into the aircraft parking area. We were also around the cargo hanger, by the VIP lounge doors and inside the terminal building. I wasn't talking to the Beatles, but I will always remember the crowds."

Standing nearby, close to the apron, were two 15-year-old schoolgirls in their uniforms, who had skipped school to see the Beatles. Having already checked the early morning boat service to see if the Beatles were on board, they eventually travelled out to the airport. "My friend and I had gone to meet them off the boat in the morning but no one got off with Beatle haircuts," Kaye Ryan remembers. "It was a miserable day, cold and wet. But we knew they had to come into Dublin somehow. So we took two buses and we went out to the airport."

Lena McDevitt picks up the story: "We were down below, at the front, looking out on the tarmac. There was quite a crowd there. We saw the Beatles' plane come in. The police were holding people back, with their arms linked. Eventually we took our chances and we ducked under the police cordon and we ran to where they were. We asked for their autographs. They sort of smiled and said hello. I remember they had very strong accents. I got mine on a sandwich bag, so I had obviously taken my school sandwich with me.

"I had gone to see President Kennedy when he came a few months before. I saw him in O'Connell Street. But I loved the Beatles the most. I didn't have their albums or even a record player. I couldn't afford any of that stuff. I didn't even have the money to buy a ticket for the concert, which is why we went to the airport. But I still have the autographs in a very safe place. I have been offered money for them but I'm not giving them up."

The Beatles had travelled on the scheduled mid-morning flight departing London at a quarter to eleven. They flew first class, which was located in the turbulence-prone rear of the prop plane. "Their Viscount was one of the few that had first class," according to cadet pilot and future captain Michael O'Callaghan, who witnessed the arrival. "First class had about eight seats and the flight took around one hour and thirty minutes. They had a full meal service available during the flight.

17

You'd be talking about a half-duck or a half-chicken or a big steak and a prawn cocktail, with big cream desserts and tea and coffee. It really was superb. But the fare was £200 odd, which was very expensive and very exclusive at the time."

Travelling on the same flight were support acts the Kestrels, the Vernons Girls, the Brook Brothers, Peter Jay and the Jaywalkers and Frank Berry. They flew economy class. "The thing I remember most about the Dublin visit was flying out with the Beatles from London Airport," Peter Jay recollects. "The crowd when we left was enormous. Brian Epstein had a way of tipping off all the fans that the Beatles were flying in or out. You often see it now on the newsreels with them either going to, or coming back from, America. It was like that when we travelled to Ireland. On the way back from Belfast to London Airport it was the same. We actually had the experience of coming down the steps of the aircraft and all these thousands of people were screaming, shouting and going mad. It was amazing, really fantastic."

Also flying into Dublin that morning was George Harrison's mother Louise, who had travelled on an earlier prop service from Liverpool. "She was very friendly," says Rita Hempenstall, who met her. "She had greyish hair with a perm in it. She had a green suit or coat. That has always stuck in my mind. She could have been about 60 but everybody looked 60 when we were just 15. She might have only been in her 40s. She had arrived before the Beatles. She was waiting on them as well. I think George's uncle was there also. Mrs Harrison was talking about George and how he enjoyed being in the Beatles. They were famous alright but not *that* famous at the time. She seemed very happy for them. She was excited about how well they were doing."

Lena McDevitt and Kaye Ryan also bumped into Louise Harrison. "I remember standing in this car park area and a woman came up and talked to us. It was Louise Harrison, George's mother. She was lovely. I was struck dumb," Kaye Ryan recalls. Her friend Lena McDevitt asked for her signature.

"I felt a bit sorry for her so I asked her to sign her autograph too, along with the Beatles," Lena remembers. "She signed it as well, in red biro. My son tells me the autographs must be quite unique, with George Harrison's mother as well as the Beatles."

Surrounded by the mayhem, the Beatles posed briefly on the tarmac for the assembled photographers. They performed what was described as a 'jig' or a 'fling'. Snappers from the *Evening Herald* and *Evening Press* immediately hurried back to base to meet deadlines for their late editions. Others weren't so happy. "It was impossible at Dublin Airport," photographer Pat Maxwell explains. "I had been commissioned by several magazines to get some sort of different picture of them. They wanted something new, an exclusive. It was too much to ask. There was very strict security and too many girls there. What I got was the same as everyone else, with the Beatles posing and bunched up together. I knew I needed something better later that day."

Although the chaos of 7 November was exceptional, the arrival of celebrities like the Beatles at Dublin Airport was far from unknown. Throughout 1963 many groups and solo artistes, from Britain and America, included Ireland as part of their tours. On one day alone in October, Helen Shapiro headed for London while Freddie and the Dreamers travelled the opposite way. That day also, Taoiseach Seán Lemass arrived from the United States to be met by President Éamon de Valera and members of the cabinet. Less than a few weeks before that, Roy Orbison passed through.

Almost every act that toured Britain also travelled to Ireland. Bill Haley arrived along with Chubby Checker, Adam Faith, the tiny Brenda Lee, Johnny Cash and Billy Fury. Jim Reeves came to play venues like the Orchid in Lifford, the Ormonde in Arklow, the Oyster in Dromkeen and the Arcadia in Cork. From September to Christmas 1963, it was estimated that 20 top names were scheduled to come Ireland's way, including the Searchers and the Springfields not to mention the Beatles.

It wasn't just pop stars that passed through. Back in June, US President John Fitzgerald Kennedy had arrived on Air Force One for his visit to Ireland. Battalions of Irish troops made their way to and from the Congo. Add in the steady flow of actors and celebrities who were arriving for holidays, promotion work or on general business and Dublin Airport, right through the 1960s, was like a parade of the famous. Hardly a flight touched down without a recognisable face on board.

So many celebrities were arriving that Dublin Airport became a popular haunt for autograph hunters. The only impediment was the airport's location. "The airport wasn't reasonably accessible," remarks cadet pilot Michael O'Callaghan. "The only way out was by bus. The airport was a little village out by itself at the time. You'd only see three or four cars parked outside and one bus and the place would be empty. Very few people even flew back then as airfares were horrendously expensive. People either came to Johnny Oppermann's restaurant or to see the odd people off. You might see 20 or 30 people, at the very most, on the balcony for the transatlantic departure in the late morning. But that was it. Very few people would have come out to the airport in those days."

The airport was so remote that showband star Dickie Rock held his wedding there in 1966, three years after the Beatles' visit. Fearful that uninvited guests might spoil the event, he and his bride booked the recently-built church of Our Lady Queen of Heaven, which was located at the airport, believing it would afford privacy. It was hoped that fans might be deterred from making the long and difficult trip out from the city. The plan worked, although an outbreak of sighing from some over-wrought girls accompanied the exchanging of vows.

Activity at the airport was sufficiently intense to warrant the establishment there of a full-time press agency. Run by journalist Derek Ball, it was busy. "I was used to meeting big-name stars," says Ball. "I met people like Che Guevara, Shirley MacLaine, Elizabeth Taylor and John Wayne. Yet, now, people say, 'Ah, you met the Beatles.' Everybody singles out the Beatles. At the time, I was less impressed by the Beatles than the others. News-wise, the others were bigger and I was getting more out of them than I got out of the Beatles, who were just passing through."

That Ball's airport press agency thrived speaks volumes for the vitality of air travel and air terminals back in the '60s. It was something that Brian Epstein was acutely aware of. As far as the Beatles' manager was concerned, air terminals were hubs of movement and perpetual motion – perfectly in tune with the fast-paced, all-action public image of his group. Flying was glamorous and exciting, with only the privileged and exclusive heading off to distant, exotic locations. Young boys dreamed of becoming air pilots. Girls aspired to becoming hostesses. Airports were also secure venues, where the fans couldn't tear their idols apart. To Epstein, shots of the group stepping off planes and waving to thousands of fans were ideal for publicity and hype.

Epstein was masterful at alerting fans to the times of the Beatles' arrivals and departures. Prior to the visit to Dublin, their previous overseas trip was a short week-long tour of Sweden at the end of October. Fans were advised of the date, time and place of their return home. Their arrival at London Airport was extraordinary. Thousands of screaming girls waited for the Beatles, bringing traffic to a halt. An estimated 50 photographers and reporters, who were also tipped off, were there to record the occasion. So loud was the screaming that the noise of aircraft engines was totally drowned out. Even the British Prime Minister was delayed in the ensuing mêlée.

News of the pandemonium reached Ireland where, especially among adults, the reaction was generally hostile. Renowned poet Patrick Kavanagh sarcastically referred to the Beatles as "simple-faced young chaps without, I am certain, an ounce of publicity guile." Their hairstyles, he suggested, were comparable to those of The Three Stooges. He went on: "So far the Irish have not produced a guitaring ensemble of sufficiently outrageous codology. I saw the Clancy Brothers on the television and somehow they hadn't that final touch of nerve and neck which is required. Of course, you have to be marketed and plugged in opposition to all the other exponents of idiocy."

A Dublin doctor added fuel to the fire. "Screaming at a pop idol is a para-sexual phenomenon," he said in a press interview. "It could, possibly, point towards a lower I.Q. and, as far as I can see, is rarely indulged in by the better educated girls. Going in deeper, this reaction could have something to do with a lack of religion or a substitution of parenthood. I don't really know. I was reading in one medical journal where certain tests were carried out on girls screaming at a particular idol of theirs. It reveals that it was a form of eroticism and could be physically damaging. It could, the experts said, be harmful to blood pressure, the heart or the brain."

With this sort of high-octane stuff as a backdrop, the Beatles' pending arrival in Dublin was well-publicised and widely reported. Newspapers built up to the event by describing how the city authorities were "standing by" or "bracing themselves" for the Beatles' shows. "If they do not have the same effect as an exploding bomb the Gardaí will be profoundly grateful," the *Evening Herald* commented. Another columnist remarked: "Many other people are getting out of town by plane, boat, bus, train and car. But we're not joining them. Oh, no. Our place is with this stricken city, with our loved ones and our faithful readers. Besides, we were too late to get an airline ticket. They're all gone."

The *RTV Guide*'s 'Showpage' also cranked up the heat, referring to the forthcoming 7 November as "Beatles day at the Adelphi cinema." Their columnist wrote: "Instead of the usual film, the building will shake to the guitars and voices of these four Liverpool lads who have so quickly pounded their way into big-time publicity, teenage adulation – and very substantial money. The hysteria which follows them can only be paralleled by the perfervid devotion that greeted Johnnie Ray in 1955. On Thursday, November 7, Middle Abbey Street will ring to the Mersey beat. One night only, two performances. And if you haven't got one of the 4,600 tickets, you've had it. They're sold out."

The *Evening Herald*'s kiddies' page – compiled by 'Uncle Bill' – was awash with news of the Beatles. In mid-October the column promoted the forthcoming shows by publishing shots of the Beatles, the Brook Brothers and the Vernons Girls. "Pop, pop, pop, right at the top sparkles the most with-it group to emerge from Liverpool. Wherever they go they bring a big beat, and their fans can't get enough of the Beatles," 'Uncle Bill' commented. Kids were offered free photos of the group. The paper was swamped with over 500 requests, which they promised to deal with as soon as they could.

Even on the day of the Beatles' arrival, *The Irish Times* added to the fever: "This morning, four young men from Liverpool will try to enter Dublin unobtrusively, spend 24 hours in the capital, and just as unobtrusively leave for Belfast tomorrow. Their efforts, however, will be a waste of their valuable time. For the Beatles, making their first appearance in this country, are as well known here by thousands of young enthusiasts as they are in their homeland and on the Continent. Everywhere they have appeared in recent months they have been mobbed by their fans both inside and outside theatres."

The Irish Times also acquired details of the Beatles' Irish itinerary, which they were only too happy to publish just hours before the group arrived. The paper quoted tour promoter Arthur Howes, of "Greek Street, London," as saying that the band would be flying from what was then known as London Airport and touching down in Dublin at quarter past twelve. Understandably, the airport authorities were concerned. With the fans in the know, anything might happen. Airport security was beefed up, with extra staff assigned for the visit. Additional Gardaí were called in. The authorities, however, were confident that there wouldn't be trouble. "They are enthusiastic, of course," an Aer Lingus spokesman said regarding pop fans, "but they keep their enthusiasm within proper limits."

With the media frenzy at a peak, even lukewarm pop fans were straining either to get to the airport, to the Beatles' hotel or to one of the shows. "We certainly knew about the hysteria that was coming," recalls schoolboy and aspiring musician Dave Pennefather. "We used to sit and talk about the forthcoming concerts. Some of us had seen the Beatles on TV, which was sneaking in at the time. We also had English newspapers coming in like the *People* and *News of the World*.

"The Irish media were looking forward to the fights outside the theatres and they were hoping there might be a bit of crowd trouble. The boys were all going to hear them and see them playing their instruments, because the sound and style on their records was so hugely unusual at the time. The girls were going because they wanted to see Paul McCartney and wanted to hug Ringo Starr.

"But the hype in Ireland wasn't really hype because hype is something that is fabricated. This was an excitement that was completely driven not by the media but by people themselves who wanted to be there. It was true, genuine, full-blooded excitement among people dying to see these guys. You had this genuine feeling that something was going on out there, something new was happening."

Immediately on entering the main terminal building at Dublin Airport, the Beatles headed for the VIP lounge. "They passed through the transatlantic departure hall, which was empty at the time," says former security officer Joe Kelly. "I was manning the entrance door linking the departure hall with the check-in area. That's where you would normally be checking boarding-cards for departing passengers. On that occasion, I was making sure that no unauthorised people came in. I was on my own. The Beatles strolled in and passed me by. They were ribbing each other, as young fellows do. They had a little bit of horseplay among themselves. They seemed to be enjoying themselves, chatting away as they walked through the departure hall."

The Beatles then went to the VIP room at the end of the hall. "Looking nothing at all like four young men who earn between £650 and £1,000 per night, the famed Liverpool Beatles strode nonchalantly into the VIP room at Dublin Airport," the *Evening Herald* reported. "At a glance journalists detected the world acclaimed hair styles; their casual, though colourful attire and their likeable approach to show business in general. Their very appearance will more than please the 5,000 admirers who will pack Dublin's Adelphi Cinema tonight and the many thousands more who will mob them in Belfast tomorrow."

Representatives of the national dailies and evenings, including the now-defunct *Irish Press* and *Evening Press*, were present. "There were not much more than half a dozen journalists in the VIP room," observes Derek Ball. "We talked to them for a good long while. There was no great rush among them to get out and wave back at the fans. They just sat around and chatted. It wasn't like the usual press interview. It wasn't sitting around with notebooks, talking to them and scribbling it all down. It was a lot of banter, wisecracks, mickey-taking and waffle. It was quite difficult to get a question in with any of them. If you did, you didn't get an answer of any kind that you could put down and make a story out of.

"It was a very light-hearted affair. I spent a lot of time talking to Ringo Starr, who I didn't particularly think much of until I met him. He was a most pleasant young man. Like the rest of them, he had no airs or graces. These were guys who had their feet on the ground and who were as ordinary as they were before they got famous."

Journalists heard how the group were "flabbergasted" by their recent success. "We feel we are appealing to the masses and the type of stuff we are giving them at present is near to their hearts," they explained. George Harrison highlighted his connections with Ireland, pointing out that his grandparents were Irish. "I was here before, you know, when I was about eight years of age. I think I stayed in Drumcondra, but I'm told I have dozens of relatives in Dun Laoghaire and other parts of the country," he added. John Lennon said they had never before played to an Irish audience and hoped the show would be a good one. "So how much are you earning?" someone asked. "About 4/3 a week," quipped Paul.

Also present in the VIP room was Fintan Russell, who was hired by his brother, tour co-ordinator Paul Russell, to pick up the Beatles' gear at the airport. "Paul was in a bit of trouble because he had to drive his own car out to the airport," Fintan recalls. "He had an American-type car that he was using for a bit of flash around Dublin. He needed to drive it to the airport, to bring the Beatles back into the city. His idea was that I would drive out the Viscounts' van to bring in the Beatles' gear, thinking that they wouldn't travel in the same van as the gear.

"It was an old black and white Volkswagen van, one of the original Volkswagens. It had 'The Viscounts Swing The Most' written on the side of it. It was used for their gigs up and down the country. So I drove the van out to meet them. I got £3 for my work that day. At that time I was working in the Hibernian Insurance as a clerk. I think I was earning about the same – £3 a week!

"When we got there, Paul discovered that the promoter Arthur Howes had arranged all that stuff. They had a kind of a semi-big bus which brought gear in the rear, which Paul wasn't aware of. So Paul said, 'Come on in, Fintan, and you can say hello to them, and after that you can head home.' I met them there, lovely guys. I had a drink with them in the VIP section.

"I sat down and had a cup of coffee. I didn't even drink alcohol at the time. I was only a greenhorn from County Kerry. I wasn't really in the conversation bar Paul saying, 'This is my brother, Fintan.' But a lot of people were coming over and saying hello to them. The guy I was most taken with was Paul McCartney, probably because I loved the piano. He was a lovely guy, down to earth, didn't say much but what he said you listened to. They were also talking to the Viscounts, who were there. I remember distinctly they were asking about the Viscounts and how the Irish scene was music-wise.

"The one thing I did notice in the 25 minutes I was there was how interested they were in meeting other people. Most people who have just arrived in on a flight want to sit down and go into a toilet and relax for five minutes and then go outside, sit in the corner and read the paper. But they were very interested in everything. I thought they had amazing stamina and interest in other people. They were lovely, refreshing guys. They looked so fresh. They were totally charismatic people. Then I drove the van back to town."

George's mother, Louise Harrison, also joined the guests in the VIP lounge. "She was an ordinary woman in an ordinary coat, standing in the background, sipping away at a coffee or a tea," journalist Derek Ball remembers. "One of my parents came from County Wexford," Louise remarked. Many years earlier, at the turn of the 1950s, she had brought George on a visit to Dublin. A devoted mother, she was already answering fans' letters on George's behalf and joining the group backstage whenever she could. "What of the Beatles' success?" Mrs Harrison was asked. "They haven't changed a bit," she responded.

The sound of girls screaming periodically penetrated the press conference. A group of 40 or so had made their way to the VIP lounge door. They congregated at the entryway, hoping for a glance inside. Aged 15 – 17 and dressed in their Sunday-best coats, they were restrained by airport security and Gardaí. The noise was deafening. At one stage, one of the fans stuck a head through the half-open door. The move precipitated a frenzied rush. Although the Gardaí were pushed backwards into the room, order was restored and the interviews continued.

Conspicuous by his absence was Beatles' manager Brian Epstein, who two days before had taken a flight to New York where he booked into the prestigious Regency Hotel on Park Avenue. His intention was to secure top billing for the Beatles on what was America's most famous coast-to-coast pop television programme, *The Ed Sullivan Show*. The subsequent historic transmissions, the following February, catapulted the boys to the top of the USA charts. Noticing Epstein's non-attendance, a curious Dublin journalist asked where he was. John Lennon, who was known for his caustic wit and scabrous remarks about Epstein's Jewish background, replied, "Oh, he's in America signing up a new rhythm 'n Jews group."

In Epstein's absence, tour promoter Arthur Howes had flown in from London and turned up at the press briefing. An intense man with a crew-cut and sporting a decidedly Romanesque nose, Howes had travelled because, as he said that autumn, "I want the boys to know that I care; that I'm more than just someone who pays their wages." His loyalty to the group was regarded as genuine and his links to the Beatles would extend right to the end of their concert careers. He had also arrived to see that all went smoothly in Ireland.

"The whole thing has been going like a military operation," Howes said at the press conference regarding the Beatles' first week on the road. "Obviously they appeal to the masses. They are doing what they want." He also outlined how he had known the Beatles for some time and how they were learning to live with their phenomenal renown. Not only had they come to terms with their fame but their recent notoriety hadn't changed them a bit, Howes stated. He finally described how he was inundated with requests for the group from promoters in places as distant as South Africa, Australia and New Zealand.

The Beatles were also interviewed by Telefís Éireann's Frank Hall. For a while it was feared that the prearranged recording might be cancelled due to pressures of time. Too many reporters and photographers were present. As ever, the Beatles had been eager to please, answering questions and posing for shots. "A hurried huddle with the newspapermen ate into a meagre time schedule," Hall, who initially thought the Beatles were "young pups," wrote later. "Not a moment to lose! Strangely biddable, the riotous quartet arranged themselves as the cameramen ordered. In this alone, they contrasted favourably with the average teenage idol, who tends to be as temperamental as an ageing prima donna."

The interview went well. Over the previous months, the Beatles had become known for their witty and spontaneous interview style. Capitalising on their Liverpool accents and humour, they delivered madcap inanities more suited to schoolboys in playgrounds than to national stars. It was refreshingly appealing. Frank Hall got what he wanted. He recorded a four-minute conversation to be televised at five minutes to eight that evening on the station's news magazine programme *In Town*, which was transmitted in a short prime-time slot preceding *Bat Masterson*.

Interrupted by the deafening sound of taxiing aircraft, the interview covered a wide range of topics including haircuts, touring, female fans, the group's Irish links and the 'Liverpool Sound'. At one stage, while discussing their personal closeness, a flurry of theatrical fisticuffs broke out, with the boys light-heartedly battering each other about. In November 1963 even the sight of the Beatles hamming it up would sell.

"I was as ready as the next man to loathe them," Frank Hall later reflected. "Why did I come away with a reluctant regard for them? I wish someone would tell me. It was the most spontaneous interview I have ever been involved in. It flowed as easily as a casual conversation with four friends unexpectedly met. A television interviewer does not expect to be entertained by his subject. At its best, the TV interview is an exercise in vigilance and skill. But the Beatles were no trouble. They had style, awareness, intelligence. They had humour too; a strange, guarded, allusive humour. It was a group feeling, I thought, springing from a deep well of shared experiences. These boys had grown up together, discovering in one another their common interest in what they called music.

"They had known – not for long, perhaps – obscurity, hard times. From this, they had learned the value of comradeship. This I discerned from the instinctive way their remarks flowed into a central channel. Though highly individual, they had discovered the strength of interdependence. Implicit in their talk was an adult awareness of the transience of fame and the waywardness of public taste. Cynical? No, but acutely mindful of their early obscurity and their ultimate return to it. They took no trouble to disguise it. Their anecdotes, jokes, remarks were imbued with the knowledge that fame is a flirt and time's a thief.

"They had no illusions, which is a different thing from being disillusioned. There is nothing wrong with the Beatles, I thought, as I packed my gear. But looking at the frantic mob that threatened to tear them apart, I said to myself, 'The question is, what's wrong with us?'"

With the interview over, the Beatles returned to the aircraft parking area, thereby avoiding a risky, high-profile exit to what was called the 'land side' of the airport. "Their car was brought around onto the apron so that they didn't have to go out into the mêlée out front," says former security officer Joe Kelly. "They waited in the empty transatlantic departure hall all by themselves while the organisers brought their transport around 'air side'. There were no transatlantic departures until later in the day. They were sitting there, chatting among themselves. The fans were all outside the VIP room waiting for them to come through. But they never did."

Paul Russell's American Chrysler Saratoga was driven around to take the Beatles into town. The Saratoga stood out, with its red and white bodywork and motto on the back bumper, 'The Viscounts Swing The Most'. Costing a fortune at £700, it had a registration number BIN 600. "It was the most obnoxious thing I ever drove but it suited my personality at the time," Russell comments. "The police on O'Connell Street would wave me by and stop all the traffic. I remember going in the Chrysler to the GPO to get the newspapers. The guy threw them in and said, 'Don't worry about it, Paul. It's so great to see you. You should get a decent car some of these days.'"

Equally unimpressed was Paul's father, the Garda sergeant and former Kerry football star. "I remember Dad saying to me after a while, 'Would you ever ask your brother to get rid of that heap of rubbish from outside the front door. It's embarrassing. Jesus, what will the neighbours think?'" Paul's brother Fintan recalls. "I approached Paul one morning, when I knew he hadn't a sick head, and I said, 'Paul, it's like this – Dad isn't too happy with that yoke outside the door.' I remember Paul was reading some music magazine. He said, 'Do you know what, Fintan?' I said, 'What?' He said, 'It looks like Dad will have to leave.' That's the way Paul was. He was afraid of confrontations, and his way out of them was to be jocose."

Ever the showman, Paul McCartney was overawed as he entered the brash automobile. "He asked me about the car," Russell remembers. "'Hello! Look at this car!' he said. 'This is a beauty!' I had a guy at the time who used to be my driver, a big heavyset guy who would knock you on your ass in two seconds. He would knock you spinning. He used to clean the Saratoga for me, shampoo it and clean it. Johnny was driving that day. He drove from the airport. Paul McCartney thought I was some kind of a millionaire. He was enthralled by it and that I had this chauffeur."

Within minutes, the Saratoga was winding its way from the airport, carrying its cargo of driver, Paul Russell and four Beatles to Dublin. "They went off, having spent three quarters of an hour or so at the airport. The big part of the story was later on, down in the city," journalist Derek Ball remarks. Before departing, the Beatles paused briefly to sign autographs for four stray fans who had come on the off chance of meeting their idols. "We haven't got tickets for the show tonight, but we expect to be in Abbey Street to lend them moral support," one of them said. She didn't foresee how, that night, Middle Abbey Street would be nothing short of a war zone.

THE GRESHAM HOTEL

The worst-kept secret in Ireland was where the Beatles would be staying on the night of 7 November 1963. Anyone picking up *The Irish Times* that morning knew the answer. Scotching speculation that the Beatles had quietly booked into the Gresham Hotel the previous day, a spokesman was quoted as saying, "They are not here yet. We expect them tomorrow for one night." Early editions of the *Evening Herald*, which covered the group's arrival at Dublin Airport, confirmed the story.

"From the airport we went straight to the hotel, which was just down the road from the theatre," says Jeff Williams of the Kestrels, support group for the Beatles who had shared their flight. "Most often we would leave a venue in one city and go straight to the next one. We were then locked in from maybe 12 o'clock until the shows were over. Dublin was an exception. In Dublin we were all able to go to the hotel first. It was unusual. It was one of the better places we went to because the hotel was that close to the theatre."

The Gresham was the perfect choice of hotel for the Beatles. Located in O'Connell Street, it was only a short walk to Middle Abbey Street where the group were scheduled to perform. Back in the '60s it was also one of the posh hotels in the city. Its stately façade and its liveried doorman hinted at the grandeur and opulence that had been the hallmark of the Gresham since it first opened its doors in 1817.

The hotel was one of *the* places to rendezvous in the city. Society figures, eminent politicians, barons of industry and visiting dignitaries could be spotted eating in the restaurant or drinking in the bar. Grace Kelly, Bing Crosby, Richard Burton, Elizabeth Taylor, Bob Hope, Roy Rogers, Laurel and Hardy and Dwight Eisenhower stayed there. Those in need of being seen sashayed through the foyer or relaxed in the lounge. It was also used to accommodate pop stars.

"The first time I came to Dublin I was put up in the Gresham," recalled pop star Adam Faith, who stayed in the same rooms later occupied by the Beatles. "It was one of the most memorable days of my life. The Theatre Royal was packed. Afterwards, kids jumped on the roofs of every car in the area. They tried to get into the dressing-room. The police got me out and got me back to the Gresham, where I had a suite of rooms.

"There were so many kids around on the morning of the next day that they had to block off both ends of O'Connell Street for fear of danger. The Chief Inspector came to my room and said, 'You've got to go to the balcony and wave to these people. We've got to disperse them because it's getting dangerous down there.' I will never forget the experience of standing on the balcony of the Gresham. That was my first real experience of that sort of a wave sensation that comes off of a crowd of people. I was only a kid of 19 or 20. It was absolutely massive to have come from a council flat and to be standing on a balcony in front of 4,000 or 5,000 people blocking off O'Connell Street outside the Gresham Hotel."

The Gresham Hotel used to be the be-all and end-all, says Brush Shiels who, as a fledgling musician, attended one of the Beatles' concerts. "It was right at the centre of things," he points out. "When we went to town for a concert in those days, we'd waltz down O'Connell Street as far as the Carlton and the

Gresham. That used to be a great area. We'd look in the shop windows. You'd arrive in town two hours before the gig just to have a look at all the things you couldn't afford. You might even head in for the afternoon and make a whole day of it. Then you could look in every shop."

O'Connell Street was also a haven for people who assembled at night to talk and meet and buy newspapers. "The Cafollas, the Fortes and the Capaldis had their cafés there and they all came out at night for a chat," Sergeant Bill Herlihy, who was on duty the day of the Beatles' visit, recollects. "Some of them didn't speak any English. The Senezios had the Pillar Café. There was also the famous restaurant at the bottom of the street, The Green Rooster. It was a thriving centre."

The Beatles and their entourage arrived at the Gresham shortly before two o'clock in the afternoon. They pulled up at the hotel entrance in tour co-ordinator Paul Russell's Chrysler Saratoga car. The *Birds* programme, broadcast by Radio Éireann, played on the car radio. *The Kennedys of Castleross*, the *Prescotts (Cleaners and Dryers)* show and the *News* at one-thirty had accompanied them on the earlier part of the trip. Few could have missed the bright, brash automobile as it drove down O'Connell Street and approached the hotel. No one could have failed to recognise the four famous Beatles and Paul Russell, star of the Viscounts and *The Showband Show*, who spilled from the car.

The Beatles entered the Gresham through the large swell of people congregated on the footpath or crammed into the entryway of the hotel. "I was standing to the right, inside the door, when they came in," hall porter Diarmuid Flood remembers. "They brought them in through a small gap in the crowd of people packed outside. I was at the hall porter's desk, concentrating on maintaining order and keeping people out. People were jammed up on the steps. I was dressed in my black tie, white shirt and blue uniform with gold braid on the sleeves and on my jacket collar. I brought their luggage up to their rooms a few minutes later. After that, they never used the front entrance again."

The four Beatles briefly relaxed in the lobby, where they were spotted resting and having a chat. Two boys, who had gone on the hop from school, approached them. "We knew the Beatles were in town and playing in the Adelphi," says Ken Ronan, who was aged 14 and a secondary school student at O'Connell School CBS. "The best hotel in Dublin at the time was the Gresham. My friend and I thought they would be staying there. So we went mitching from school to see if we could find them or if we might get a ticket to the show, which there wasn't a hope in hell of getting.

"We were walking up and down O'Connell Street trying to be anonymous in the crowd because there were truant officers about in those days. We got to the Gresham at about a quarter to two. We went into the hotel, straight into the foyer. We walked in past the doorman. And there, straight in front of us, were the Beatles sitting down. I thought, 'Oh, my God, there's the Beatles.' They were reasonably close to the door, about 20 feet away. They were sitting on two big couches, which were beside a table. Two were on one couch and two on the other. They were flopped down and looked like they were just taking a relaxing couple of minutes. There were people around them engaging them in conversation, probably some of their entourage.

"I saw a paper on the table. It was an old *Sunday Review* newspaper, which is long since out of circulation. I grabbed it and asked them would they sign it. They all signed it. They just signed their Christian names. Ringo Starr had the best handwriting; his signature was the most legible. I then heard George Harrison say something to someone else about Drumcondra. I said, 'Are you going to Drumcondra?' He looked at me and said, 'Do you know Drumcondra?' I said, 'Oh, yeah, I do.' He smiled but he wasn't really giving out information. He then said something about going to see cousins. I think their name was French. We were then given a kick up the backside by security people and we had to run out of the place.

"I went home that evening and it was discovered that I hadn't been in school. I was so thrilled with myself that I gave away what happened. I got a few clatters for going mitching, which is what happened in those days. The bigger issue, however, was, 'How long have you been mitching from school?' To be truthful with you, it wasn't that often. I showed them the autographs. My mother didn't seem to mind but my father wasn't impressed. He thought a day's education far outweighed the Beatles' autographs. They were of a totally different generation and I think the Beatles were abhorrent to them. They probably thought they had long hair but they really didn't. Eventually, however, they saw the brighter side of it all.

"I was thrilled, of course, to have got the Beatles' autographs although, to be perfectly honest with you, I was a Rolling Stones' fan. At this stage, the Rolling Stones weren't quite as big as the Beatles. But I did have an old Elizabethan gramophone player at home, which I saved for and bought, and I had some of their records. I had 'Love Me Do' and 'Please Please Me'. So I was a fan and, as a 14-year-old in those days, you couldn't help but be overawed by the fact that you stood beside the most famous band in the world."

Unwinding in the busy Gresham lobby that lunchtime, the Beatles waited as their tour manager checked them in. Beside them was a table with a selection of newspapers affixed to long sticks to ensure they wouldn't be stolen. The headlines that day made for grim reading. The *Irish Press* led with tension in Berlin between the Americans and the Russians over the movement of convoys. "War Was Possible," the headline proclaimed, quoting a remark made by Khrushchev the previous day. *The Irish Times*, with its eye on foreign affairs, also led with the worsening Cold War relations. "West Protests At Convoy Incident," the paper announced. The *Irish*

Independent looked elsewhere for its lead, settling on the rescue attempts to save miners trapped in an iron mine in West Germany.

The Beatles themselves featured in a tongue-in-cheek column in one of the early editions of the evening papers. "Down the blood-stained decades this old city has looked on many fearsome things," the columnist wrote. "But, when the Beatles move in this evening, another grisly chapter in its history will be written. As we write, a sound of tapping rises into the foggy November air. It's the hammers of white-faced citizens nailing up extra-strong barricades.

"Prepared for the worst, we're waiting here in Abbey Street for Beelzebub, or Beatlebub, call it what you will, to descend on the Adelphi Cinema only a few yards from where we knock out this putrid, sorry prose. We have bought extra-heavy shin-guards, a crash helmet and an iron waistcoat which, we hope, will withstand the most merciless elbow-digs from hysterical Beatle-nuts. We'll be somewhere in the Adelphi buried beneath all those screams … If we don't come back, you'll know we died fighting."

The newspapers' advertisements also contained references to the Beatles. Beatle boots, readers were told, had arrived in shoe shops, with the first Irish-made prototypes going on sale that very day. Their début in the provinces was planned for the following week. Manufactured by O'D Shoes in their Basin Lane factory in Dublin, the company's strikingly-coloured promotional posters proclaimed, 'It's A Must To Be Mod' followed by the words 'Beatle Boots' in modernistic printing. Initially available in black leather, plans were afoot to manufacture one of the Beatle boot models partly in suede. The company advised that "the toes are sharply pointed," giving the foot a slim look. Boasting a two-inch high Cuban heel and measuring a full eight inches from bottom to top, demand from shops was insatiable, with the factory working around the clock to fill orders.

Had the Beatles scanned the entertainment pages they would have found them equally engrossing. Contrary to the perception of Dublin as a 'morgue' during weekdays, the city was a hive of activity that night. Playing just down the road at Clerys was Mick Delahunty and his Orchestra. The Mighty Avons were appearing at AGS. The Melody Aces were booked into the Crystal while the Altonaires were playing at the Ierne. South of the river, Micheál MacLiammóir, playing a moustachioed Adolf Hitler, joined Hilton Edwards in *The Roses Are Real* at the Gaiety. With the weekend beginning the following day there were dances scheduled with the Dixies, Casino, Victors and the ever-popular Eileen Reid and the Cadets. And if your tastes didn't stretch quite that far, there was always bingo at Gael Linn.

The Beatles were eventually led to their rooms by Charles Bentley, Assistant General Manager of the Gresham, who was second-in-command to legendary Manager Toddie O'Sullivan and, in his own right, a well-known and respected figure in hotel circles. The unobtrusive Mr Bentley was referred to in one newspaper at the time as a man "whose public appearances are as rare as a white blackbird." Crossing the elegant front hall with its Donegal carpet and blue and gold décor, he guided the Beatles to their suites via the back stairs so as not to unsettle the rest of the guests. An Englishman with an old-fashioned demeanour and style, he frequently stopped to ensure that they were close behind and not lost in the maze of corridors and stairs. "This way, Mr Beatles," he would repeatedly advise them, causing hilarity among his accompanying guests.

Coming from an entirely different social milieu, Charles Bentley was bemused by the sight of the Beatles, especially their hair. In that, he wasn't alone. The style was simple: collar-length at the back, over the ears at the sides and with straight-cut bangs. The fashion was, to put it mildly, controversial. For once, men cared about their hair. Teenagers brought with them magazine cuttings of the mop tops when selecting a hairstyle.

Electrical shops began stocking newfangled hairdryers. Some barbers, open to change, started calling themselves hairdressers. Others resisted the trend, horrified by men's fascination with the new Beatle cuts, or what many referred to as "women's hair styles." The day prior to the Beatles' arrival, one Dublin hairdresser told *The Irish Times*, "We got two young lads in about 10 days ago asking for a Beatle cut. We explained that our prices would have to be increased for such a speciality and that was the end of that. Too much trouble involved."

The 'Duck's Ass', with greased hair piled high at the top and swept back at the sides to form a seam at the rear of the head, was passé. Everyone who wished to be cool wanted a Beatle cut. "The kids went absolutely mad for it," hairdresser Alex Brophy remarks of the new style, for which he charged half a crown. "It was a revolution in the sense that young people started to take an interest in their hair. The older generation resented it because it wasn't what they knew and they resented change. I suppose the old always resent the young.

"I can remember one kid coming in at the time who was very into the Beatles. His father was very strict and I have a feeling he and his son didn't get on. I had, at the time, a magazine in the shop called *Picture Post* and it had a big spread on the Beatles. The kid asked me could he take it away. Then he started to sport this Beatle style. There was a kick against authority there from the word go. He was known far and wide as 'the Beatle'.

"It wasn't a difficult style to do. It was kind of a pudding-bowl style to the front and sides with the back left long. The problem was it didn't suit everybody. Somebody would come in with a photograph in their hand and say, 'I want that.' But they mightn't have the hair for it. If your hair was very thin and straggly you couldn't have it. They mightn't have the shape of head that was suited to it. Their head might be shaped like a kicked-in petrol can! You had to try and hit a balance between what the guy wanted and what was possible.

"Not every barber liked it or did it. Some wouldn't tolerate it. You got what they gave you, short back and sides, and you'd be very glad of it. If you didn't like it, you would be on your way. Others of us would have been open to fresh ideas. I suppose throughout the country there would have been a resistance to it, because any change from the type of trade they were normally catering for would be seen as a threat to their livelihood. Looking back, it was revolutionary but when you compare it to the free-for-all today it was actually a very conventional style."

It was after two o'clock by the time Charles Bentley had settled the Beatles into their suites. Tired from the trip, they relaxed on their beds. The housemaids weren't impressed. "The housemaids were complaining that they were lying on their beds with their clothes and shoes on," says Peter Hynes, a 15-year-old pageboy who was on duty that day. "The housemaids said it to me. Many of them were country lasses and they weren't happy. They were very particular. That was not the done thing at the time. Beds were for sleeping in. They knew the Beatles were VIPs but they were being bold."

From outside in the street came the sound of fans shouting for the Beatles. "There were hundreds of people outside on the footpath, in front of the door," hotel porter Paddy Fogarty remembers. "They were youngsters, about 16 years of age. They were looking up at the windows, hoping for a wave. They also hoped the Beatles might come in or out the front entrance. We had a man on the door and he wouldn't let the fans pass. His name was Harry Gray. He played hurling for Laois and Dublin. He was the commissionaire. He had a gate there on the steps and he kept them out as much as he could. The crowd were like bees after honey, trying to hunt them. But the Beatles were regular guys, very friendly and no bother whatsoever. They never refused an autograph if there weren't too many people around. They were very nice guys."

Within a radius of a few hundred yards of the Beatles' hotel suites was a city transformed by the music they initiated and inspired. Called the 'Liverpool Sound', its impact was everywhere to be seen. Resident dance bands, particularly in hotel ballrooms, were becoming a thing of the past. In their place, showbands and beat groups were thriving. Out went waltzing and swing. 'The Twist', 'Bossa Nova' and 'Hully Gully' were dead. As a jaundiced contributor to the pop magazine *Spotlight* put it, "In is the Shake, the Blues and all the other Beatle inspired variations of that peculiar jerking 'dance' which is the rage of all British dance halls and quite a few Irish just now." In a press interview at the time, Paul Russell added, "At the moment, the Liverpool sound is almost replacing country and western music or, as one ballroom owner said last week: 'If you play the Beatles and the Clancys, you're made.'"

Sales of Beatles' records were booming not only in the capital but all over Ireland, achieving for Parlophone EMI a succession of high-volume hits. Of the four major recording conglomerates – Pye, Decca, Philips and EMI – Pye led the field in Ireland with a line-up of showbands that included the Miami, Capitol, Drifters, Cadets and Dixies. Sales of 80,000, or more, for recordings like Dickie Rock's 'There's Always Me' and Butch Moore's 'I'm Walking The Streets In The Rain' weren't uncommon. EMI, however, with a tight line-up that included Brendan Bowyer and the Royal on their HMV label along with the Beatles on Parlophone, were tough opposition.

EMI also ran Ireland's only record factory, which was located near Ferrybank, just over the river from Waterford city. A staff of ten pressed, packaged and dispatched some 9,000 – 10,000 singles and extended-play records each week for sale in record shops throughout Ireland. Although owned by EMI, the factory also pressed discs for the other major labels, including Decca, Philips and Pye. The facility produced an average of 1,600 discs each day on its four pressing machines, which cost £3,000 each. Records arriving in retail stores throughout Ireland were literally 'hot off the presses'.

Despite limited retail outlets in Ireland, the Beatles sold well. In March 1963 'Please Please Me' crept into the Irish charts and stayed there for two weeks, reaching a high of number 10. In May 'From Me To You' went to number one and stayed in the charts for three months. In September 'She Loves You' only reached number two but, happily for EMI, was kept from top spot by another of their artistes Brendan Bowyer with 'Kiss Me Quick' on the HMV label. 'She Loves You', however, remained in the charts for 19 weeks including the lucrative period over Christmas.

"EMI had a wholesale place at the back of Granby Row and I would do business with them for Beatles' stock," recalls Peter Ryan, who worked with both Liam Breen's record shop and at Waltons. "You couldn't go wrong with Beatles' records. Coming up to the weekend, we would buy 50 to 100 of a new Beatles' recording for people coming into town on the Saturday. We would put out a Beatles' window display to bring in the customers. If someone wanted to come in and hear a Beatles' record, there was no problem.

"Beatles' sheet music sold also. Every showband in the country played Beatles' songs. They had a two-hour show and they always included the Beatles. They would come in to buy the sheet music and listen to the latest top-selling records, to learn the songs. All the top bands – Dickie Rock, Joe Dolan, Brendan Bowyer and the Royal Showband – used to practise around the corner in Barry's Hotel when they were doing gigs in the city-centre. They would come in to buy instruments. There was a big boom at the time."

Shortly after the Beatles went to their rooms, showband queen Eileen Reid came to meet them. Known for her bouffant hairstyle – described by one newspaper columnist as being "as elaborate as anything ever seen at the court of Louis XIV" – she was, at the time, one of Ireland's leading music stars. The previous July, Eileen and the Cadets became the first Irish group to perform on ITV's *Thank Your Lucky Stars*, sharing the bill with the Rolling Stones. Mick Jagger had been particularly impressed with the group's snappy uniforms, especially the braids and epaulettes. The Cadets had appeared on BBC TV's *625 Show* along with Telefís Éireann's *The Showband Show* and Radio Éireann's *The Seventeen Club*. They also had their own show on Radio Éireann, *Carnival Time With The Cadets*. Their manager's idea was for a meeting between 'The Queen of the Showbands' and the Beatles, photographed of course for distribution to the national press.

"I had set it up with Paul Russell," says Tom Costello, manager of the Cadets. "I used to give him some work and he was returning a favour. He used to play in the Crystal when I ran it and I would hire him as support. He was with the Viscounts at the time. I remember we went up to their floor of the hotel to meet the Beatles. It was very big for Eileen to have the photograph taken with them. I distributed it everywhere for publicity purposes. It was easy once you had the photograph and it was a great publicity coup."

Eileen picks up the story: "If Tom Costello couldn't get us to meet them, nobody could. He made the arrangements. We went upstairs to their bedroom. We didn't have to wait or anything. Someone went in and told them and two of them came out. Paul McCartney and John Lennon emerged into the corridor and we had a photo taken there. The other two boys were inside, but we were delighted we got the right two. It was a big corridor and there was nobody else there. I was in the middle of the two of them for the photo. Paul McCartney put his arm around my waist and he squeezed my waist a little bit. Later on, I was telling everyone, 'Girls, I got a squeeze from Paul.'

"We were with them a good bit and we were talking to them. John Lennon was talking to the boys. Paul McCartney was asking me, 'What sort of band have you got?' I was explaining that we had uniforms. He was asking, 'What sort of uniforms?' I explained they were blue and white, with gold braid and gold buttons, and the women all loved them. He

43

thought that was a great thing. He said, 'That sounds fantastic.' When the Sergeant Pepper thing came out I wondered if that had put a little idea in his head.

"McCartney asked, 'What sort of music do you play?' I said we did country, Dixieland, ballads, you name it, and we covered everything in the British charts. He was really open and nice and he looked interested. He was saying, 'That's fantastic.' I was telling him that we did all their stuff as well. John Lennon butted in and said, 'You know, you can't record our stuff.' He was a bit of a downer. He wasn't really nice. All of the boys even said it. You could live without him.

"That was it, and then we left. The photo was in the papers, it was everywhere. That's what Tom Costello wanted it for. It was terrific. I didn't see any other photos of them with anybody else and I was saying, 'We must have been very lucky that we got that.' We used the photograph in a sort of calendar thing that you could open up. There were a number of photographs in it, us with the Beatles, on *Thank Your Lucky Stars* and so on. It's a terrific picture.

"I had to laugh because everyone on the scene, especially the women, were saying, 'I don't believe you met the Beatles!' They were asking, 'What did they wear?' 'What were they like?' 'What was their hair like?' They were all dying to know. I couldn't understand that. We just looked on them as successful musicians. We were in the same game although they were mega. They were musicians who got the break."

So popular were the Beatles that all of the showbands spent hour after hour rehearsing their hits, which they then reproduced note-perfect onstage. The punters expected it. When a Beatles' song was released, the single was bought, copied, rehearsed to perfection and performed night after night in ballrooms and dancehalls from the Majorca in Crosshaven to the Cloudland in Roosky, the Flamingo in Ballymena, the Redbarn in Youghal and the Arcadia in Bray.

Beat clubs opened throughout Dublin, mimicking the

Cavern in Liverpool and offering venues for beat groups and the beat generation. "The Beatles created a whole new scene here," observes young drummer and band member Dave Pennefather. "They inspired clubs like the Club A Go Go and the '5' Club. The '5' Club was at the bottom of Harcourt Street. It was two cellars in a tunnel-like shape. At the end of one cellar you had a stage. But the first big one was Club Arthur, which was opened down in Burgh Quay. It nearly didn't open on the first night. In the afternoon the high tide in the Liffey shoved all the manholes up. The boys were there frantically trying to clear the place out, waiting for the tide to go down so they could open the door. It was a fantastic club. Before that it was all dancehalls but now you had something entirely new. These were all inspired by the Beatles."

Beatles' fashions were appearing on the streets, in dancehalls and clubs. Traditional men's suits were giving way to casual outfits and the latest gear. "You had to look the part," according to Brush Shiels. "Everything was coming in. At that particular time, Cliff had *Summer Holiday* out and he wore those short-jacket suits and the Beatles had a variation on that. I'd go to Premier Tailors or Hughes Brothers. We'd go up to Belfast once a month because they had different clothes up there. If you wanted to get what was happening in London's Portobello Road you had to go to Belfast where the shopping was much better. We'd also go over to Liverpool probably once every three months and have a look at what was available."

Dave Pennefather also travelled to the home city of the Beatles. "We all trooped off to the Cavern at some stage, to see it," he recalls. "We travelled over by boat, puking our hearts out all the way over. It was worth it when we got there. They had maps showing where all the clubs were. We went off on a club-crawl, so to speak. We tried to get gigs in Liverpool because we thought that was the magic wand. If you played Liverpool, you were going to strike it rich. Then we realised that 5,000 other bands were doing the same thing. Everybody

45

wanted to buy Ludwig drums. Everybody wanted to have a Hofner bass, like McCartney. Fellows were even trying to play left-handed.

"There was also an extraordinary wave of music coming from Liverpool and Manchester and the north of England. We were all carried away on this. All the bands over here started delving into rhythm 'n blues. We were looking to America as well and looking at the catalogues of Atlantic Records and Sun and so on, especially some of the black labels that were coming out of the south of America. So we were listening to John Lee Hooker and Screamin' Jay Hawkins and those other people who were creating the sound of the Rolling Stones and, to a lesser extent, the Beatles."

Also checking into the Gresham on 7 November, along with the Beatles, was the eminent Welsh playwright Alun Owen. He had just been commissioned to author a screenplay for an as-yet-unnamed movie featuring the group. A master of Liverpudlian dialogue, Owen was well-known for his ground-breaking TV play *No Trams To Lime Street*, which the Beatles had loved. He was also familiar with Dublin, where his play *A Little Winter Love* had been the highlight of the recent Dublin Theatre Festival.

Although born in Wales and brought up in Liverpool since the age of eight, Owen was regarded by many as Irish. "I was born in South Wales, of a Welsh father," he was quoted as saying. "But I was classed as Irish not just because my mother was from Leitrim. The area in which I lived, the fact that I went to Catholic schools, how I looked, all classed me as Irish." Owen was successful writing screenplays for TV. He had also, for the two years prior to the Beatles' tour, been collaborating with Lionel Bart – of *Oliver!* fame – on a spectacular new musical called *Maggie May*, which dealt with the tribulations and joys of a Liverpool-Irish family. Bart had attended the opening night of *A Little Winter Love* at the Gaiety not long before the Beatles arrived.

In the lead-up to the autumn tour, at meetings held in London between United Artists film producer Walter Shenson and Brian Epstein it had been decided to produce a comedy starring the Beatles. Epstein asked Shenson to meet with the group. They were impressed. They were even more taken with Shenson's suggestion that Richard Lester, who had worked on the TV series *The Goon Show,* should direct them in the project. *The Goon Show* was a favourite of all four Beatles, especially John Lennon. The final piece of the jigsaw fell into place when both Shenson and Lester proposed Alun Owen as scriptwriter for the film.

At a get-together in London just days before the Dublin concert, it was suggested that Owen should travel to Dublin to get a feel for the Beatles' frantic lives. Producer Walter Shenson said, "I told Alun that we wanted to do a comedy and I thought it might be good to do an exaggerated day in the life of the Beatles. Alun asked me what was a day in the life of the Beatles? I said, 'I haven't a clue but go up to Dublin, move in with them – they are playing there in a theatre – and come back and tell us.'" The visit, in effect, allowed Owen a fly-on-the-wall view of Beatlemania, especially the hysterical behaviour of girls. His subsequent script became the basis of the groundbreaking film classic *A Hard Day's Night.*

"I was prepared for the usual pop singers," Owen, who had also travelled from London that morning, remarked. "Many are nice people but have nothing inside. It's very difficult to communicate with them. I discovered at once that the Beatles aren't like that. I knew they were my kind of people. They knew the streets I was brought up in. We shared the same kind of humour. They have a mocking but kindly outlook on life. This means that most of their conversation is a send-up.

"I hardly left the boys. I stayed with them hour after hour, standing quietly in the wings watching them work, or sitting in their hotel rooms, absorbing their personalities. As soon as we got to know each other, which was remarkably easy, they began to call me Al. Then came the send-up. It was 'Make way for Al, the distinguished author and playwright,' delivered with mock bows. After the hypocrisy that goes in so many stage circles, I dig that stuff. Underneath all their semi-cynical send-up, there's an honesty which I hope they never lose."

Following check-in, Alun Owen joined the Beatles for afternoon tea in their suites. With the arrival of room service, Owen got his first introduction to the madness surrounding the Beatles. "She was a parlour maid," he later recalled regarding the young lady who entered the room. "She had brought in a tray of coffee and cakes in a nice, normal, sensible fashion, walking across the room and setting down the tray. Suddenly, she flung off her cap, dropped to her knees and cried, 'I'm going to pray for you, boys! I'm going to pray for you!' They weren't shocked. They didn't laugh. They weren't embarrassed. Paul just helped her to her feet and talked to her as if they had been nicely introduced at a party."

The drama over, the food consumed and the meeting concluded, the Beatles headed back downstairs and entered the ballroom. There, for the purpose of recording an interview with the group, a Telefís Éireann outside broadcast unit had already been installed. The national broadcaster and the hotel had a friendly working relationship. Less than two years earlier, on New Year's Eve 1961, the station had launched its new television service in the beautiful wood-floored ballroom. As snow fell, cameras outside captured revellers celebrating the event. This time the hotel ballroom was booked to accommodate the Beatles, who arrived ahead of schedule.

"I wandered down towards the ballroom," says broadcaster Ken Stewart, who was contracted by the *Evening Press* to write a colour piece on the visit and who dropped into the Gresham to check out the action. "I remember noticing a lady sitting on a seat nearby. Nobody seemed to notice her because of the excitement of the Beatles and maybe because in a busy hotel there's plenty to notice otherwise. She was Gene Tierney, the

American actress. She looked composed and glamorous sitting there.

"I was there to see what was happening generally around the hotel and I went into the ballroom. The ballroom was empty except for TV cameras. While I was there, the four Beatles wandered in. They walked around making jokes in a light sort of way to each other, as they were known for at the time. They were just being the Beatles. They were moving around and restless, looking at the cameras. They were chatting among themselves. I didn't want to intrude. It was a private moment for them. They were ahead of some appointment, by the look of it. They were checking things out. I just watched them. I didn't go over and I didn't say anything to them. They didn't say anything to me. The moment passed and I left."

Paul Russell and his Telefís Éireann crew eventually arrived at the ballroom to record the prearranged sketch with the Beatles. The fee agreed with NEMS Enterprises for the appearance was £5. The recording was to be inserted in a forthcoming edition of *The Showband Show*, which was broadcast prime time. The series showcased Ireland's top showband stars along with beat groups and visiting acts. On air since the previous June, the programme was a top-of-the-ratings success. Among the visiting acts featured were Chubby Checker, the Springfields, Johnny Cash, the Searchers, Eden Kane, Brian Poole and the Tremeloes and Brenda Lee.

The Showband Show was frequently condemned for the quality of the live performances and for the miming done by visiting acts. It was also criticised because girls in the audience danced together, ignoring the boys at the back. Russell, however, had his defenders. "Will you please stop knocking Paul Russell around," columnist 'Steve' demanded in the October 1963 edition of *Spotlight*. "He's doing a first-class job. Remember this! He's the one who started this TV series, and is also responsible for the guest artists who appear on it. And when Brian Poole, Gerry and the Pacemakers, Jimmy Justice, etc., come over here, he brings them in." Certainly, when it came to media coverage, Russell had it all wrapped up.

Paul Russell's interview with the Beatles, conducted on the stage of the ballroom, consisted of the group's usual inanities, with lots of wisecracks, witty remarks and manic activity. "The whole thing was a disaster," says Russell. "It was very giddy. Ringo got on my back. John took my handkerchief and my tie off and tied them around my neck. And, of course, I had the mike and I was trying to do a voiceover. Only McCartney stayed out of it. They were going to mime but they didn't. This was their way. It wasn't the greatest thing I ever did. I did better interviews with Johnny Cash and Brenda Lee and everybody else."

Watching the interview was a stills photographer from the *RTV Guide*, the listings magazine owned by Telefís Éireann which later became the *RTÉ Guide*. Photographer Roy Bedell had arrived at the hotel at one o'clock to shoot promotion stills for the forthcoming transmission. "My name was down at the door of the Gresham but when I arrived there I was told that I had already gone in," Bedell remembers. "Someone had done an impersonation of me. I know who it was. He was a freelance man who had been turning up around town. He saw me inside and he had to apologise.

"The Beatles had come down to the ballroom, which was down the back of the hotel, to do their piece for *The Showband Show*. They looked like four lads who needed a haircut. They were quite exuberant lads. They just ran around the place. It was one of those lively, bouncy things. They were great at banter. Yet it was hard to get more than a sentence out of one before one of the others interrupted. They were just like wound-up springs. If I remember rightly, mostly what they did onstage was to run from left to right with Paul Russell in the middle trying to intercept them. They were quite unruly in a nice way.

"I was busy trying to get some shots with this ancient

camera of mine. It was a £30 Mamiyaflex, which I got from my father. Telefís Éireann was only getting set up at the time and we were mostly using our own equipment. I asked them for a few poses and they were all, 'Oh, no, we have no time.' One of their tricks was to say, 'I'm sorry, there's no time for pictures.' Yet they would do any stunt that you asked them to do. This was one of their little quirks. They used to arrive at theatres in a very plain van. They would park outside the stage door and run in. The thing was they would never park very close to the stage door. This was part of their gimmick. They wanted to be seen to be rushing and running. But everybody got enough time.

"It was my idea to get a shot of them with the television camera, to incorporate Telefís Éireann. They were, at that stage, still very much on the up and were very co-operative. I just got a few shots, one with the television camera and a few others including one of them with Paul Russell. They were very nice. I was there on my own for about 20 minutes at the most and then I was gone."

Shortly after Roy Bedell's departure, the Beatles left the Gresham and made their way to the Adelphi to prepare for the shows. "I was in the kitchen, where we were starting our preparation for dinner," says Charlie Lyons, who was working as a hotel commis chef. "Suddenly, the Beatles passed by. There wasn't any security, just the four Beatles and a couple of managers with them. We were sweating away in the kitchen at the time. They went through a big, long passageway out the back of the hotel, down around the cellar and the kitchen areas. They went out into Thomas Lane and headed off to the Adelphi."

Given the threat of a build-up of fans, the Beatles' four o'clock departure from the Gresham to the Adelphi was cutting it tight. Already, Dublin was abuzz with excitement. Crowds were beginning to form. The reason was simple – at the Adelphi the management had cancelled that night's regular feature.

Peter Sellers would be back in his role as a country vicar in the satirical comedy *Heavens Above!* the following evening. But tonight, for one night only, at half past six and nine o'clock, the Beatles would be cramming them in.

THE ADELPHI CINEMA

Just after four o'clock the Beatles arrived at the Adelphi for a press conference and to prepare for the shows. A small group of fans, waiting outside, began screaming. Gardaí held them in check as the Beatles were bundled inside. Attracted by the commotion, more fans came rushing from other locations. Mostly young girls, they pressed themselves against the cinema doors, attempting to gain entry. An estimated 15 Gardaí kept them at bay.

"I saw the Beatles going into the Adelphi," says Joe Nolan who, as a 20-year-old apprentice in Arnotts, was working close to the rear of the building. "They smuggled them in the Prince's Street entrance while everybody was out the front waiting for them to arrive. People suddenly started shouting, 'There's the Beatles.' The door opened and they were gone. There were about ten or twelve people there. Other people, mainly girls, came running around and autograph hunters went up to the door. They waited and waited and waited. But they were gone inside before anyone realised what had happened."

The Beatles were welcomed to the Adelphi by manager Harry Lush. "He was a very fine man, a very handsome individual with a very relaxed, easygoing manner. He was a fairly laid-back guy," is how Noel Rennick, Assistant Secretary of Adelphi-Carlton Ltd, describes him. A respected and well-known figure

53

on the Dublin business scene, Harry had transformed the Adelphi into one of the leading entertainment venues in Dublin. John Wayne and John Ford used its projector to view rushes of *The Quiet Man*. Actors like Ronald Reagan, Noel Purcell, Van Johnson and Van Heflin paid visits.

With a combined cinema and catering staff in excess of 100, the Adelphi had taken over as the city's premier live music venue since the closure of the Theatre Royal in June 1962. It had a ready-made stage and adequate backstage facilities. The stage was elevated high enough off the ground to be safe from the fans. Its house capacity of 2,304 was regarded as ideal to accommodate demand for a Beatles' concert. Just as important, the cinema had already hosted live performances with considerable success.

Among those who appeared at the Adelphi were Ella Fitzgerald, Marlene Dietrich, Louis Armstrong and, later on, Beatles' contemporaries such as Gene Pitney, Roy Orbison, Bob Dylan, Val Doonican, the Bachelors, Cilla Black, the Rolling Stones, Tom Jones and Cliff Richard. It was, in effect, the Point Depot of its day. Its restaurant, The Hideout, advertised itself as 'Dublin's luxury barbecue rendezvous'. A popular meeting-place in the city-centre, it was known far and wide. Regular customers included authors Brendan Behan and Benedict Kiely, poet Patrick Kavanagh and broadcaster Eamonn Andrews.

The highlight of Adelphi manager Harry Lush's career was the arrival of the Beatles. A former schoolteacher and an expert at Irish, he rated them highly and regarded them as the sort of boys he would have liked in his class. "Harry always said that, from the moment he met them, the Beatles were gentlemen, very nice, pleasant, easy and great fun," according to Norman Lush, the last remaining member of the five Lush brothers. "They were not a bit spoilt. They had charm and were one of the nicest groups he ever encountered. They were mannerly and unassuming. They called him Mister Lush. He was most impressed."

The group headed upstairs to the boardroom, which was located at the front of the cinema, overlooking Middle Abbey Street. Journalists, photographers and guests were already assembled there, awaiting their arrival. Light refreshments were provided. Admission was restricted to those with official passes. "What Harry Lush did, by way of giving people press badges, was he sent one of his staff around to Easons on the day of the Beatles' shows," recalls journalist Éanna Brophy. "They came back with a paper bag full of badges that said things like 'Treasurer' or 'Steward'. I think I got 'Treasurer'. When you compare it to the range of passes today! Once you had one of these badges on, the ushers let you in and out of the cinema."

Like other Beatles' press conferences, the event in the Adelphi was a mad, chaotic affair. The boardroom was stuffed with people who weren't invited. One fan, masquerading as a journalist, argued at the door that she was a junior reporter with the 'National Syndicate of Papers'. Aged 16, she was granted admission. A copyboy with the *Evening Press* by the name of Donal McCann stepped in for a reporter who was sick. McCann, who wrote a colour piece describing the night, eventually became one of Ireland's most celebrated stage and screen actors.

Poet Patrick Kavanagh, who disliked the Beatles, wandered about the room, telling stories of the time he was 22. A journalist described how the Beatles sat or stood about, "their hair down over their sunken eyes like African thatched huts." Someone quipped, "Aithníonn ciaróg ciaróg eile," which directly translates as "one beetle recognises another beetle" but indirectly means "it takes one to know one," whereupon Ringo looked up uncomprehendingly from a record sleeve he was signing. Flash bulbs popped. Strange Liverpool accents intermingled with Irish brogues. And so it was that the most bizarre press conference in Adelphi history proceeded.

"Paul McCartney was definitely the PR man," says Éanna Brophy. "He was charming everybody. He was cracking all these *Goon Show* jokes. I was in a group asking him questions. You'd ask him, 'What do you think of Harold Wilson?' He'd say, 'We are just good friends.' I remember asking him, 'What's the name of the new album?' He went, '*With The Beatles*. It wasn't our idea.' Obviously, at that stage they didn't have power over titles and things like that. *With The Beatles* had clearly been wished on them by EMI.

"I asked John Lennon, 'What's the difference between rock 'n roll and rhythm 'n blues?' I think he looked at me slightly pityingly and said, 'Rhythm 'n blues is black.' I also asked him, 'Is it not frustrating for you up there onstage with all these girls screaming and roaring and you know they can't even hear you?' I think it was a bit of prescience on my part as they eventually stopped touring because of that. John Lennon gave me some PR answer and said, 'As long as we're entertaining them!'

"When the Beatles posed for photographers, they were so sharp. They were saying, 'Do you want a four-column photograph or a one-column pose?' If you wanted a four-column shot they would put their arms and legs out and go 'dah, daah.' If you wanted a single column, they'd actually put their heads so that one head was on top of the other. I thought, 'God, they are impressive, how media-savvy they are.' There were all these older photographers there. Some might have even been about 30! I think the photographers, who were hardchaws, a bit blasé and not ready to be overawed by anybody, were highly impressed."

Among those infiltrating the press conference was 16-year-old Lynn Geldof who was accompanied by her brother Bob, aged 12. Bob later became famous with the Boomtown Rats. "My pal and myself, and Bob, crashed the press conference," Lynn explains. "The father of a friend of mine at school worked in the newspaper business and he was assigned to be there. We were all madly jealous because my friend was going to be brought in with him. We had no such luck. However, a pal and my brother and I were in the baying horde outside the door before the first concert. I had the brother by the hand. There was some sort of a side entrance that I spotted. It was a sort of porch entryway for bins and whatever else. Somehow we leaned against it and the door gave. I looked in and turned around to the others and said, 'Come on.' It led to a staircase. We went up and up and up until we could hear the clinking of glasses. We saw the pressroom. In we burst and we were completely and utterly freaked-out with excitement. There they were!

"I think Ringo had a pink check shirt on, a small check, much smaller than gingham even. This was completely outré really to be wearing a pink shirt at all. It was either policeman's blue or white at the time. I liked the vibe of George Harrison the most of all of them. I was in a state of angst and guilt because I felt I had jumped ship from the Shadows to the Beatles. The guilt was consuming me. I was reassuring myself that it was alright. I said, 'They're a great bunch as well.'

"I got three autographs. I got them on the *Please Please Me* LP, which my uncle had bought me for my birthday. I didn't get John Lennon's. He was doing an interview. I remember he had one leg up on a bench or a chair and was just standing there in the pinstripe. I went to all the others. They kept saying, 'Quiet, quiet, you'll get thrown out of here.' They were really sweet. Eventually, a bouncer came over after what seemed like ten minutes but it was probably two. We were turfed out. We came back down the long and winding stairs and out into the crowd and went to the concert. It was just fantastic. We couldn't believe it."

Although the Beatles were initially besieged for their autographs and accosted by all sorts of stragglers, order was eventually restored with the ejection of most of the non-press. Returning to the business of the day, McCartney was, as ever, the star of the show. He was pleasant, polite, considerate and always respectful. No matter how ill-informed his questioners were, he engaged them with courtesy and deference. Ringo, as the recent replacement for Pete Best, felt awkward especially when asked about the group's early years. He presented himself instead as affable, agreeable and good natured. George hated the limelight and resented intrusions to his privacy, although when interviewed he was serious and informed. Despite being present for the photographs, Éanna Brophy observed that he "made himself scarce" for the subsequent chat with the press. John was the time bomb; edgy, freethinking, sometimes intolerant and capable of savaging a journalist he disliked or believed to be ill-informed.

"The most cynical person would have been Lennon – cynical and a little bit of a conniver," according to Paul Russell, who stayed close to the Beatles at the press-call. "Lennon had an inferiority complex. George Harrison was the quiet one, not really a great personality but very charming. He was probably the better looking of the lot of them at the time. He was always conscious, like Paul, of the public. Ringo was not the greatest drummer but he was a good bluffer and he was popular. The most gentlemanly and the most businesslike was Paul. Of all the Beatles he made a lot of sense to me. He always had a smile and I would say he was a little bit of a dreamer. I needed a friend and in the other three I couldn't find one. It is Paul who has always stuck in my memory to this day as the one most likely to succeed.

"This was a bunch of guys from the Cavern. These were kids. The word is 'naïve'. They were frightened. They were very nervous, very giddy. One of the things I noticed about them was that they really had to be chaperoned. Derek Taylor, who became Epstein's assistant and the group's press officer, had a terrible job. He was filling in for Epstein in Dublin. It wasn't that important a gig but then all the gigs at that time were not that important to them. If you asked them where they were going they'd say, 'We're not sure.'

"It was like a homecoming thing for them. There was a lot of Irish in them. They talked like I was a newfound friend and Ireland was their favourite country. That was genuine. They were down-to-earth kids. However, they had a little bit of snootiness that I noticed in Dublin. A couple of times I was called by Lennon, 'Hey, Paddy.' It pissed me. This wasn't the most likeable guy in the world. Lennon was not my favourite, by any means."

Outside, word spread that the Beatles had arrived at the Adelphi. Numbers swelled, with those turning up for the first concert being joined by ticketless fans hoping to spot the Beatles as they arrived for the show. Over and over they chanted, "We want the Beatles." With eyes fixed on the upstairs windows, they hoped that one or two Beatles might emerge to give them a wave. "A photographer who was there had hair like me, which was starting to grow a little bit longer," journalist Éanna Brophy says. "I had naturally got my hair into a fringe and so had he. I remember opening the curtain at one stage and we looked out quickly and got girls to scream down on the street. I think the Gardaí on the street sent word in asking would people get away from the window."

The press conference bounced along at a madcap pace. Asked about his hobbies, Ringo replied, "Girls, drums and cars." His name, he explained, was derived from the rings on his fingers. He complained about difficulties signing his name because of the two rings on his right hand, one of which was "the size of a small apple," *The Irish Times* reported. "Yes, we like to hear the kids screaming. It makes us feel good," he agreed. He was, nevertheless, at a loss to explain what made the Beatles so popular.

"Someone told me I could get an Irish McCartney tartan," Paul said. "Did you ever hear the like?" He was unaware of their earnings although up to £2,000 had been paid for one night's performance. What car does Paul drive? "None," he replied, "thanks to Mr Marples I've been had-up three times for speeding," referring to his recent driving ban and fine for exceeding the speed limit. How long might the good times last? "It could end tomorrow," he said, "but I hope it won't."

Paul Russell, who was observing the press briefing, was less than enthused. "I was disappointed," Russell remarks. "There wasn't the enthusiasm that I had or that Arthur Howes had. I noticed at the press conference people saying, 'I never actually heard of them but what exactly is this all about?' It's a feature of the Irish people. I was disappointed that we didn't get that much real press. When I say real press I mean, 'Could I do an interview with Paul McCartney? Could I sit down with him to see about his background?' No. It was, 'What exactly are they doing here?' They asked questions about the riots and stuff. The press conference was a disaster."

Meanwhile, Harry Lush had invited a few close business contacts to the cinema to meet with the Beatles. Among them was Michael Ball, assistant manager of the Carlton, which was located just around the corner in O'Connell Street. The Carlton, which was the sister cinema of the Adelphi, had assigned staff to help with the pressures of the night. Harry and Michael had their photograph taken with the group. Paul McCartney once more played the charmer and spokesman, chatting freely while John and George looked uninterested. Ringo, as ever, was amiable.

Lush had also invited Bunny Carr, the popular radio and television presenter famous for programmes like *Quicksilver* and *Teen Talk*. He turned down the offer. "It was my heartbreak that I didn't meet the Beatles," Carr says. "Harry Lush and I used to train in Trinity College every day at lunchtime. We ran around the cricket pitch there. Harry asked me, 'Do you want to come down? There's this group called the Beatles coming.' I said, 'No.' I was probably chasing a girl or something, which I thought was a lot more important."

For scriptwriter Alun Owen, what he witnessed that afternoon at the Adelphi was ink for his pen. Owen attended the press conference to watch the Beatles, observe their dialogue and mannerisms, and get a feel for the frantic environment they worked in. He was himself instantly recognised by the press, who recalled him from his recent play at the Dublin Theatre Festival. Admitting that he was working on a film script with the Beatles, he described them as, "A great bunch of lads. Why not? We all come from the same area of Liverpool." Asked why he was scripting a film for, of all people, the Beatles, he answered, "Because I happen to like the Beatles. I hope this film will be like nothing that has been done before. At any rate, I am enjoying myself thoroughly working on it."

Owen was accompanied to the press conference by Cathal O'Shannon, reporter with *The Irish Times*, who knew him well. "Alun was a friend of my parents," O'Shannon points out. "Because of him, we had more access to the Beatles than most of the other papers. He was a nice man. I remember going up with him to meet the Beatles and drinking lemonade and Coca-Cola at the press conference. The Beatles were very pleasant. The one who intrigued me was Paul McCartney. He was the one who I felt closest to. He was extremely nice. Lennon struck me as a tricky sort of character. He was very cynical, whereas McCartney was doing his utmost to be pleasant. Otherwise, Alun Owen was just doing his research and I stuck with him."

Owen was astonished by the pressures the Beatles faced. Two press conferences, two photo-calls, two TV interviews, the trip from the airport to the hotel, check-in and a rendezvous with an Irish showband star – and only four and a half hours had passed! There also was the signing of autographs and the pressures of dealing with or avoiding the fans. And the concerts hadn't even begun! That pattern had been replicated the previous day Wednesday in Northampton, Tuesday in Slough, Monday in London and on the three days before that in Leeds, Sheffield and Cheltenham. The day prior to Cheltenham they had returned from their concert tour of Sweden.

"We went right from the hotel to a press reception, straight to the theatre and at no time were they actually allowed to enjoy what was supposed to be success," Owen reflected. "They live in a series of boxes all the time, a hotel room box, a car box and a dressing-room box. They can't move away from these boxes in case they are recognised and mobbed. I thought, 'God, this goes on every day of their life.' There's a price to pay for that sort of success. You see them running from place to place doing things but at the same time being in peril ... and the only freedom they ever actually get is when they start to play music and their faces light up and they're happy ... but mostly they are confined.

"I happen to like the Beatles. They haven't a hard-shell star quality. If their road manager is a bit late, they put microphones onstage and arrange the sets themselves. It doesn't occur to them to do anything else. The thing about the boys is this great joy of being alive that they put across. They're so ebullient it knocks me out. They aren't a sleazy image of pimply adolescence. These boys really live. They swing. They're with it all the way."

Just yards away, in the auditorium, preparations were in train for the imminent shows. Equipment belonging to the Gael Linn newsreel *Amharc Éireann* was put in place. The weekly Irish-language cinematic gazette was modelled on *Pathé News* and broadcast in cinemas all over Ireland. Up to the establishment of Telefís Éireann, the newsreels – for the most part distributed by British-owned Rank Film Distributors – were understandably popular. They were the only way most ordinary people could see moving pictures of the week's major events.

"I was with the Gael Linn newsreel at the time," says Morgan O'Sullivan, who later became a broadcaster and film-maker. "Val Ennis was the cameraman and I was kind of the assistant. We went into the Adelphi to cover the Beatles, whom I had very little knowledge of. I drove in using Jim Mulkerns' car, which was a beautiful white Opel. He was the head guy in the newsreel. He always took great pride in his car. It was in pristine condition. I parked it right outside the door, at about four or five o'clock in the afternoon.

"We took all the equipment in and we were setting up the

cameras and sound and all the rest. After we had finished, I went out to move the car. I couldn't get outside the door. Harry Lush said, 'You'll get killed if you go out. You'll get trampled to death.'

"I stood there looking out and saw that all of these girls in high-heeled shoes, stilettos almost, were standing on the roof and on the bonnet of the car. They were dancing and all the rest of it. The car was dished. We couldn't get out at all so we went back in and worked throughout the concerts. We had to abandon the car outside. We got busy.

"I remember when I came out after the second show the street looked like a battle zone. It was phenomenal the amount of rubbish and stuff on the street. The car was still there but it was wrecked. It did drive but that was about it. I had to give it back to Jim Mulkerns the next day. He was horrified. At least, he was so interested in the story that he was happy we got it. God love him, it was a terrible thing to do to his car."

Elsewhere in the auditorium, the cinema's lighting system was checked for the forthcoming shows. Doing the lighting was Tommy Nolan who, unfortunately, got into a bit of a spat with John Lennon. "Before the show I went to the toilet up the backstage," Nolan remembers. "It was upstairs, close to where the Beatles were. There was only one toilet in that particular area. While I was in the toilet, the next thing there was banging on the door. I said, 'I will be out in a minute.' I didn't know who it was, hadn't a clue. Whoever it was wasn't happy with that. He was banging on the door. He was chipping on the door and all that. I finished my business and came out and it was John Lennon standing there.

"I said, 'You are very impatient.' 'Hold on,' he said, 'do you know who I am?' That was the worst thing he could have said to me. I had met them all. I said, 'Do you know who *I* am? I'm doing the lighting here.' So we had a few words. I told him where to go. He wasn't being exactly polite at the time either. I went about my business and he went about his. But I met up with Lennon later on and we had a laugh about it. When they were pulling down the Adelphi, a big fan of the Beatles asked me could I get that door for him and I did."

Also gearing up for the night were the spotlight operators located in the projection room at the back of the theatre. "There were two spots," explains Tony Foran, aged 15, who was a first-year trainee cinema projectionist in the Adelphi's sister cinema in Dun Laoghaire – also called the Adelphi – but who was helping out on the night. "When a film was being shown, we used to use the spots to highlight the sales girls during the interval between the supporting feature and the main feature. The girls would stand on either side of the stage. When live shows were on, we used them to spot the artistes. They had fantastic big portholes for the spots, so we had a great view looking down on the stage.

"Two people worked the spots and two others kept an eye on the carbon arcs. Then there were the two apprentices – Brian who was the apprentice in Middle Abbey Street and who was called 'Big Adelphi', and me from the Adelphi in Dun Laoghaire who was called 'Little Adelphi'. We would listen for the cue from the lighting monitor – pink, yellow or whatever. You had different colours for different songs. For a faster song like 'She Loves You' you might have a flicker with magenta and for a slow song you might have a dark blue. We'd tell them what we heard on the monitor. The guy that was maintaining the carbon would then drop in the colour. It was like the old slide-lamps years ago. Everything was manual in those days."

The Beatles Show crew likewise prepared for the imminent shows. Central to the action was Neil Aspinall, a former trainee accountant and Beatles' driver who was eventually promoted to road manager. Responsible for setting up the Beatles' gear in Ireland, few would have predicted that Aspinall would one day become head of Apple Corps. Aspinall was assisted by Mal Evans, a 6 ft 2 in telephone engineer who was hired as a second roadie. Mal would later add his voice to 'Yellow Submarine', blow through a hair comb on 'Lady Madonna', work the alarm clock on 'A Day In The Life', hit the anvil on 'Maxwell's Silver Hammer', play the tambourine on 'Dear Prudence' and contribute to the brass on 'Helter Skelter'.

Programme sellers cut open boxes full of specially-designed, metallic silver souvenir booklets which made history by promoting and selling endorsed Beatles products. An official Beatles sweater – 'high fashioned black polo sweater in 100% botany wool' – was promoted on page ten. Available by mail order from 'Weldons of Peckham', the ad promised a 'top-quality two-tone Beatle badge' and guaranteed 'precision-finished embroidery' in gold and red. Selling for 35/-, the sweater was upmarket. The Weldons – Raymond and Peter, who were Epstein's cousins – sold 15,000 of the sweaters worldwide including in Ireland. The programme also promoted high-quality Nempix photographs of the Beatles, Billy J Kramer and Gerry and the Pacemakers, all part of Epstein's stable of stars.

As the pace picked up, a few special guests came to visit. In Dublin, three young fans had the honour. Phyllis and Josephine Tyrrell, aged 16 and 15 respectively, along with a friend Nuala Mullen, aged 15, were provided by Brian Epstein with a special introductory letter inviting them backstage prior to the first show. They were also given free tickets. The access was arranged by a third Tyrrell sister living in England, who had contacts in the music business. "This is great," Josephine was reported as saying in a press interview preceding the shows. "We are really looking forward to meeting them. They are the greatest." The girls arrived at half past four.

"My legs were like jelly at the thought of meeting them," says Josephine Tyrrell today. "I had been up half the night talking to my mother because I couldn't sleep. My mother was saying, 'Don't be so silly, they are only ordinary guys so don't be getting yourself worked up.' But we loved the Beatles and I loved Paul from day one so I was in bits." Older sister Phyllis picks up the story: "I was working in a butcher's at the time and my sister and her friend were working in a bakery. We skived off work for the day. We went into town in the morning to buy clothes. I bought a black leather skirt and a jumper and put them on at home. Unfortunately, the black leather skirt looked stupid afterwards. We went into town, by bus, to the Adelphi and knocked on the stage door at about half past four. We were then taken backstage to where the four Beatles were."

Josephine adds: "We were telling them that they were very popular in Ireland but they knew that already because every one of their records was a hit and everyone bought them, including ourselves. I can't remember much else of what they said because I was so jelly-kneed. But I remember the real Liverpudlian accent which they had in those days. When I hear Paul talking now on the television, I don't think there's much of it left." Phyllis continues: "Their gear was already set up. I saw the drums and I said to my sister, 'Come on, we'll play the drums.' But they said, 'No, you won't.' I then said, 'Show me how to play.' So Ringo gave me the sticks and showed me how to play. I just banged away for a little while. There was a photographer there and he took a picture of me playing the drums with the Beatles. My sister and her friend were also in the shot. It was in the paper the following day.

"We were also brought into a little room nearby where we had tea and biscuits. It was just the three of us and the Beatles, with one other man. Eventually, two guys called them and they had to go off to prepare for the show. We were then brought down through the lobby and came back in for the first concert. It was like a dream. We were the only ones in Ireland at the time to get to meet them and to have that sort of access. They were lovely to us, very friendly. They shook our hands goodbye and gave us a couple of kisses. It was fabulous, unforgettable. It was one of the biggest moments of my life."

Between five o'clock and five-thirty the early-evening darkness descended on Middle Abbey Street and the crowds grew dramatically. Large groups of concert-goers, there for the half past six show, assembled outside the cinema. They clutched their tickets as if they were gold-dust. Priced at 6/6, 8/6 and 10/6, the full complement of 4,608 seats had gone on sale almost four weeks in advance at the Adelphi box office. Queues had built up from early morning, with the box office opening at one o'clock lunchtime and closing at seven that evening. "No tickets exchanged nor money refunded," was written on the stubs. It was a most unnecessary condition of sale.

"I had queued for almost eight hours to get my ticket," says Sandra Grant, aged 16. "I must have gone into town on the eight o'clock bus and I started queuing outside Easons in O'Connell Street. I wound my way down to the Adelphi. I shuffled along with everybody. It being autumn, I remember being warmly dressed and having nothing with me to eat or drink. It was the first time anything like this had happened in Dublin. It was all very polite. People just stood quietly, moving along. I paid 6/6 each for two tickets, one for my friend and one for myself. I had been saving since it was publicised in the paper. My friend was willing to go but she didn't want to put in the slog. We were up in the gods for the 6/6. I was thrilled. I floated home."

City relations helped country cousins and bought tickets. "A first cousin of my father's was a buyer in Clerys," John Olohan, who lived down country, remembers. "She went down when the tickets went on sale and bought me one for the front row of the balcony. I had relations to stay with in Dublin so I decided to take off from school. I planned to say nothing. Of course, when the time came someone at school asked, 'Where is Olohan today?' 'He's gone to see the Beatles,' some little shite told him. I was in trouble."

Influential friends were brought into play in the scramble for seats. "Harry Lush, who was the manager of the Adelphi, was a fantastic man and he taught me Irish," according to Gillian Freedman. "He gave me Irish grinds. I have a funny feeling that was maybe how we got tickets. Another friend who was with me was doing Irish grinds with him too. He was a brilliant man and we did well in the Irish. He got me through my Junior Cert and Leaving Cert. But I suspect he also got us in to see the Beatles."

Supplies of tickets turned up in the strangest of ways. "A crowd of us used to hang out in the Coffee Inn in South Anne Street," says Dave Pennefather, who was a 16-year-old schoolboy but soon-to-be-member of a band called the Kult. "We were all sitting there despairing about how to get to see the Beatles. There was a wonderful character around at the time called Randy White, who was a man about town. He was an amazing drummer, a very jazz-influenced drummer. We all knew him. He arrived in one day, out of the blue, in a big coat. He came down to the table and he took out of his pocket a wedge of tickets. In his great voice he said, 'Anybody want to buy some tickets for the Beatles?' He was descended upon. I got a seat in the stalls for the first show, in the third row from the front. It couldn't have been better. They were great seats and we were all there in a row."

A remarkable number of musicians from bands like the Chessmen, the future Greenbeats, Skid Row and Thin Lizzy also booked seats for the shows. "You had to go to the Adelphi concert," argues Brush Shiels, who was playing with Dickie Rock's brother, Brian, in a band called The Boys. "If you were in the entertainment business or in a big band, a little band, a showband, anything, you had to see the Beatles. This is where it was going to go. Their songs were very intricate compared to what I had been listening to, like Elvis and the Shadows. They also had a great way of playing with that Chuck Berry driving beat. Up to then, the only harmonies I was used to were the Everly Brothers or maybe the Shadows behind Cliff on 'Bachelor Boy'. But the Beatles' harmonies were terrific. It was certainly a big night ahead. For a lot of people it would change their lives, especially when you were that young and you knew that if you worked at it you could be up there too."

Interspersed among the fans were ticketless young teenagers, with no hope of entry, who had turned up to see the Beatles' arrival or to catch a glimpse of their idols. Mostly girls, they moved between the front of the cinema and the stage door. They were noisy, boisterous – some even hysterical – as they focused on the upper floors where they expected the Beatles to be. They hoped that the Beatles might wave or perhaps a signed photo-card would be dropped from the windows above. If they were lucky, one or two band members might emerge to sign autographs or chat.

"I remember the crowd milling around in the lane at the back of the Adelphi," says Sandra Grant. "There must have been a couple of hundred people there. Everybody had high hopes that they would come to one of the windows above. Maybe, as Gerry and the Pacemakers did, they might throw down photographs into the crowd and there would be a wild scrum. I remember we were speaking to a policeman who was on duty. He would have been an older policeman. We kind of edged in beside him for security because there was a bit of jostling. He was scandalised that the young people of Dublin were out screaming and roaring and shouting. Unfortunately, nobody appeared at the windows."

Catherine Cahill, who came from the nearby flats in 'Monto', had better luck. Aged 16 and from a family of 12 children, she couldn't afford the price of a ticket but she did get to see the Beatles. "We were so mad about the Beatles that we just had to see them," Catherine remarks. "There were three of us went together, two friends and myself. We had the hair backcombed and the short miniskirts and the plastered pan-stick on the face and the black eyes. I had all of that, dyed blonde hair and all. But we hadn't the money to go to the concert. I was working in Jacobs at the time, earning something like 15/- a week. The cheapest ticket was almost half my weekly wage. We could never afford to go even to the pictures. If we wanted to go to the pictures we didn't have to pay, we knew how to get in. One of us would go in and then we'd open the side door and let the rest in. Or we'd climb up a drainpipe. We knew the place well.

"We hung out at the front of the Adelphi. The whole street was packed. Eventually, we decided to break in. We climbed up the drainpipe at the back and we got in the windows. We had done it before, to go to the pictures. But we couldn't go down into the cinema because it wasn't a picture, where the lights would be out. It was very active. We snuck into this room. We couldn't put on the lights in case we'd be spotted. We heard someone coming so we hid behind two boxes and a chair. Lo and behold, the four Beatles and somebody else came in!

"It was breathtaking. My top lip was going. One of them walked to the window and looked out. I could swear it was Ringo. He talked about the number of people outside. We said nothing. They never knew we were there. Then they talked about going for something to eat so they left. That's when we scarpered out. They never saw us. They would never have caught us anyway because we were too fast for them and we knew the run of the place. We then came out and I don't know how I didn't fall off the pole coming down.

"After a while, we were showing the other kids the window where we had been. There were these black railings around the window, maybe for plants or for standing out in. The next thing, the window opened and two of the Beatles – Paul McCartney and I think it was John Lennon – looked out and waved down at us. That's when I realised it was most likely the dressing-room we had been in. Then I climbed up one of those big poles with kind of wings coming out of them that held the lamps. I sat on top of it with my legs hanging. I was level with the window trying to see them but I couldn't. We eventually gave up when the show started and all the doors were locked."

Frank Grimes, aged 16, who didn't have a ticket, also recalls waiting outside: "I remember running down the laneway near Prince's Street because girls would shout, 'The Beatles are here,'

'They're coming out,' 'They've stepped out.' We'd run around to see if we could catch sight of them. But they were never there. There was loads of action, with girls screaming and getting excited. We were running back and forth. It was just exuberance, youth.

"My friend 'Moggy' Collins and I weren't able to afford tickets. I was a messenger-boy in Dublin at the time. We had gone down mainly to see the crowds. I was a great Beatles' fan and used to sing all the songs on my messenger bike. Eventually, we were up against the doors of the Adelphi and they just gave way. A whole gang of us found ourselves in the foyer. 'Moggy' and I looked at each other and made a beeline to the gents upstairs. 'Moggy' had the nous to ask a fellow if we could have the stubs of his tickets. He gave them to us. And that's how we got in. We stood at the very back, upstairs in the balcony, with lots and lots of people. Eventually, ushers came along the back row turfing people out. I remember saying, 'Look, I've got a sore knee, I can't sit down. There's my ticket.' He allowed us to stay. So we saw the Beatles and it was unbelievable."

Photographer Pat Maxwell also witnessed the build-up of fans outside the front of the theatre. "There were a few thousand people there and a row of about 20 cops holding them back," he remembers. "It was full from side to side, going back about 40 feet, tightly crammed with people all screaming and shouting. I got a great shot of the crowd. I walked upstairs and I went over to the windows that overlooked Abbey Street. I opened one of the windows, leaned out and took a shot. Just as I did, a girl broke through the ranks of the thin line of police and she was racing madly to get to the door. A cop turned around and grabbed her coat. There was this wonderful picture of her with her clothes fully stretched out and the cop holding onto her. It was a marvellous picture, which summed up the excitement. But it was still not what I wanted."

Back in the dressing-room, the Beatles locked themselves in and prepared for the shows. A rare interruption came from the selfsame photographer Pat Maxwell, who had chanced his way backstage to secure an exclusive shot of the group. In a masterful piece of opportunism, he snapped the Beatles drinking tea. This time, "it was what I wanted," he declares. "The Beatles went to their dressing-room and nobody was allowed near them," Maxwell recollects. "I went out of the theatre and walked around to Prince's Street, which was the back way into the Adelphi. I dropped some money to the doorman, a fiver if I remember correctly, which was a lot of money at the time. I knew you couldn't have got near them for a pound. That got me up to the next floor.

"I knocked on the door there and Lennon opened it. It was a typical, tatty dressing-room, but then again it was a cinema. Their suits for the show were hanging up on the wall behind them. There was a small mirror. They were just lounging around. I couldn't think of anything to say. I didn't want to say, 'Can I have a picture?' and have the door slammed on me. I said, 'Good evening, I'm wondering could I just come in for a quick chat. I'm related to the owner of the cinema.' That, of course, was a lie. 'Yeah, come on in, Chuck,' Lennon said.

"I went in. It wasn't a big room. They were sitting around in various places with big gaps between them. They weren't dressed yet for the show. I saw a teapot and cups. I think they had just finished some tea but there was still tea in the pot and I said, 'Do you know what I really want, lads? I want to get a picture of you having a cup of tea, like aristocratic people in England. Is there any chance?' Ringo said, 'Yeah, no problem. John can pour out the tea and we'll do the necessary.' They were exceedingly friendly about it. So I got the picture. John poured the tea as he stood behind Paul, leaning over his shoulder. You can see their stage suits hanging behind them. It was perfect. It was a really happy picture, a lovely informal one, not the least bit stilted.

"They were terribly nice to me, although you could see they were tense before the show. Ringo then said, 'Listen, you've overstayed your welcome, you'll have to let us get ready now.' I said, 'Well, thank you very much. I appreciate what you've done and I'll tell my uncle about how good you were.' As I went out the door, John Lennon looked at me and said, 'I hope your uncle is feeling well.' He knew I was telling a yarn. I think he thought it was a very original one. I got out after only about two minutes there, whistling all the way down the stairs with my exclusive. I wired the picture off to the magazine, which was a German one I think. I also got it off the next day to *Time* magazine and some other magazines. Once I got the exclusivity over with, I could send it anywhere."

Soon after Maxwell departed, the backstage buzz intensified as the acts geared up for the first of the shows. The sense of urgency came in phases, with the early performers the first to panic and those on later the last to tense up. As the final act, the Beatles took their time, tuning their guitars and changing into stage suits. They also applied theatrical make-up, which they had first heard of in December 1962 during a disastrous one-night stand with Frank Ifield in Peterborough. Ted Taylor, the leader of the Ted Taylor Four, who was also support on that bill, had introduced them to the benefits of applying pancake make-up. Ever since then they wore it onstage and in photo-shoots.

John inserted contact lenses, which he was introduced to by American singer Bobby Goldsboro. In the early summer, Goldsboro, who was then playing guitar with Roy Orbison and had yet to become famous with songs like 'Honey', showed him the revolutionary new lenses. It was a godsend for Lennon, who normally wore 'Buddy Holly' glasses. Seriously short sighted, as a child John used to wonder, on trips into Liverpool, how his mates were always aware of the time. Only when prescribed wire-rimmed National Health Service spectacles did he realise that they were reading the time from the Royal Liver Building's clocks. He had never before known they were there.

"I couldn't be seen in horn-rimmed specs onstage. That would never do for a Beatle," John said. The alternative in the

'60s, bar no glasses at all, was contact lenses which were primitive, painful, unreliable and hard on the eyes. They constantly fell out. Large amounts of time were spent on hands and knees, especially in hotel bedrooms, trying to find them. They frequently dropped out onstage. "Can you imagine what it is like," Lennon asked, "hearing all that noise and playing, and not seeing a thing? It's frightening." Given what the Beatles faced that evening, John Lennon might have been better off leaving his lenses at home!

THE SUPPORT ACTS

Canadian comic Frank Berry strode onto the stage at Dublin's Adelphi cinema to be greeted by a hostile reception. As MC for the Beatles' autumn tour, he had what must have been the worst and most hopeless job in entertainment history. His role was to provide humour, perform magic and introduce the various entertainers. Unfortunately, each time he walked onstage he was greeted by adolescents chanting that they wanted the Beatles.

No one wanted to listen to what he was saying. He was booed and hissed. Every appearance he made was interpreted as being one step closer to the only thing the kids wanted to see, which certainly wasn't the support acts or Frank Berry. "On the poster he was called 'Your Favourite Canadian'," says Peter Jay, drummer with Peter Jay and the Jaywalkers. "I used to think, 'This is the '60s. I don't think anybody knows anybody else from Canada!' He was a nice guy but he had the most impossible task in show business, going on there and trying to talk to people."

Frank's comedy spots, interspersed throughout the show, were subjected to loud derision. His magic tricks were at best ignored. Far from smoothing the transition between different performers he was perceived as being the man who was holding things up. "Every time an act finished, this unfortunate comic

75

had to come out to fill," recalls one of the future Greenbeats, John Keogh. "People were roaring for the Beatles. He couldn't get a word in. The poor guy was fighting an uphill battle. He tried several gags and we were close enough to hear him. When it wasn't working, I remember he said, 'That went down like a pork chop at a Jewish wedding.' I will never forget that line. I thought it was very radical at the time."

The programme notes listed his talents. "Frank has built up quite a reputation for himself ... for not only is he a top rate comedian and magician, he is an excellent ventriloquist. In fact, wherever the tonic of laughter is needed Frank is the man to provide it," the notes proclaimed. Today, virtually no one can remember Frank's jokes. Nor can anyone remember his feats of ventriloquism. Perhaps he would have been better employed as a hypnotist – at least he might have kept the audiences quiet!

"Half the time, Frank wasn't even able to do his act because of the commotion," observes Mal Cook, who worked with promoter Arthur Howes. "He would just go onstage and rattle on about something. It didn't matter if they didn't listen. He'd stand there with a piece of cord and a scissors, cut it in half and join it up again. He rang me once and said, 'Mal, are you going to watch *Sunday Night At The London Palladium* tonight?' I said, 'Yes.' He said, 'I'm on tonight.' I said, 'OK.' He said, 'I'm going to give you a tip – watch the carnation.' I watched the carnation and it shot from his left buttonhole to his right. And no one noticed it. He was very funny and a lovely man."

Frank performed with the Beatles on another occasion – on *Blackpool Night Out* in 1964. With the ABC Theatre in Blackpool as the venue, the show was transmitted across the ITV network. That night Frank and the Beatles appeared with Mike and Bernie Winters, Lionel Blair and Jimmy Edwards. He was also known to audiences for his appearances on the live entertainment circuit. Unfortunately, however, history recalls him as the man who died a death night after night as he built up the crowd for the Beatles.

"He was a really nice guy, a genuine guy," Jeff Williams of the Kestrels concludes. "He was quite a young guy, about the same age as us. He was quite switched on. He could do a good act if he had the opportunity. He would do some good magic tricks. Like most other comedians, Frank could tell a few stories but he had enough sense not to do that. Before the Beatles came on, all he had to do was to build up the tension while they were setting up backstage. Anything else and he'd be wasting his time."

Up first on the night was the Rhythm and Blues Quartet, which was essentially the backing band for the Brook Brothers. "They were four musicians – two Welshmen and two Scotsmen – and they were really good," says Geoff Brook. "We had them along as our backing group but the other acts – the Vernons Girls and the Kestrels – used them as well on the tour. The drummer was fantastic. The guitarist was very good also. They did an instrumental piece at the top, which I think was 'You Can't Sit Down'. It was an appropriately-named piece for the shows."

Following a brief introductory set from the quartet, Frank Berry got down to business. The next act he introduced was the Vernons Girls, who had interesting beginnings. They started out in the 1950s as a choir sponsored by Vernons Pools of Liverpool. Initially part of the social activities of the company, the original line-up was eventually reduced in size and streamlined into a commercial act.

"Vernons Pools had a social club and it started as one of the things that you did as part of the leisure activities," Maggie Stredder, who joined in 1957, recalls. "The social club had a choir just for the females. Its size was whittled down bit by bit. We had to say that we all worked in Vernons Pools. We were all Merseysiders and we used to rehearse in Liverpool every day. When we weren't in London doing a television show we'd rehearse in Liverpool, go home to our own beds at night and then we'd come back down to London for more television shows."

By the time of the Beatles' autumn tour, the Vernons Girls had been trimmed to a complement of three. Their names were Maureen Kennedy, Jean Owen and Frances Lea. Two of them, Maureen and Jean, were 'auburn-haired', the programme notes for the concert told us. The other, Frances, was a 'blonde'. The girls were accomplished, glamorous and recognised for their successful recordings 'Lover Please' and 'You Know What I Mean'. They were appearing on all the top TV shows of the time, *Oh Boy, Boy Meets Girl, 6.5 Special* and *Thank Your Lucky Stars*. They were also touring with the likes of the Everly Brothers, Frank Ifield, Marty Wilde, Helen Shapiro, Del Shannon, Eden Kane and Cliff Richard.

"We met the Beatles first when we were on the Cliff Richard tour," Jean Owen, who later became known as singer Samantha Jones, remembers. "One day Bruce Welch, of the Shadows, got on the coach and he said, 'Have you heard the Beatles' new record?' We discussed it for a while. He said, 'There's a party at my house tonight. Do you want to come?' I said, 'Yes'. Then he said to me, 'The Beatles are coming.' Maureen sort of turned her nose up. She liked all 1950s stuff but wasn't interested in pop and rock. But I liked it.

"We arrived at Bruce's house. Cliff was there. The Shadows were there. The Beatles came in. John Lennon came up to Maureen and he said, 'It's great to meet you. We really love your "You Know What I Mean".' Maureen looked at him down her nose. He said, 'We've written songs that you might be interested in.' She sort of just smirked and walked away. She said, 'Their hair!' When I look back, their hair wasn't really long at all but we all thought it was. 'Oh,' she said, 'they are horrible.' Eventually, we met them again. This was some time later. I remember Maureen went up to John and said, 'What was that song you wrote for us?' He said, 'You can bugger off now. You didn't want it when you thought we were nothing.' But we became great friends."

The Beatles and the Vernons Girls got to know each other well. They appeared together on *Thank Your Lucky Stars* in April 1963. It is said that the title of the Vernons' hit song 'You Know What I Mean' was incorporated by John Lennon as one of the lines in 'I Saw Her Standing There', replacing another line of McCartney's. In late 1963 the Vernons recorded one of the first Beatles' tribute songs, 'We Love The Beatles'. In 1964 the girls appeared on the TV special *Around The Beatles*. In '64 they also played support at the *Pops Alive!* shows at the Prince of Wales Theatre, London. And, of course, both acts toured together on the Beatles' autumn tour in 1963.

"The girls didn't like touring very much but I absolutely loved it," says Jean Owen. "I loved getting on the coach and going to another gig. The tour itself was great. We had a ball on it. The shows were wonderful. I think we got something like £125 a week. That was between all three of us. We still had a deal with Vernons Pools. They paid our expenses. They paid us £20 a week subsistence, if I remember rightly. It was like pocket money. On top of that we got whatever we earned. It wasn't a lot.

"We had been around quite a while and the boys were still just four little lads. Maureen used to say, 'Oh, for God's sake, John, go away and leave me alone.' We treated them like kids really, even though we were of an age. But we had been doing it for longer than they had. When the boys did the Royal Variety show we sent them a telegram. We were the only people on the tour to do that. They said, 'Nobody else even bothered.' They were really pleased. I also played a lot of poker with them. I can't remember whether it was John or Ringo who taught me to play. Frank Berry and either one or two of the Brook Brothers and the Beatles and I used to play poker regularly.

"I remember standing onstage when we were rehearsing 'I Want To Hold Your Hand'. The Beatles asked us would we do the claps offstage. Maureen said, 'No. Gerroff.' I remember when they were rehearsing it Tony Burrows of the Kestrels said, 'My God, they are so flat.' Of course, we all were. I remember saying, 'You are too, sometimes.' But when we went out there it was a whole different ballgame.

"When we did 'We Love The Beatles' we were so embarrassed. We went back on the tour after we recorded it. We had an article out as well. I think it was in the *Express*. It had come out with the record. It was something like, 'The Hell Of Being On Tour With The Beatles' or 'How Hard It Is To Tour With The Beatles' or something like that. After it came out, George Harrison came knocking at the door and said, 'Could I talk to you?' I said, 'What do you want?' He said, 'I don't know how to say this but "Eppy" is suing you.' Maureen said, 'What?' He said, 'It's that article you printed with your song "We Love The Beatles".' All day we kept thinking that we were going to be sued. They let us off the hook that night. But we were so embarrassed having to sing 'We Love The Beatles'. It was terrible and it bombed completely, thank God.

"I remember another occasion when George came knocking on our dressing-room while we were putting on our make-up. He knocked on our door and came in. He said, 'All right, girls?' Maureen said, 'George, get out of here.' He said, 'Girls, come on, we can't get any women. You could just stand there. You wouldn't have to do anything.' 'Get out!' We threw him out. It was all very good-natured."

The Vernons Girls went down well in Dublin, helped by the fact that as show openers the hysteria was as yet somewhat restrained. "Liverpool's attractive Vernons Girls contributed 'Ain't Gonna Kiss Ya', a somewhat faster but no less imaginative treatment of 'Be My Baby' than that of the Ronettes' original," future Radio Éireann star Ken Stewart commented in his newspaper review the following day. "A deftly executed version of the plaintive 'Passing Strangers' was succeeded by 'Funny All Over' and their current single

'Tomorrow Is Another Day'," he continued. The audience lapped it up. They roared and cheered. Then, almost as quickly as they had appeared, the Vernons were gone. Such was the speed of variety shows!

"They were great audiences in Ireland," Jean Owen concludes. "I remember the kids screamed for us as well as screaming for the Beatles. It was wonderful. We loved it. They screamed for all the acts. The audiences were absolutely fantastic. In Dublin we came offstage and started walking back to the hotel. We were going out the stage door and a pile of little girls said, 'Oh, my God! It's the Vernons. You've touched the Beatles. You've touched them.' And they chased us all down the road. They were good-natured, great kids. The next morning I remember sitting with Maureen in the Gresham, waiting to leave. She went, 'Oh, my God!' I said, 'What?' She said, 'Look who is over there.' She recognised faces very easily. It was Gene Tierney, the movie star. I said, 'Only you would recognise her!' We had a great time in Dublin. We really enjoyed it."

Bouncing back onstage, the irrepressible Frank Berry introduced the next act of the night – the Brook Brothers, from Winchester, Hampshire. Like the Everly Brothers, Ricky and Geoff Brook cultivated the cool, clean, Brylcreem look of the late 1950s. Their musical style was similar to that of the American heartthrobs. They even recorded some Everly Brothers' standards like 'When Will I Be Loved'. "They were a very good act and we used them on a lot of tours and shows," recalls Susan Fuller, personal assistant to promoter Arthur Howes. "They were very attractive young men with dark hair and were very smart, as artistes were in those days. They were very polite and good fun. They certainly were in the Everly Brothers mould – a very good act onstage, a very polished duo."

By the time of the tour, the Brook Brothers had won healthy acclaim as performers and recording artistes. In their early 20s, the two boys had scored in the charts with 'Warpaint' which peaked at number 5, and 'Ain't Gonna Wash For A Week' which reached number 13. Other recordings, including 'He's Old Enough To Know Better', 'Welcome Home Baby' and 'Trouble Is My Middle Name', had stalled in the lower reaches of the Top 40. They had performed with the Beatles the previous summer. The duo had also appeared in Richard Lester's début film *It's Trad, Dad!* in which they performed 'Double Trouble'.

"We had already toured with Cliff Richard, Gene Vincent, Helen Shapiro, Brian Hyland, Little Eva, Chubby Checker, Tom Jones and Gerry Dorsey who later became Engelbert Humperdinck," says Geoff Brook. "The Beatles' tour was by no means our first. We were old hands by the time we linked up with them. But the Beatles' tour was certainly the most outstanding. It was just fantastic to be on."

The Brook Brothers also toured Ireland, where they experienced some highs and some lows. "We went to the Opera House in Belfast with Gene Vincent," Geoff Brook recollects. "Our manager Peter Walsh, who was always into publicity, got us to turn up at a department store in Belfast and sing a couple of songs. It went so well that a sort of riot started. The store manager phoned the police and his message was not very clear. He said, 'There's a couple of brothers causing a riot here.' Policemen turned up and arrested us, took us to a police station and put us in a cell. Peter had to come and get us out.

"We also did a sort of ballroom tour, supported by a lot of showbands. I remember one ballroom with a gravel car park around it and lots of ploughed fields. We turned up at half past seven or eight o'clock. By half past ten we were getting really worried because there was nobody there. We thought, 'What a failure!' By eleven o'clock everybody poured in, arriving by cars, buses, on their bikes and everything. They had been at the pub! I also remember going to Ballyhaunis. We stopped for a drink on the way and the lads put some balloons on the van to drive down Ballyhaunis high street. When we arrived we were greeted by nobody but a whole herd of cows!"

Described by journalist Éanna Brophy as "two guys in suits," the Brook Brothers did as well as they could at the concerts. Reviewer Ken Stewart found them appealing. "The Brook Brothers opened with Neil Sedaka's former hit, 'You Gotta Learn Your Rhythm And Blues,' 'Warpaint,' the number most associated with them, and the duo's thoughtful interpretation of a country flavoured 'Seven Daffodils' proved outstanding," Stewart concluded.

"We were very lucky," Geoff Brook reflects. "The fans were full of excitement before the show started. During the Vernons Girls, the anticipation was so high that the fans wanted to have a good old scream. We were in a slot where they were still prepared to listen. We were in a sort of lull. It gave us a chance to do our stuff. The people who I really felt so sorry for were the Kestrels, who were on before the Beatles and didn't have a chance to get their stuff across because anticipation was at such a high level at that stage."

Once the Brook Brothers were through, Frank Berry strode onto the stage to introduce the final support act prior to the break. A hugely popular, much-travelled group with a big fan base, Peter Jay and the Jaywalkers were described in the programme notes as being "rock 'n roll fans, some even verging on being addicts." Once their equipment was in place, they were ready for action. Predating the beat boom, this "happy, hippy crew of guys," as they were referred to in one pop magazine, had a seven-piece line-up that included guitars, piano and brass. Their stage performance was all-action, electric and entertaining. They also had a new rhythm 'n blues vocal release on the Decca label, called 'Kansas City'.

"Their act is probably the most polished in the world," one teen publication declared back in the '60s. "The man responsible for that is Peter Jay. Not only do all the group wear fabulous suits (once they had every member of the group wearing a different coloured suit) but Peter has introduced many, many 'gimmicks'." Frank Grimes, aged 16, who attended one of the concerts, recalls the gimmicks which included sparks from the cymbals and lights from the drums: "Peter Jay on the drums had a great lighting effect. When the lights went down each big bass drum lit up separately and pulsated with the rhythm. It was a great theatrical effect. They were fantastic."

By the time they arrived in Dublin and Belfast, the Jaywalkers had appeared on *Thank Your Lucky Stars*. They had also toured with Billy Fury, Eden Kane and Marty Wilde, who they admired. Back in November 1962 they featured on the cover of *New Musical Express*. Fans following their career would have seen them on *Ready Steady Go!* and noticed their billing as opening act for the Rolling Stones in 1966. They also overlapped with the rise of the Beatles.

"When I first heard of the Beatles, my initial reaction was, 'That's a crap name. They are never going to make it with a name like that,'" Peter Jay, the group's accomplished drummer, recalls. "Everybody was so-and-so and the so-and-sos. I was also told that they didn't do foot movements. I remember sitting there for about an hour thinking, 'How can a band get anywhere without doing foot movements?' Everybody did foot movements like the Shadows. You all had to do it or you weren't a pro band. The Beatles didn't sound promising at all.

"We eventually got quite friendly with the Beatles. They told us that they used come and see us when we came with the big pop tours to Liverpool, to play at the Empire. We had got these Cuban-heeled boots from Anello and Davide, in Charing Cross Road, London. You could only buy them there at the time. It was a theatrical shoe shop. We had some made especially for us. The Beatles said, 'We would come and see you, and we said if we get any money we'll go down to London and buy some of them boots like the Jaywalkers.' They were made originally for Danny Williams, who was really small and the Cuban heels made him look taller. Eventually, everybody had them."

Well-established by the time the Beatles were emerging, the paths of the two groups crossed on a number of occasions. Back in February, on the Helen Shapiro tour, the Jaywalkers stepped in for two shows in Peterborough while the Beatles travelled down to London to record their first LP. Just a month before arriving in Dublin, both groups were part of the line-up on *Ready Steady Go!* They also, of course, toured side-by-side during the autumn tour in 1963.

"We got to know the Beatles," Peter Jay says. "When we played in Leeds, the Beatles couldn't stay in the city at the top hotel because all the fans would think, 'Oh, they are staying here.' They went to Bradford and stayed there instead. At one stage on that tour they had to dress them up as policemen to get them in. Another time they came in a baker's van. The national press picked up on the way they got them in every day. We used to just sit there and play cards. That's all we could do.

"No matter who you were, once you went outside the stage door they all jumped on you. It was dodgy. We had one guy who worked for us, who we used to send out for food. He used to come back covered in Chinese takeaway because they used to jump on him. At that stage we had the Beatle haircuts and the Beatle jackets. As soon as we set foot outside we'd get torn limb from limb. Once we put our foot out of the stage door we were attacked by the girls at the front and the boyfriends at the back, putting the boot in. It was a strange combination. It was an incredible experience.

"We had heard hysteria before. I had seen something similar with Billy Fury. He got the same reaction from girls. He did his act and they went mad. He did a lot of sexy, writhing around on the floor sort of stuff. He used to get 1,200 or 1,400 people all screaming their heads off and standing up and going crazy. It was more intense with the Beatles. There were thousands more people. Every time Billy Fury would go to a town, there were 500 people outside when you arrived and 1,000 outside at the end. They were screaming and going mad. But with the Beatles there were maybe 3,000 people and the roads were closed off. It was crazy.

"As soon as they finished 'Twist And Shout', the Beatles were gone, smuggled out. Then, all the fans went out of the theatre. It was virtually impossible for us to get out. We'd pack our gear up quite slowly. We would try to leave it at least an hour or two hours later before we would emerge. Sometimes it would take us two and three hours just to get out of the theatre. We'd try to avoid going out while it was in riot mode. By the time we'd come out, there would still be a lot of people looking for autographs. It was mayhem.

"We played one place with them and we came out in the end in a little van. For some reason, the fans thought that the Beatles were in the van. It was scary. We were stuck there for about half an hour with everything completely black and everyone banging on the van and trying to turn it over. Eventually they brought policemen on horseback, with great big batons, and they literally chopped at these people. We drove off and I thought to myself, 'Now I can see why the Beatles go to all the trouble of dressing up in disguise and trying to avoid this.' It was frightening actually.

"We thought in 1963 that this was their year and next year it would be us. It wasn't until we got to Bournemouth, where quite a few American film crews turned up, that I thought maybe this was going to be bigger than the normal Cliff Richard and the Shadows. But the Beatles were changing during that autumn tour. John was just starting to get a little more withdrawn, sitting there reading books and getting a little bit more arty. George was the boy of the band. Paul was that sort of upfront character which he always was. He was a bloody good drummer as well. But I was friendliest with Ringo because I knew him before when he was with Rory Storm and the Hurricanes."

Bursting into the popular 'Do You Love Me?' the Jaywalkers stopped the audience in their tracks and received widespread applause. They soon followed with a slick medley of titles popularised by the Temperance Seven, Acker Bilk, Russ Conway, the Shadows and other British acts. The group also performed their hit recording 'Can-Can '62', which was a chart hit. Their rendition "spotlighted the group's skilful drummer," reviewer Ken Stewart commented the following day. They also had a follow-up, 'Totem Pole', which sold well.

"It sounds incredibly corny now but part way through our act we also did an impression of the Beatles," Peter Jay recollects. "We actually went out and bought some Beatle wigs. And, even though it sounds so cheesy now, they did a blackout, I did a drum roll and I said, 'Ladies and gentlemen, now, what you've all been waiting for … the Beatles!' The lights came up and, for that moment, we got the reaction the Beatles got, with all that screaming. People gradually realised, 'Oh, it's not them. It's only the Jaywalkers with wigs on.' But it was the most incredible experience. We got that reaction every night on the tour.

"We also closed the first half of the show. We did 'Can Can' with a big drum solo. We did a big dramatic piano number called 'Exodus'. At the end of that we stood in a line and did a bow. We used all go in a line, count 'one, two, three, four' and we'd all bow. The Beatles used to always stand on the side of the stage, taking the piss out of us. We'd count 'one, two, three, four', look across and they'd be all doing this fake bow. They were great. They were just like the famous quote, 'Everybody else changed; they stayed the same.'"

Following the intermission, tension heightened with the anticipated arrival onstage of the Beatles. The fans cranked up the noise. The unfortunate Frank Berry headed out into what can only be described as a wall of sound. Although seemingly upbeat and exuberant, he must have been crestfallen. From the moment he walked on, it was one long uphill struggle until the Beatles appeared. "The first half was OK," Jeff Williams of the Kestrels recalls. "The people at that stage hadn't got themselves into a frenzy. As soon as the first half was finished, they all knew the Beatles were coming on. Whatever came on before them was in trouble." John Keogh, who was watching from downstairs in the Adelphi, agrees. "In the earlier part of the show the other acts got a bit of a response, but as the show went on it boiled up," he remembers. "When the show moved into the second half, people were really going mad. People were screaming and shouting. Every time an act finished, people started roaring for the Beatles."

Apart from the Beatles and contributions from Frank Berry, the second half consisted of a performance by the Kestrels. Hailing from England's West Country, at the time of the tour they were often referred to as 'Britain's top vocal group'. The Kestrels were a four-part harmony act with a repertoire of songs ranging from rock 'n roll to jazz. They had recorded with people like Billy Fury, Tommy Steele, Cleo Laine and Lonnie Donegan. Described by one of their members Roger Greenaway as "a doo-wop group," they were good. Not unlike the Platters, their name was in keeping with similar vocal groups of the time such as the Penguins and the Crows. On the road since the second half of the 1950s, they had appeared on *Sunday Night At The London Palladium*, *Putting On The Donegan* and *All That Jazz*. They also had a long succession of singles which threatened to break into the charts.

"We got paid double our normal fee to do it," Roger Greenaway says of their role as penultimate act on the autumn tour. "Nobody else would go on before the Beatles. We had already done one tour with Helen Shapiro and the Beatles. That was pretty chaotic. When our manager came to us he said, 'Do you want to do another Beatles' tour?' We said, 'Of course we do, but please don't put us on before them.' That's exactly what they wanted to do. They said, 'We'll double your fee.' We said, 'OK, we'll do it.'

"We were scared by the mania. It was frightening. The fans just wanted a piece of you. They would rip, tear or bang. It was

The Beatles arrive at Dublin Airport on 7 November 1963.

Crowds on the public viewing balcony at Dublin Airport watch the Beatles arrive.

Paul Russell pictured with the Beatles while recording an insert for The Showband Show at the Gresham Hotel.

Eileen Reid and the Cadets, with their manager Tom Costello (left), photographed with Paul McCartney and John Lennon at the Gresham Hotel.

Phyllis Tyrrell (on drums) with her
sister Josephine (middle) and friend Nuala
Mullen (left) pictured with the Beatles
backstage at the Adelphi.

The group pose
backstage at the
Adelphi.

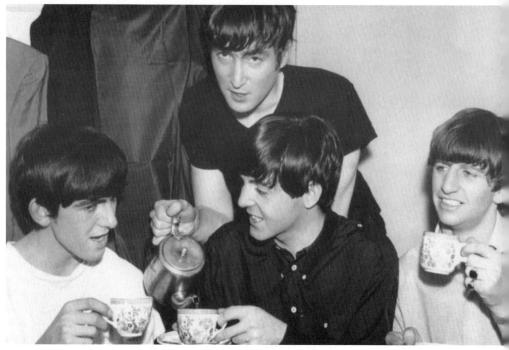

Pat Maxwell captures the Beatles
drinking tea prior to their Adelphi
concerts.

Playwright Alun Owen (left) pictured with
Lionel Bart (middle) and Beatles'
manager Brian Epstein (right).

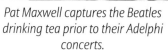

George pictured with his mother
Louise Harrison.

The Vernons Girls (l-r) Jean Owen, Maureen Kennedy and Frances Lea toured with the Beatles in autumn 1963.

Peter Jay (centre, back) pictured with the Jaywalkers.

The Brook Brothers were also on the autumn tour.

The group onstage at the Adelphi cinema, 7 November 1963, in a still taken from the Gael Linn newsreel filmed at the shows.

Jeff Williams, Tony Burrows and Roger Greenaway of the Kestrels.

Crowds build up outside the Adelphi cinema.

Gardaí battle fans outside the Adelphi.

Paul McCartney is the first to emerge from the ABC Ritz following the 1963 Belfast concerts.

The Beatles perform at the ABC Ritz, Belfast, in a shot taken by 16-year-old Chris Hill.

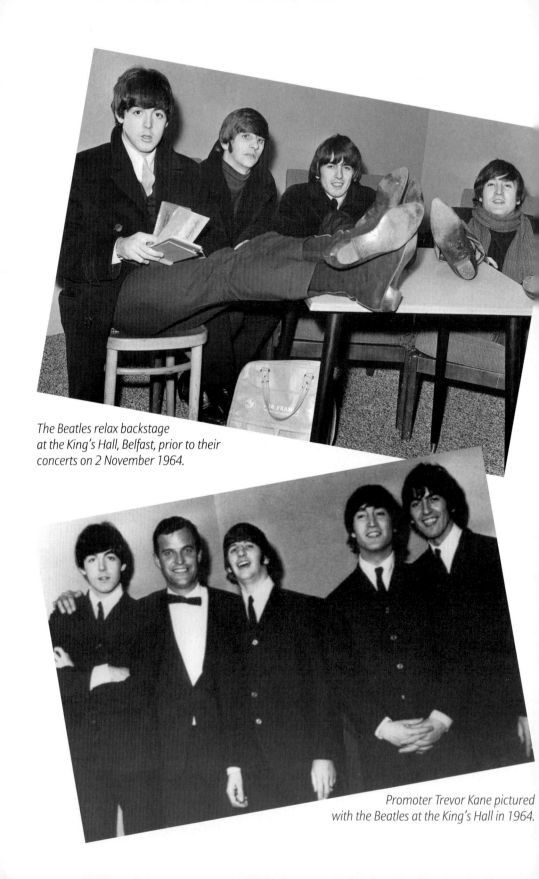

The Beatles relax backstage at the King's Hall, Belfast, prior to their concerts on 2 November 1964.

Promoter Trevor Kane pictured with the Beatles at the King's Hall in 1964.

crazy. We used to stick our hands out the windows of the dressing-room and people would go mad. The screams outside were incessant. They didn't know whose hands they were. It could have been anyone. But it could have been a Beatle. We did it for the fun. Someone would say, 'Watch this.' They'd stick their hand out. And you'd hear, 'Aaaaaagh!'

"When we toured with them on the Helen Shapiro tour, they had the suits and the ties and the long but cropped hair. They were becoming more cabaret although they wouldn't want to admit it. We taught them how to bow. Coming from the old school, we were doing 'one, two, three ... down' and 'one, two, three ... up'. I remember Ringo saying, 'How do you all bow together? How do you get it in sync?' We said you count it out. Next night he was going 'one, two, three ... down' and 'one, two, three ... up'. They had never bowed before that because they had come from Germany where they were doing rock 'n roll."

By the time of their appearances in Dublin and Belfast the Kestrels were known for their versions of 'Wolverton Mountain', 'Walk Right In' and 'Love Me With All Your Heart'. Their *Smash Hits* LP, which included a cover version of 'Please Please Me', was released in 1963. They also released a cover of the Lennon-McCartney composition 'There's A Place', which they performed on the autumn tour. "It was John Lennon suggested it," Roger Greenaway remarks regarding 'There's A Place'. "We just heard it and our recording manager said let's do it. I remember the Beatles were quite excited about it because they thought it was going to be a hit. It ended up almost being one."

As the Kestrels ran through their set, the audience counted down to the Beatles. "We used to do our set and when we came to the end of it the place used to erupt," says the Kestrels' Jeff Williams. "It was the same in Dublin. As we were going off, the compère Frank Berry would come on. He used to call us back on again. As we came back on, the place used to go deadly silent. When we went off again, the place used to erupt once more. The other people on the show used to say, 'Golly, you went down well again tonight.' In the end we had to tell them the truth, which was that we had died a complete death. Nobody wanted to hear us. All they wanted to hear was the Beatles." The audience might have been pleasantly surprised if they had listened. "The Kestrels have personality, poise and a compelling, pulsating style, especially evident during 'There's A Place' and the infectious 'Green Green'," wrote reviewer Ken Stewart. Unfortunately, on the night, no one cared.

"You felt like you were just nothing," Roger Greenaway ruefully remarks. "The whole thing about show business is that you're up there and if you please people they'll clap you. Instead, this roar would go up as we went off because now they were going to see the Beatles. That and the roar greeting the Beatles were the biggest roars of the night. They didn't want us to come back; they wanted us to stay off. We worked with people like Billy Fury before. That was pretty chaotic but never as mad or as fraught as it was with the Beatles. The fans were only there to see them. It was funny and tragic at the same time.

"Going on before the Beatles almost destroyed us. We nearly split after that tour. One of our guys almost lost his eye. In those days we had a threepenny bit in the UK, which was a little coin but very heavy. They were tossing these things at us and it caught him right in the eye. The fans didn't want to listen to us. We were keeping them from the Beatles. To have people scream and throw things at you to get off was absolutely soul-destroying."

Sometime around eight o'clock the Kestrels' torture was over. The curtains closed. Behind them the Beatles' equipment was put in place. There was bedlam. Frank Berry walked to the front of the stage. He was about to introduce the last act of the night – the Beatles!

AND NOW ... THE BEATLES!

The shrieking, piercing cacophony of young girls' voices produced a resonance so loud and high-pitched that the fans couldn't hear themselves screaming and the Beatles, backstage, couldn't hear their own voices speaking. The noise was the equivalent of a jet engine, registering well over 100 decibels of shrill, sharp, ear-splitting, nerve-jangling sound. It could seriously damage eardrums. Only dogs could pick up some of the frequencies.

Hysteria front-of-house was at breaking point. A pungent, steaming heat rose from the 2,304 ticketed fans, not one of whom remained seated. The overflow of observers, intruders, cinema staff and un-ticketed guests lined the side aisles and the vacant spaces at the rear of the balcony and stalls. A row of determined-looking ushers stood in front of the stage. First aid volunteers braced themselves close to the exits.

"The atmosphere was hot and sharp; full of powder and perfume and a frightening excitement," observed journalist Donal McCann, who described the fan mania in the minutes prior to the show. "They screamed at the pictures in their programmes, or if someone shouted 'Beatles' they screamed – long, loud screams that cut through the heavy air. The house erupted into one mad, thunderous, piercing noise that it would be impossible to forget."

Frank Berry walked to the front of the stage wearing a dress suit and bow tie, looking every bit the part of the variety show MC. "I remember Frank Berry coming out and whipping up the crowd even more than ever, as if they needed it," says journalist Éanna Brophy. "He was trying to prolong the moment before the Beatles arrived onstage. He was out in front of the curtain, trying to say something. 'We want the Beatles' got louder and louder. You couldn't hear anything as we waited for the Beatles to come on. He kind of gave up."

The MC had an impossible job, according to Jeff Williams who, with the rest of the Kestrels, was in the wings recovering from his recent ordeal onstage. "He had to do a little warm-up to give them time to get the scene set for the Beatles behind the stage curtains," he remarks. "The musicians backing us had to get their stuff off the stage and the Beatles' drums and everything else had to be brought on. He had to fill. The fans just screamed and screamed and screamed. All he was waiting for was the word 'go'. It might take two or three minutes but that can be a lifetime if you are up there on the stage dying on your feet. He obviously was dying, the same as us. He might as well have not been there really."

Behind Frank Berry was the half-curtain and behind that, as everyone knew, were the Beatles and their road crew going through their final routines. With well-rehearsed precision, Ringo's drums were assembled, guitars fine-tuned, microphones repositioned and amps put in place. "We could hear 'dong, dong, dong, dong, dong' from the guitars behind," recalls John Olohan, aged 16. "Everybody knew what was going to happen. Frank Berry kept jabbering on. Everyone wanted him off. They were chanting, 'Out, out, out.' You could hear George Harrison tuning-in behind. The more you could hear the guitar, the more the place went ballistic."

Berry took his time, stalling, delaying and dragging his feet, seemingly oblivious to what everyone wanted. He prodded and taunted the crowd into a fever as he waited for his cue from the side of the stage. The fans went mad. "It was mayhem," says Phyllis Tyrrell, also aged 16, who was seated in the third row from the front, downstairs, in the middle aisle. "We were all standing up. It was really, really loud. We all wanted the Beatles out."

Upstairs in the balcony girls wept uncontrollably, roaring their heads off while pulling their hair to bits. "I remember Frank Berry saying, 'Who do you want to see?' 'I don't hear you,' 'I don't hear you,'" remarks Sandra Grant, another 16-year-old, who sat alongside her friend. "He kept asking us the same question. Everyone was screaming back the answer, 'The Beatles,' 'The Beatles.' The noise was decibels high." John Olohan, seated a few rows away, recalls how eventually Berry received his cue to introduce the Beatles: "Frank Berry then went, 'Guess who we have now?' The crowd went bananas. He left the stage. The lights went down. You could still hear 'dong, dong, dong, dong'."

The Adelphi stage metamorphosed into a *mélange* of colour and sound. The first sensation to hit home was the music. "Just before the curtains opened, they started off with 'She was just 17.....'. The intro was going before the curtains parted. It was a great opening number. The crowd went wild. It lifted them off their feet," Éanna Brophy remembers. Next came the visual impact as the Beatles suddenly appeared into view. "When the curtains were pulled back three of the Beatles walked forward one or two steps," Sandra Grant says. "Ringo was raised up on drums at the back of the stage. Where I was you only heard the first note of the song and the twang of the guitar. Immediately, the place erupted with screams."

The four Beatles stood on the Adelphi stage in their trademark pose. To the right of the stage was John with his Rickenbacker guitar. Bought in Hamburg in 1960, he used the same American-made Rickenbacker in all the group's live shows up to 1964. In the centre was George with his Gretsch Country Gent, bought in Sound City, Rupert Street, London. At the back was Ringo sitting up on a riser, behind drums emblazoned with the Beatles' logo featuring a capital 'B' and dropped 'T'. It had been designed for a fiver just six months before by a signwriter in London.

Paul McCartney was positioned on the left with his Hofner bass, which he appeared to be playing. He also appeared to be singing. Had anyone heard it, the song he performed was 'I Saw Her Standing There', which had been conceived by Paul after a concert in Southport and completed at his family home in Forthlin Road, Liverpool. Recorded the previous February, it was the opening track on the Beatles' début album *Please Please Me*. As Paul sang, thousands of screaming voices accompanied him in unison, drowning him and his fellow Beatles in a sea of noise.

"I screamed because everybody else was screaming," explains Phyllis Tyrrell. "When you are younger you just go with the flow. A lot of the girls were crying around me. They had their hands up and were roaring and shouting. They also went mad when Paul and George put their heads together and shook their hair." Sandra Grant was hysterical too: "I was screaming and I was standing up on my feet. I hadn't a clue what they played. You simply couldn't hear it. You couldn't even lip-read from the distance where I was. But the excitement was electric. The ushers were trying to keep order. But you couldn't stop the exuberance."

Journalist Éanna Brophy had never witnessed anything like it before. "The girls were unable to help themselves," he remembers. "I could feel my eardrums reverberating. The pitch was incredible. They were crying. There were tears in their eyes. When they shouted the Beatles' individual names, the lads would look in the direction the shout came from and the screams got even louder. They didn't know what was wrong. They had no control over what they were doing. They wanted the Beatles to come down and take them away."

The Beatles were dressed in their grey collarless suits.

Inspired by one of Pierre Cardin's designs, the outfits were made for the Beatles by London tailor Dougie Millings at a cost of £31 a suit. They wore high Beatle boots with Cuban heels and elastic seams at the sides. They also sported mop top hairstyles, which were either invented by Astrid Kirchherr, the girlfriend of 'fifth Beatle' Stuart Sutcliffe, or copied from Jürgen Vollmer, an acquaintance from their days in Hamburg, depending on which story is to be believed. The sight of them was too much for the teenage girls in the crowd.

"I was mad about Paul so I was roaring my lungs out for him all the time," says 15-year-old Josephine Tyrrell, who was seated near the front, downstairs. "I kept shouting, 'Paul,' 'Paul.' The noise was fantastic. We were standing up on the seats. The people behind couldn't see so they got up on the seats to see better. The people behind them then tried to get even higher. Some girls were even on the shoulders of their boyfriends so they could get a good glimpse of the stage. There were a lot of people in the aisles and a lot of people from the back started running forward up the aisles, towards the stage. They were being sent back by the ushers. A lot of girls were crying, their heads in their hands and passing out. They were being given glasses of water."

Many people fainted, agrees John McGrath, one of the St John Ambulance volunteers who attended to overwrought fans: "People were fainting because of the excitement and hyperventilation. And when some girls fainted they all fainted. It was like a domino effect. We took them out to the foyer and eventually out to the street, where we had more room. We had smelling-salts and all that with us. I remember the police were very nice to us and gave us a cordoned-off area in the street where all the first aid people were. We could bring the patients to that spot. Nowadays it would be drugs but in those days it was more innocent."

Up on the stage, John, Paul and George stood in front of the black Vox AC-30 amps that powered the rhythm and lead guitars and the Vox AC-30 bass head and T-60 bass cabinet. Although primitive by today's standards, they were state of the art at the time, producing the loudest, cleanest, punchiest sound around. Since 1962 the Beatles had an exclusive promotion deal with Vox of Dartford in Kent. In return for free amps, they provided what would eventually become priceless publicity. Even as the Beatles rose to megastardom, Brian Epstein stuck to that deal.

Also onstage was the Ludwig drum kit which, by late '63, had become a trademark of the Beatles. It was acquired the previous April at Drum City in Shaftesbury Avenue, London, after Ringo had grown sick of his Premier set. Like the Vox amps, it was a promotional deal, with Drum City and Ludwig getting lots of publicity. Modelled in oyster black pearl finish, the set was the best you could buy at the time. It was designed to make Ringo look like he was sitting conspicuously on top. There were, after all, four Beatles, not three, to be seen.

"There were two microphones out the front – one for Lennon on the right and one for McCartney on the left," observes 20-year-old musician John Keogh who, accompanied by his girlfriend, was seated downstairs, near the centre aisle, about ten rows back. "If John Lennon was singing, George would lean into McCartney's mike. The girls loved the two lads' heads together at the one mike. They also had a very particular body language onstage. Lennon stood in a wide-legged, straddled stance with his head thrown back. George Harrison stood slightly back and he pawed the ground like a horse. McCartney jollied along, jogging from side to side. Ringo was bopping away and threw his head to one side when he'd hit the cymbal to punctuate something. When he flipped his head, the mop of hair would flop all over the place. People went bananas for it."

The Beatles moved briskly through their repertoire. Their second number, 'From Me To You', was written on the coach from York to Shrewsbury during the Helen Shapiro tour.

Inspired by a letters section in the *New Musical Express* titled 'From You To Us', it was a genuinely co-operative effort by Lennon and McCartney. Composed and recorded within the space of a week, it had gone to number one in the charts.

"After each song there would be a split second of silence," Sandra Grant recalls. "After a number finished, the crowd would be exhausted from the screaming and the applauding. You would hear the first guitar note of the next song and you would be into this maelstrom of noise. When there was that little bit of silence in the theatre you could hear the shouting of the crowd on the street outside. You could actually hear it inside the theatre, it was that loud. There were so many people, the sound travelled inwards. They were shouting, 'We want Paul,' 'We want George,' 'We want the Beatles.' You could identify what they were saying. Our noise was going out and the noise outside was coming back in. They were getting excited by what they could hear. They could probably hear the music better than we could."

Among those standing outside was Brian D'Arcy who, as an 18-year-old student priest from County Fermanagh, was living at the Passionist monastery in Mount Argus, Dublin. "I stood outside and heard the wailing and screaming. I could hear everything," he says. "I sneaked out the window of the monastery to see the Beatles. If I had been found out I would have been sent home immediately. I got my little bicycle and found where the centre of Dublin was, hoping I'd find my way home. I parked my bicycle somewhere near O'Connell Street and found the Adelphi. I thought I'd get in. But I only got as far as Abbey Street, to the barriers.

"What to me was a massive crowd was there, definitely in the thousands. I sneaked in through bodies, trying to get to the top. I got so far that I could see the Adelphi doors. I could hear the songs but what you could hear most was screaming. It was the most exciting thing I ever heard in my entire life. Did I see the Beatles? No. Was I at the Beatles? Yes. Eventually I took fright and said, 'If anybody sees me here, I'm finished.' I got on my bicycle, went back up, found Mount Argus and sneaked in the window again. I went up to my room and I never told anyone until 2006.

"It was a very life-changing thing for me. I knew then that there was a world out there that I wasn't being prepared for. You knew that the quiet world of the '50s was gone. I did go to Confession to confess what I did but I chose a blind priest who wouldn't recognise me. He had never heard of the Beatles and wondered how looking at insects could be a sin!"

Next on the set-list was 'All My Loving', which had been written by McCartney during the Roy Orbison tour. The song's 'boy-meets-girl' lyrics went right to the hearts of the bewildered girls in the balcony and stalls. Undying teenage love was on offer. Thankfully, as far as parents were concerned, the over-tures were coming from four clean-cut, well-groomed Liverpool lads, packaged and presented by manager Brian Epstein as non-smoking, non-drinking and non-swearing. Apart from their unusual hairstyles, they looked 'safe' and respectable – unthreatening enough to soothe anxious parents worried about their young daughters attending the back-to-back shows.

Among the young teenagers in the Adelphi was 14-year-old Gillian Freedman, who was taken to one of the concerts as a birthday treat and who was seated upstairs near the front. "I went with my mum and a number of my best friends," she remembers. "We were very excited because we were dying to see the Beatles and we had never been to anything like this in our lives. I will never forget the feeling of being part of something so exciting, part of something happening. We were part of the noise.

"We could see the Beatles although they seemed quite far away. The lights were on them. They were physically there and you could hear the beginnings of any of the big numbers. But the screaming was so loud that you couldn't hear them playing the songs. We couldn't hear them singing. Everybody was throwing their arms around, yelling. We were absolutely ecstatic to be part of the lunatic noise and jumping up and down. I can still feel the excitement when I think of it now."

Lynn Geldof, aged 16, was also overcome by the show: "We had seats that were fairly close, about the eleventh row down below. There was a 'vroom' when they played songs like 'I Saw Her Standing There' or 'She Loves You'. There was a sudden charge of energy, which no one was used to in those days. The songs came at you. The whole youth of it and sense of excitement was marvellous. I had already seen Chubby Checker and Brenda Lee and Cliff and the Shadows, but they weren't the same."

Unlike the girls, the boys in the audience looked unsure and slightly uncomfortable. Although also caught up in the frantic emotions of the night, screaming just wasn't their thing. Some clapped their hands and tapped their feet, or moved to the rhythm of the music. Others watched, puzzled, as the girls beside them went to pieces. The night provided an insight to the opposite sex which the boys found hard to comprehend or digest.

"The girls were holding their faces as if their heads were going to burst," 16-year-old Jonathan Ryan, who was sitting downstairs at the back with a group of his school friends, points out. "We couldn't really hear the Beatles at all. Whenever they shook their heads and did that 'oooh' thing, the girls went mental. When McCartney did it they went ballistic. The girls were there with their '60s hairstyles, going mad. It was non-stop bedlam. I can remember it actually hurting my ears. It was painful."

The girls seemed to be sexually aroused, according to Ted Carroll, a 21-year-old bank clerk and part-time promoter who was up near the front. "The girls were jumping up and down looking as if they were having orgasms," he says. "The noise was pretty permanent. But when the Beatles shook their heads, with their fringes going, that obviously inspired an additional intensity of screaming. If a new number started that they recognised, it got worse. I do recall some girls being carried out, who had fainted. But we were just focused on the Beatles."

Three girls in beehives and heavy mascara caught the attention of John Olohan. "They were Dusty Springfield look-alikes," he remarks. "They had the biggest beehive hairdos. They had dyed-black hair and black eyes. With the make-up on they looked 26 but could have been 13. They were screaming non-stop. After a while I turned around and the three girls were totally unrecognisable. They were like something out of the *Rocky Horror Show*. They had been pulling at their hair and it had gone into big peaks. It was like big peaks of candyfloss. The mascara was running down their faces. They were like something out of a Hammer horror film."

The girls were comical, says Brush Shiels, who was seated downstairs: "You'd be just laughing at them. They had gone crazy. Their screaming was fairly piercing and it was non-stop. I remember I was trying to get closer because it was hard to hear the numbers. I was always at that, walking around and trying to get closer. There was always a chance that one of your pals' sisters was working as an 'orange maid' and they might bump you up a few chairs or let you walk around. There's no doubt about it, the downstairs was mad."

Twenty-one-year-old Denis Deegan couldn't have cared less what the girls were up to. Instead, he was preoccupied with photographing the Beatles. "I was sitting in the stalls about half-way back and I had my camera with me," he explains. "I had bought it in Clerys. It was a Kodak Retinette 1A. It was a very popular camera at the time. I had put 400 ASA film in it, which was for poor light. I reckoned that if I used the flash I wouldn't get near enough for the photos to work. I brazenly walked down the aisle. There was a lot of shouting and screaming from the girls but there was nobody crowding around the stage. The whole front of the stage was clear.

"I went down the side aisle and then I crossed over close to the centre. Nobody stopped me. I was only about 15 or 20 feet away from the Beatles. They were playing away, sounding exactly like they did on record, and I took a few photographs. The crowd behind me were screaming, 'Get out of the way. We can't see them.' They weren't rowdy but they were roaring, 'You're blocking the view.' I got out of there pretty quick but I got some great shots. I still have the camera to this day."

Another young man was annoyed primarily with the girls but also with the general noise and commotion. "I said to myself, 'If they paid money to come to this, why don't they listen?'" remarks college student Myles McWeeney, who was sitting near the front. "If you didn't stand, you couldn't see a damn thing because everyone was up on their seats. It was the first pogoing I ever saw because people were jumping to try to see everything. I had gone to see Bill Haley in *Rock Around The Clock* in the cinema in Ballsbridge. They stopped us in the middle and told us to sit down. So we weren't allowed rock 'n roll in the aisles. But the carry-on in Ballsbridge was nothing compared to the Adelphi."

Warmed up and sweating, the Beatles slid effortlessly into their fourth number 'You Really Got A Hold On Me', a Smokey Robinson composition that had been a Top 10 *Billboard* hit for the Miracles. The song was the very first track recorded by the Beatles for their second LP. With John Lennon on lead vocals and George Harrison on close harmony, it was a favourite of the group throughout much of 1963. It also turned the spotlight on Lennon who, as always, looked bored and indifferent as he went through his routine.

"Lennon looked as if he was in a really bad temper," Frank Grimes, aged 16, observes. "He was being extremely uncom-municative. He had this stance with the guitar high up on the chest and the jaw jutting out. He was myopic. He had an absolute hostility, I felt. It was amazing at the time for an artiste to go onstage and not try to win you over. He was up there and making a statement very, very clearly that he hated being there and he despised some of the stuff he was going through.

"For me, as a 16-year-old kid, I thought, 'Oh, that's a real rebel. I feel like that sometimes.' He became a hero of mine. He was a working-class hero even though he was less working-class than all of them. It was only years later that I discovered he was extremely short-sighted and quite blind. It was a bit intimidating for him at the time, I think, because he couldn't see properly."

An older favourite was next – 'Roll Over Beethoven' – showcasing the vocal talents of George. Written by Chuck Berry, it was performed by the Beatles from their very early days as a group. The four boys loved it, slowing it down, lowering the key and massaging its driving beat. "Beethoven and Tchaikovsky are yesterday; rhythm 'n blues is today," its message proclaimed. From the first notes, the song was drowned out by waves of brain-mangling screaming. At the Adelphi it brought the house down.

"It was manic," says Morgan O'Sullivan, who was filming the concerts for Gael Linn. "It was like as if the girls there were in another world. Had you said something to them I don't think they'd have responded. It was like as if they had put themselves in this trance. I was quite close to the Beatles actually. I was up on the side of the stage for part of it and I saw the Beatles coming on and off. I think that the Beatles found the whole thing a bit frightening and unnerving.

"The extraordinary thing was that nobody was listening. You couldn't hear anything. For me, it was like being sober in a pub with people who were drunk. I was working but everything around me was mayhem. Everybody was in a state but I was quite calm. I was looking at it and wondering, 'Why are all these people behaving like this?' It looked like they were under immense stress. Maybe they were happy inside but they didn't look it."

Lighting-man Tommy Nolan, who was located to the side of

the stage, also had a bird's-eye view of proceedings. "Looking out into the audience was an unforgettable experience," Nolan remarks. "I was up on the lighting platform about eight feet off the deck, on the right-hand side of the stage, just next to where John Lennon stood. I could see that the audience were really carried away. They didn't invade the stage. The only time I saw that was when the Rolling Stones came the second time. Even where I was, you could see the Beatles but not really hear them. They didn't have the amplification they have now and there was a wall of noise. Yet it was a fabulous concert."

With George Harrison already showcased on 'Roll Over Beethoven', next it was over to Ringo. He sang 'Boys', the B-side of 'Will You Love Me Tomorrow?' by the Shirelles. An old drummer's favourite, it had been performed by Ringo as far back as his years with Rory Storm and the Hurricanes. From the album *Please Please Me*, the number was popular with the girls, concerning, as it did, an issue close to their hearts. The pace was frantic. The crowds danced in the aisles. A wedge of beefy ushers forced them back to their seats. It was all heat and explosive energy. The Adelphi was rocking – surprising many of the adults attending the shows.

"I was standing in the aisle on the right side, up near the stage," says Tom Costello, manager of the Cadets showband, who was present at both the press conference and the first concert. "There were about ten of us. We had come directly from the press conference into the theatre. We had about four or five complimentary tickets between us, that we were given. I remember one of the attendants wanting to check them. He'd start at the beginning but we'd pass the tickets back. He knew there was something wrong. He checked us a number of times. He was going out of his tree. He gave it up in the end. We were lucky because the show was terrific."

An equally mature Noel Rennick, who was Assistant Secretary of Adelphi-Carlton Ltd and who had an office in D'Olier Street, also turned up for the first performance. "I was over at the restaurant in the Adelphi having lunch and there was a road manager there from ABC who said to me, 'Why don't you come over and look at the show?'" Rennick recollects. "I said, 'Ah, I don't know if I'll bother. I'm not much into that type of music.' Anyway, at about half-five I said, 'I'll walk over and see what's happening.' I walked in when the show started. I was close enough to the Beatles. They were playing at the time. It was very hard to hear the music and I could barely hear their voices coming out. I was in a little alcove quite near them. Normally you would hear very clearly from that point yet it was impossible to make the Beatles out, the noise was so loud. But it certainly was an experience."

Photographer Pat Maxwell was overwhelmed. "I only went into the theatre for about ten minutes of the concert," he points out. "I was surprised. The set-up was amazingly simple in the cinema, totally unlike what you would get nowadays for a pop group with flashing lights and massive sets. They just had a drum set, a couple of guitars and they were in the middle of a bare stage. They had small speakers and they still could just about be heard. The screams were ear-piercing. I waited for about ten minutes and I couldn't take any more. The noise was unbelievable. It wasn't the fault of the artistes. The noise went through your head. It was the most exciting night ever in Abbey Street."

Next, Paul introduced 'Till There Was You', a lilting love song borrowed from Meredith Willson's *The Music Man*. Although a track from the group's forthcoming LP *With The Beatles*, it was also one of the numbers performed by the band at their failed Decca audition the previous year. Paul dedicated the song to Mags Graham, the young 'reporter' who had attended the afternoon press conference while masquerading as a journalist from the 'National Syndicate of Papers'. She had owned up to McCartney that she was an impostor. Mags was overwhelmed by Paul's dedication onstage.

"'Till There Was You' was thrown in at the right time to bring the excitement level down a little bit and chill the thing out before hitting them again with another upbeat number," Ted Carroll remarks. "The Beatles were very experienced in stagecraft because they'd been doing it solidly for three or four years at that stage. Obviously, with a show like that you have to have light and shade. You can't maintain a high level all the time. You need to bring the excitement down and build it up again to be effective."

John Olohan remembers 'Till There Was You' primarily because of a mistake made with the spotlights at the end of the song. "There was a double spotlight on McCartney," Olohan says. "They were going to another number after it which involved himself and John Lennon. The two spotlights stayed on McCartney. There was a bit of a hiatus. John Lennon was kind of waving to the spot guy. He jumped into the double spotlight and danced out with one of the spotlights on him. It looked like as if it was planned but it wasn't. He trusted the spot operator that he would know what was going on. It was real John Lennon. He did the little kind of quirky dance he used to do. The place went crazy. It was great."

Frank Grimes recalls a similar error at the second show. "During 'Till There Was You', when they went to George's solo they mistimed the spotlight," Grimes recollects. "When he was doing his solo, the spot had moved over onto him from Paul. When he was finished the solo, it didn't go back. He had to point to the man on the spot to send it back over to Paul. There was a big laugh."

Both miscues were caused by chaos in the projection room, where the spotlights were located. "The noise was ferocious," 15-year-old Tony Foran, the trainee projectionist who was helping with the spots, offers by way of explanation. "We couldn't hear the cues for the colours from the lighting monitor. We couldn't hear a thing with the screaming. We couldn't hear the music either. Young ones even got into the projection room and all they did was scream, scream, scream. We had to guess what was happening on the stage.

"We kind of knew, looking down on the stage, what they were going to perform. If the stage lights went to normal settings, you knew they were talking and introducing a song. If the lights went dark and were dimmed, then you'd know you should put in a magenta light or a pink light or something like that. You just changed your colours on the spots with what was happening on the stage. Unfortunately, even though we had rehearsed it, at the end of the day it was just guesswork."

Cranking it up, close to the end, the Beatles launched into 'She Loves You', which had been written after a concert in Newcastle the previous June. The pace was upped as the Beatles belted it out, the song's pumping rhythm surpassed only by the lyrics and the 'yeah, yeah, yeahs'. The fans danced in the aisles. They bounced on their seats. The balcony of the Adelphi shuddered with the pounding it received. 'She Loves You', as one newspaper critic reported, "was virtually obscured by unrestrained cheering." Those in attendance from the worlds of music and entertainment were spellbound by the quality of what they were hearing.

"McCartney said at the press conference, 'Bring your earmuffs tonight,'" says Tom Costello, manager of the Cadets. "They were going to blow us out of it and they did. The crowd were going mad for them. It was probably the first real screaming we ever heard. The crowd were well-behaved although they were screaming and clapping. They were enjoying themselves. They were no trouble. It was ahead of the wild times and it was great."

Part-time promoter Ted Carroll was similarly enthused. "The Beatles were a very tight rock 'n roll band and they were playing at close to full volume," he remarks. "The Adelphi was a big enough place and they needed to crank everything up as close to full as they could. There was a lot of mid-range so it was quite a loud sound coming from the stage. Sitting where I was, you had the sound of the band, which was as loud as it could be, coming at you from the front. From behind, you had an equally deafening roar and non-stop screaming. It was like being in a maelstrom of sound, very exciting and lots of fun."

Brian Lynch was surprised by the standard of musicianship. "I was impressed by the fact that they actually could play," he explains. "I had gone to see people like Marty Wilde and Billy Fury and these kinds of people. They were the school of English rockers. A lot of them were hired for their looks. But the Beatles had been gigging in Germany and it knocked an awful lot of corners off them. Their sound was quite pure. They used a bit of tremolo. But it was before guitar distortion. That came later. It was a genuine live performance, before backing-tracks and light shows. What you heard was a very clean kind of sound. You could hear that they were playing properly. It must have been very hard for them in the face of that kind of compressed wall of sound coming up at them. There was far more sound coming up onto the stage than going off it."

Equally enthralled was the young Jimmy Magee, compiler of *Ireland's Top Ten* for Radio Éireann, who attended one of the shows. "The Beatles were something completely different. They were new," he says. "We were used to rock 'n roll, with its particular beat and rhythm. You couldn't resist dancing or tapping your foot. If a Presley record came on, the place was jumping straight away. But the Beatles had a different rhythm, like in 'I Want To Hold Your Hand'. You couldn't jive to it. It wasn't jive music. You had to think about it. People had grown tired of Bill Haley and 'Rock Around The Clock'. Later, the Beatles went to do 'Norwegian Wood' and 'And I Love Her' and all these beautiful songs. But not that night!"

The spotlight picked out John Lennon for the final two numbers of the night. First up was a track from the group's forthcoming LP *With The Beatles*. The song, 'Money (That's What I Want)', was an old Barrett Strong hit from the late

107

1950s and a *Billboard* chart success for Motown's first label named 'Tamla'. Featuring John's rasping, leathery voice as lead vocal, it was one of his favourites.

Lennon also sang the last song on the show, the classic 'Twist And Shout'. Written by Phil Medley and Bert Russell, versions had already been released by the Top Notes and the Isley Brothers. The last track to be recorded on the *Please Please Me* LP, it was a number Lennon delivered with legs astride, eyes focused on the far distance and his mouth in close on the mike. With his vocal cords straining as he spat out the words, the volume of sound in the auditorium peaked as the group brought the show to an end.

"'Twist And Shout' was the only song we heard because they cranked it up," recalls Jonathan Ryan. "You might hear the opening notes of something like 'I Want To Hold Your Hand' but then there were shrieks and you wouldn't hear a thing after that. But 'Twist And Shout' was different. My other abiding memory of John Lennon was of him standing over on the right side saying, 'Shut fucking up!' He shouted that out at one point. It was in that marvellous high-pitched Liverpool accent."

From then on, mayhem reigned until the Beatles finished. The *Irish Independent* described the scene: "When the show was almost over and the Liverpool group was singing one of its more famous hits, 'Twist And Shout', hundreds in the stalls rushed from their seats and ran to the stage. The attendants were powerless and were crushed. An aggressive teenager snatched a torch from one of the ushers and threw it onto the stage. Papers and programmes were also thrown. Many more stood on their seats, clapping and stamping their feet."

Ann Huet, aged 25, who was seated close to the front, was caught in the stampede: "People ran over our backs to get to the stage. They were running over the seats. They must have been collecting in the gap that was there after the first five or six rows. They just took off. The ones near the front all had to put their heads down. I remember putting my head down between my knees, with people running over me. I had a new duffle-coat on, from Milletts. It was a nice creamy colour and very fashionable. It had little knobs on the front and red tartan lining. I bought it myself out of my hard-earned money. I thought I was the bee's knees. All I remember thinking was, 'My bloody new duffle-coat!' I think it survived another few weeks."

By that late stage the air was moist and the atmosphere heavy, according to Sandra Grant: "It was hot and wet. It was moist from the energy given off by people. There was no air, basically. The little air there was had a moistness in it. You were bathed in a film of perspiration. It was possibly hotter upstairs where I was because heat rises. There was just this hectic excitement."

As the final note of 'Twist And Shout' faded away, John, Paul, George and Ringo bowed and, all of a sudden, the concert was over. Short and sweet, in the traditions of variety, the Beatles had performed ten numbers – 'I Saw Her Standing There', 'From Me To You', 'All My Loving', 'You Really Got A Hold On Me', 'Roll Over Beethoven', 'Boys', 'Till There Was You', 'She Loves You', 'Money (That's What I Want)' and 'Twist And Shout'. It had passed in a flash, like a bolt of lightning, a sudden earth tremor or a spontaneous explosion. After just 25 short minutes, the curtains had closed and the Beatles were gone.

"We didn't want it to end," says Phyllis Tyrrell. "All we kept shouting was, 'More,' 'More.' It was fabulous." John Olohan adds: "After it finished there was a kind of calm and everybody reverted to normal. However, the girls behind me with the beehives, because they had been hysterical and because of the make-up and hairspray, they couldn't revert to the way they were. I thought, 'Oh, my God, what a transformation.' There was no way back."

Josephine Tyrrell started crying: "Yes, I was crying. Many other people were crying coming out as well. There were a lot of people who went around the back to the stage door trying to get a glimpse of them leaving. We didn't. But a lot of the young girls did. I heard them say, 'Come on, we'll see them coming out. Maybe we'll get their autographs.' It was an event never to be forgotten."

Gillian Freedman felt exhilarated: "I felt wonderful. There was a profound feeling of being alive. It was a sense of identity, of belonging to something, to be young and to have seen your absolute heroes. They had played these songs I knew, that were so different from anything else. They were singing songs about the way I felt. I just couldn't believe I saw them and was with them in the same room. Then I realised I hadn't heard the songs. But the whole thing was the experience. I loved every second of it."

Co-ordinator of the Beatles' visit, Paul Russell, was also there to the end: "I had been with Arthur Howes at the back of the theatre. I'm 6' 2" and Arthur was about 5' 8". He was eating cigarettes, not smoking them. Arthur said, 'Paul, this was a great idea, looking back at it.' Peter Walsh wasn't at the concert but Arthur Howes said, 'I must tell Peter it was a very successful show.' It was the chance of a lifetime for Ireland. If it didn't happen it would never happen again. It was only when they hit Ed Sullivan that it suddenly dawned on all of us that we were blessed because we would never have seen them again."

As they departed, the fans left a scene of desolation in the cinema. The floor was littered with debris – crumpled programmes with their metallic-silver front covers and back covers torn and melted from the heat and the mayhem, cigarette packets, sweet bags, combs, make-up bags and even school-books. And there probably was worse! "They used to say that if you came into the second house the seats were wet," says Jeff Williams of the Kestrels. "The seats would be wet from the first house. They wet themselves with all the screaming and excite-ment. People used to bring their coats in so they could sit on them."

That aspect of the matter wasn't lost on cinema manager Harry Lush, adds Morgan O'Sullivan: "I can see Harry Lush's face to this day. He adored the Adelphi. It was like a shrine to him. The cinema actually suited the concerts. It was a very gracious place. The upstairs was quite rich in furnishings. It was quite sumptuous, like a hotel. The seating was absolutely magnificent. The cinemas then were sort of Art Deco. To have all these youngsters in doing what they were doing devastated him. He couldn't understand that young people would behave like this."

It was still a wonderful concert, concludes Jimmy Magee: "Perhaps all these kids were opposing the rigid thinking of their parents, guardians and elders who thought that Frank Sinatra, Bing Crosby, Elvis Presley and Mel Tormé were the bee's knees with their nice hairstyles and nice suits. They were rebelling against that. This was completely different – the 'mop heads'. I'm not so sure the average Irish girl would be allowed bring one of them home on a date. They were noisy but it was good. They could have been singing anything. It was scary. It just shows how you can work people up to do anything."

Shortly after half past eight – as the first house emptied and half an hour before the second show began – journalists walked the short distance from the Adelphi to their newspaper offices nearby. 'Tempo', music critic of the *Evening Herald*, crafted his report for the following day: "Fine show – if one could only hear it. Because of the noise, which apparently goes hand in hand with the Beatles' stage shows, many were last night inclined to gloss over the entertainment value of the Adelphi show altogether. It can be said, however, that of its type this was one of the best stage productions to come to our shores for some time. The incessant screaming, clapping and feet-stomping inside the theatre however resulted in it being impossible to hear but snatches of the artists. The Beatles were just as I had expected. They sang their numbers with rare enthusiasm, their colourful appearance adding immensely to the overall presentation."

At the *Herald's* rival paper – the *Evening Press* – fledgling newspaperman Donal McCann penned his first-ever journalistic report. Perhaps it was his age – just 20. Maybe it was the novelty of writing his first piece of copy. It could have been that blossoming affection for all things theatrical which would soon draw him to a career on the stage. Whatever the cause, what he produced was the finest piece of writing of his short journalistic career.

"'I'll dream them tonight,' said a fat little girl of fifteen," McCann wrote. "Her eyes were shining and her forehead was damp and she tottered out into O'Connell Street like a girl possessed by something strange. Possessed by something stranger than the skinny youth who held her hand and sniffled and said 'Yeah'. And all because of the Beatles – four young men who proved at a press conference earlier that they're a very likeable bunch. And really ordinary fellows really – offstage."

THE RIOT

Shortly after half past eight, 2,304 excited, red-faced Beatles' fans burst from the Adelphi as the first concert cleared onto the streets. They were in a state of emotional arousal – a simmering, seething flow of mainly white-hot adolescents intoxicated by what they had just been part of inside. Their clothes and hair were dishevelled. Flushed and glowing, they were drenched in sweat. Many held their heads in their hands, overcome by what they had witnessed. Girls' faces were smeared with mascara. They stared into the faraway distance, unable to refocus their gaze.

Two thousand three hundred and four bodies exploded from the theatre to be confronted by another two thousand three hundred and four bodies waiting to enter for the second performance. The excitement was contagious. No one outside wanted to miss what those inside had been part of. No one waiting in the street wanted to lose out on even one second of the nine o'clock show. The two irresistible forces smashed into each other with unyielding power, with neither of them willing or able to give way. Like a pair of jumbo jets on the same flight path, they faced imminent disaster.

"As I was coming out, the crowd from the next show was coming in," says John Olohan. "The crowd from the show that had just finished didn't want to go home. What happened was

113

that everybody came out of the cinema and lingered. The crowd that were queuing for the nine o'clock show couldn't get in. There was a moment when I said, 'Oh, oh, I'm in a war zone here. Something terrible is going to happen.' This crush started. I got terribly claustrophobic. All you could see was heads and bodies right up Abbey Street. There was talk of cars being overturned. People were saying, 'Where are the Beatles?' 'Where are they?' 'We'll wait,' 'We'll wait.'

"People were desperate to get into the Adelphi. There was a kind of hysteria happening on the street. I thought, 'How is this going to end?' I looked up Abbey Street. I noticed a direct line to O'Connell Street where the kerb and the road met. People were either on the path or on the road. I put one foot on the path and one foot on the road and I eased my way up. I just walked straight up to O'Connell Street and got out of it."

Standing outside, waiting to get in was Sandra Grant, aged 16, who had a ticket for the second performance. "Ticket-holders for the second show didn't want to miss the beginning of the performance," she recollects. "They were excited and trying to push their way inside. There was a mêlée. There were two elements pushing against each other. I remember someone saying, 'You won't be allowed in unless you queue in an orderly fashion.' They hadn't a hope of getting it to happen."

The electricity among the emerging fans reminded Ted Carroll of the Bill Haley concert in 1957. "I went to see Bill Haley when I was about 14 and that was a hot ticket, with great excitement," he recalls. "People came out of that as high as kites and they rioted. They were so high they had to let off steam. They overturned cars. There were people in the middle of the streets and O'Connell Street was completely blocked with people walking about. Younger people came out of the Beatles in the same way."

Adding to the panic and chaos were an estimated 2,000 ticketless fans standing in the streets, with zero chance of getting to see either performance. Some had arrived solely to catch a glimpse of the Beatles. They stood there watching the upstairs windows and stage door to see if a Beatle might appear. Others hoped to come by a spare ticket or work their way into the theatre without having any ticket at all. More wanted to be able to say, "I was there." These casual spectators formed a resolute and immovable force. All they wanted to do was stand still. In a sense, they too attended the Beatles' concerts, as the sound spilled from the cinema out onto the street. A compressed, muffled noise of distant guitars and screeching was better than no concert at all. Unfortunately, as they stood still they blocked both the crowds attempting to exit and those trying to get in.

One of the ticketless fans, Joe Nolan, had arrived at close to nine o'clock to observe the excitement and to hopefully work his way into the second show. "Middle Abbey Street was packed," he remembers. "All age-groups were there, including 21-year-olds and 25-year-olds. It was a big crowd and the whole street was blocked off. People were up on the cars parked in Middle Abbey Street. They were walking on the roofs of the cars with stiletto heels. They were trying to get up close to the cinema or to get a view. There must have been 30 or 40 cars there. There were stiletto heel marks all over the roofs."

Unknown to the fans, shortly after the start of the first show two of the Beatles and two of the Kestrels had slipped quietly from the Adelphi, making their way to a pub close-by for a pint of Guinness. They timed their exit to perfection. Dressed in disguise, Ringo and John casually left the cinema soon after the early acts went onstage and walked down the street in the company of Roger Greenaway and Jeff Williams. At the time, the crowd for the first concert were safely inside while the build-up for the second show had yet to develop. With concert-goers expecting the Beatles to be in the cinema, no one paid the slightest bit of attention. Their visit to what was most likely the Oval in Middle Abbey Street is a story that, up to now, has never been told.

"The big thing I remember about Dublin was going to the

pub close-by to have a Guinness," Roger Greenaway, of the Kestrels, says. "We went with Ringo and John, who were heavily disguised. I don't think Paul and George drank at that time. God knows how we got to the pub but we did. We got away with it. I remember it vividly. I know the pub was very, very close. It was on the same side of the road as the theatre. The only reason why we got away with it was because they wouldn't recognise us. If it had been the four Beatles they would have been spotted."

Jeff Williams of the Kestrels also recalls the adventure, once more identifying the pub as being just down the road from the venue. "We did go out for a pint of Guinness with the Beatles," Williams agrees. "I went as well because I wanted to taste it. We weren't great drinkers but everyone had been telling us that we had to taste the Guinness in Dublin. They said it was totally different to what it was anywhere else in the world. We slipped out during the early part of the first show. All the people would have gone in. We weren't on until the second half of the show. The second house wouldn't have fully turned up yet.

"If you think about it, it wasn't that difficult. If you're in the theatre or in the hotel, where people would expect to see you, you would be recognised. But you can get away with just walking up a road. People don't expect you to be there. They believe that the show is on so you must be in the theatre. Sometimes you could even walk back in through the foyer. You had to tell the staff so they would know who you were. You could come in that way because the crowd would be around the stage door and people wouldn't expect to see anybody coming in through the front door. I remember doing it so well."

The foursome of Guinness drinkers returned to the Adelphi in time for their allotted slots in the second half of the early show. During their performances, the crowd outside continued to grow. Those lining up for the second house did so alongside the growing mob of casual spectators. Both groups, in turn, were soon confronted by the exiting fans after the first show finished. At its peak, some 7,000 bodies were crammed together into Middle Abbey Street, forming a heaving, swaying, agitated, panicking mass. The scene was a potential disaster. It was like an accident slowly unfolding, a catastrophe waiting to happen.

"There was a worry that someone might get seriously hurt," remarks Bill Herlihy, who was a Garda sergeant attached to Store Street station and who was present on the night. "There was pushing and shoving. It was almost like a stampede. It was a fine, big cinema but there were these swing-doors leading into it, probably seven or eight of them. They could have caused damage. Also, cinemas were a kind of place where people used to come and go. People would go in during the middle of a show and eventually say, 'This is where we came in, we'll leave now.' There was no need for large exits. If you were over in the old Theatre Royal there would have been far more exits."

Noel Rennick, who was Assistant Secretary of Adelphi-Carlton Ltd and who attended the first concert, was also concerned over the unfolding events. "When the first show was over, there was a big mêlée out in Abbey Street. It was literally impossible to go out," he recalls. "I went up to the old boardroom where I chatted with some people. There was a lot of commotion outside. We could hear it. I remember seeing someone being brought in off the street to the foyer with a broken ankle or something similar. With the mêlée that was going on in the street, there didn't seem to be any point in going out so I stayed there, chatting to people until it cleared.

"The boardroom overlooked the street. The crowds assumed that's where the Beatles were. When we went over to the curtains to look down, there would be a big roar. There would be a big surge. When they saw something moving up above, there was a cheer and a reaction. You didn't exactly pull back the curtains and stay looking out. What happened, to a certain extent, was that the press reported that this sort of thing was happening in Manchester and Liverpool and wherever. When it came to another venue, the audience reacted in the same way. It was an inconvenience to me because I wanted to go home but I couldn't."

Recognising the potential for trouble, the Adelphi management opened the cinema's rear doors into Prince's Street, hoping that some of the crowd would depart that way. It was a shrewd move, designed to steer bodies away from the crush developing at the cinema's front entrance. Unfortunately, the noise and excitement coming from Middle Abbey Street encouraged many who exited into Prince's Street to head around to the front.

"Harry Lush was on duty that night and as the manager on duty he was, if you like, responsible for the house," Noel Rennick points out. "He had to make the decisions as to what way it was emptied and how to get the Beatles out. They opened the exits into Prince's Street to let people out after the first show. That was the strategy – to let some out into Prince's Street because the other crowd were outside in Abbey Street." Unfortunately, the move didn't work, says Garda Sergeant Bill Herlihy. "People then went around by Easons and came back into Abbey Street and added to the turmoil," he remarks.

One of the fans exiting into Prince's Street was Charles McCarthy, who was aged 11 and at the first concert with his two brothers. "We came out the back door after the first show," he recalls. "There were a lot of people in the back lane when we left. A lot of the people turned around and went back into Middle Abbey Street. They wanted to get a glimpse of the Beatles. There was a mass of people around. It was like a sea of people. There was mayhem. We could hear the crowds. There was like an echo. We weren't too far away from the scene. They were all shouting, 'John,' 'Paul,' 'Ringo' or 'the Beatles,' 'the Beatles.' There was great jubilation because it was the group's first time in Dublin. They were kids like myself. We were young and cheerful. Many of them stayed there half the night thinking the Beatles were still in there and might come out. But they didn't."

Responding to the unfolding chaos, the Gardaí pushed the crowd down Middle Abbey Street with the intention of sealing it off. It was a 'slow retreat' manoeuvre. They paid a heavy price. A battle between police and fans ensued. Three Gardaí were shoved to the ground. Others had their hats knocked off. Another was hit by a stone in the eye and required stitches. Youths pushed a parked car into six of the Guards. They also pelted Gardaí with large lumps of coal. Reinforcements were called in from all parts of the metropolitan area. The total number of Gardaí in attendance rose to 250. "One Garda, hardier than some of his colleagues, rushed the mob alone, to be 'dust-binned'," observed an *Irish Press* reporter. "A bin of rubbish left out for Corporation workmen to take away was planted on his head to the delight of the frenzied rioters."

It was getting quite rough, recalls Cathal O'Shannon, reporter with *The Irish Times*: "At one stage, we had to get into a telephone box on Middle Abbey Street and we slammed the door shut. We waited until the people flooding by had passed. They were fleeing towards O'Connell Street. There was a feeling of violence around. But the Guards were reacting very heavily, slightly outrageously, to tell you the truth. My recollection is that they overreacted."

The Gardaí eventually forced most of the crowd down to the intersection of Middle Abbey Street and O'Connell Street. A double line of police then sealed the street off. Immediately, pockets of youths launched themselves at the Gardaí, attempting to breach their lines. Scuffles ensued and people were injured. Violence spread up and down O'Connell Street. One youth received stab wounds. Wooden barriers, placed on the street by workmen, were knocked down.

O'Connell Street was reduced to one lane. Gardaí struggled to keep even that single lane open. Traffic was blocked between O'Connell Bridge and Nelson's Pillar. A bus driver, stalled in the traffic back-up, was almost dragged from his cab. Crowds hissed at couples in evening dress who were making their way to a dance at the Metropole. Windows, including some in the *Irish Press*, were smashed.

Several of the rioters climbed onto the monuments in O'Connell Street, where they clung to the life-sized images. "Gardaí grappled with pointed-toe shoes and narrow pants to ground the climbers – all the while hissed, booed and sometimes physically obstructed. Said a Garda sergeant who had his cap whipped off with a flying object: 'I have seen everything now. This is really mad. What can have got into them?'" the *Irish Press* reported.

An estimated 20 squad cars and a Black Maria were called to the scene. Twelve people were arrested and taken to various Garda stations. Some 50 boys and girls needed treatment. At least three were taken to hospital with fractured arms or legs. More had suffered panic or claustrophobia as they were trapped in the mass of bodies. The arrival of three fire engines added to the confusion. Fans feared they were about to be hosed. Rumours spread of a false fire alarm at the Adelphi. The Gardaí eventually explained that they had called in the fire tenders in the hope that their bells might subdue the crowd.

"There were lots of youngsters creating a bit of mayhem but they were mostly good-humoured," Garda Sergeant Bill Herlihy observes. "The fans were singing Beatles' songs and tormenting one another. Some were, I'm sure, having a bit of banter telling us to 'go back to the bog' but we were used to that sort of mild abuse. There were a few people hurt. People got pushed against railings and against doors and things like that. I remember we had to get the ambulance to take some people away. I'd say the people who were arrested probably wouldn't be arrested today. We should have been more tolerant of them and let them get on with what they were doing."

St John Ambulance volunteers set up a holding area in Middle Abbey Street. It was sectioned off by police. They used it to treat those who were injured. They also removed some girls who had fainted in the theatre and took care of them there. John McGrath, who was one of the St John Ambulance volunteers, estimated that 20 fans required treatment for fainting. Approximately 50 volunteers were on duty, he said. One ambulance driver was reported as saying, "We are running a shuttle service to Jervis Street – this is shocking. They're gone mad."

Shortly before 11 o'clock, a further 2,304 people emerged from the Adelphi at the end of the second show. Fortunately, there was no third house waiting out on the street. Instead, in their place were fans hoping to catch sight of the Beatles. They pushed, bumped, shoved and jostled each other, all the time wondering how the group might exit. Would it be by the front or back exit? Would they leave by limousine or police transportation? Not for the first time that night, the streets surrounding the Adelphi were in chaos.

"When we went to go out of the theatre, the street was crammed," says Sandra Grant, who was accompanied by her friend at the second concert. "We came out into a sea of bodies and there was no way through. You couldn't get up to O'Connell Street to get the bus. It was frightening. I mean, we were only 16. There was nothing then like crowd control or putting up barriers so that people could filter through. You were caught in this situation where people were still pushing towards the theatre and others were trying to get out.

"The Guards were pushing people aside to try and clear the way. I remember a Guard's hat got knocked off. He hit out and while I can't say I was hit, I felt the force of whoever he connected with. He gave a forceful push because somebody had tipped his hat off. He had kind of retaliated. I was in the two or three people that felt the lash-out. I felt the Guards overreacted. I thought, 'I have to get out of this.' My friend and I made for a lane across the road. With the Guards pushing, we got roughly shoved to the far side of the road. We then went down the lane that cuts to the back of Bachelor's Walk. We got out that way and made our way home by bus."

Although the fans were unaware, by the time the second house was exiting the Beatles were long gone from the Adelphi. Within a minute of the end of the concert they were already on their way back to the Gresham Hotel, inside an *Evening Herald* van. For hours, Adelphi manager Harry Lush together with tour personnel had puzzled over the safest form of escape. A quick phone-call by Lush to Independent Newspapers, located next door, solved the problem.

"The Guards told Harry that it would be dangerous to bring the Beatles out because they would be mobbed," says Norman Lush, Harry's brother. "The crowd was way down Abbey Street and up O'Connell Street waiting for them. He knew people from the *Evening Herald* and *Irish Independent*. In fact, he knew people from all of Dublin – business people and news-paper people. He was great for giving out free passes to people to go to the pictures, to the extent that I often wondered how the Adelphi made any profit. I'm sure he had given out many free passes to the *Evening Herald* people so they were probably only too happy to co-operate. It was typical of him to think it up. He always knew a way around things. He was also very good at keeping things like that to himself. He wouldn't have even told the usherettes in case the word got out and the mob would have been around to cut off a lock of hair or whatever."

With approximately 30 minutes of the concert still to go, the *Evening Herald* van quietly pulled up into the shadows outside the stage door of the Adelphi. As driver Jack Flanagan relaxed at the wheel, it remained parked there as if waiting for the first editions to roll off the presses. Fans checked it out but dismissed its significance. Eventually, the signal was given to start the engines. The Beatles rushed from the stage door and were bundled inside.

Crouching inside the van, the four very pale, frightened-looking Beatles, with their make-up still on, were transported from Prince's Street the short distance back to the Gresham. Also in the van were *Evening Herald* photographer Jack Murphy and young journalist Liam Kelly. 'Rescue Beatles Operation' was one of the paper's scoops of the year. "With the precision of a commando operation and within ten musical beats of their closing number – 'Twist And Shout' – the Beatles were whisked to the safety of their hotel in an *Evening Herald* delivery van last night," the paper announced triumphantly in its next day's edition.

"I was on night-duty," explains journalist Liam Kelly. "I was a young reporter and wasn't very long in the place. I came on duty at around eight o'clock. The management of the cinema got in contact with us and asked could we put a newspaper van at the Beatles' disposal to get them out and back to their hotel. They were concerned about their safety. We were delighted because it was a chance to get a good story. I was asked to get into the van and go with them.

"We were waiting in the van at the back of the cinema in the dark, just where Arnotts is now. The van's lights were off. Finally, one of their entourage gave the word to start the engine. They came straight out the door and jumped into the back of the van, which was open at the time. No one saw them go in. It was like a commando-style operation. They just opened the door of the theatre, everybody plunged out and went straight into the van and off we went to the Gresham Hotel.

"It was just them in the back with me and a photographer. They were sitting on bundles of old papers, probably the previous day's edition which had been brought back from newsagents. They were amazed with the reception they got but they were anxious to get back to the hotel without any incident or confrontation. We could hear everything through the van. The fans were shouting for the Beatles while we were just edging along. There were shouts of 'We want the Beatles.' It was only a short journey, which took roughly five or six minutes. In retrospect, there could have been a very nasty incident. If the fans knew the Beatles were in there, they could have overturned the van or anything. It could have been a different story. By pure luck, it didn't happen.

"There were hundreds of fans milling outside the hotel as we headed for the back entrance. I emerged from the van followed by the four lads. We went straight to the hotel kitchen, much to the amazement of the wide-eyed staff. We headed into the Aberdeen Hall, again much to the amazement of the staff and residents of the hotel. We then went to one of their bedrooms. They were all very high after the show and were totally stunned at the reception they had got in Dublin. They kept saying it was 'Fab!' 'Fab!' and we chatted and took pictures. They were all very giddy, except George who remained quiet and, to my memory, stayed very much in the background.

"They were all talking at the same time with the exception of George, who just sat on the bed wide-eyed and shaking his head at the antics of his mates. They were in a great mood. The one I got most sense out of was John Lennon. I asked George about his Irish background but there was no response. He didn't say a word. One thing I do remember, he appeared to chain-smoke. In the 60s everybody smoked and there was nothing antisocial about it, not like today. But, even for that time, he seemed to constantly have a cigarette in his hand, pulling heavily on each weed. He seemed to love each fag. He paid a heavy price for this addiction. The cigarettes finally got him. After that, I left. I had to get back to write a piece so I didn't delay. I went back and did the piece on how we rescued the Beatles."

Outside the Gresham, fans waited for the Beatles unaware that they were safely settled in their rooms. Crowds numbered in the thousands. Many were bunched up against the hotel's main door. Groups of young teenagers walked up and down, wondering when, and where, the group would appear. Some were stationed at the rear of the hotel. "I can remember the crowds outside the Gresham Hotel," says Jeff Williams of the

Kestrels. "There were thousands of people outside the hotel. Everyone knew that they were staying there. There were as many outside the hotel as there were outside the theatre."

Numbers had been building for an hour or so, with fans knowing that the second concert would be over by 11 o'clock. Questions were being asked about what sort of transportation the group would arrive in. Some speculated that the Beatles wouldn't return to the Gresham at all. The surrounds of the hotel and also Middle Abbey Street were, for a Thursday night, scenes of frenzied activity. The rest of the city was empty.

"I was going home on the half-ten bus from Busáras," John Olohan recalls. "The city-centre was like something from a surreal movie. It was all deserted, like a curfew. There was nobody on the streets where I was, just an odd car going up and down. I remember heading off down Marlborough Street. At one stage I heard screaming. It was getting nearer and nearer and nearer. I was walking along with my bag. This crowd of about 100 people came along, screaming at the top of their voices. They ran past at full speed. Seemingly they had heard that the Beatles weren't staying in the Gresham but were staying in the Shelbourne. They were running at top speed from the back of the Gresham up to the Shelbourne. I backed into a doorway because they would have trampled me to death. Immediately, the place reverted to desolation. It was really weird. The atmosphere was really strange."

Within 20 minutes of the end of the concerts most of the last stragglers began moving away from the Adelphi and the crowds in Middle Abbey Street fragmented. Groups of revellers headed off over O'Connell Bridge or down the quays. Cars and shop windows bore the brunt of their wild enthusiasm. One car was tossed into the street with its windows smashed. Another had its roof bashed in. Reports came in that some hysterical girls were flinging their shoes at people who were quietly making their way home.

"After the concerts in Dublin, the thing that sticks in my

mind was the overturned cars in O'Connell Street and that people set fire to cars," Peter Jay, of Peter Jay and the Jaywalkers, remarks. "There was a riot, a good-natured riot but still a riot going on, which we thought was fantastic, really cool. I can remember seeing the car going up and thinking this was wild. You didn't see cars being set on fire in those days. Ireland was always this magical, mystical place, and the burning of the car stood out. It was all more like good-natured exuberance, a crazy fan thing."

By half past eleven the rioting had all but ceased, with only a small number of teenagers left on the streets. What just hours before had been a scene of mayhem was now a litter-strewn wasteland. Left behind were tons of rubbish, shoes, umbrellas, concert programmes, cigarette packets and ticket stubs, along with stones and shards of broken glass. But the rioters were gone – off on the last buses from Nelson's Pillar to their homes scattered around Dublin.

"We were hoping that the thing would peter out and we'd all get home," says Garda Sergeant Bill Herlihy. "It eventually petered out by half past eleven. Public transport was the way of getting home at that time. If you missed the bus, you'd have to walk. The last bus was at half-eleven. The inspector blew the whistle at half-eleven on the dot and all the buses would start off in unison from their terminus in O'Connell Street, in front of the GPO. He would give the signal and everybody would have to be on board by then." And that was the end of the riot!

In the following days, reaction to the rioting was mixed. The *Evening Herald* blamed the crowd. "Most citizens have been quick to point the finger of condemnation at the unruly mob that might have got completely out of hand had it not been for the efforts of the Gardaí," the newspaper declared on its front page. On the issue of fire hoses, it was argued that their use might have been effective in curtailing the trouble. A spokesman for the Gardaí responded that "hoses could not be used unless in the case of dire necessity and by direct Government order."

The Irish Times posed questions about the role of the Gardaí. "In some quarters yesterday there was criticism of the police for the way they handled the situation," the newspaper commented. "But a police officer said a situation developed where they had to clear Middle Abbey Street and it was thought better to do so by splitting the crowds. Force was used only to restrain people from breaking cordons, and every consideration was given to girls and youths who obviously were not of the 'teddy-boy' type. The Garda spokesman added: 'We did our best under the circumstances and we do not think there was too much force used.'"

The Gardaí probably did try their best, especially considering the era in question. Those were innocent, largely crime-free times. Respect for authority was commonplace. Outbreaks of mob violence were virtually unknown. Crowd control procedures were primitive. But change was occurring. The first signs of a breakdown in law and order were appearing. Social bonds were loosening. Civil unrest and paramilitary violence were less than five years away. The supposition that a Garda presence, on its own, would maintain order was old-fashioned. Something was destined to give, and it did with a vengeance on the evening of 7 November 1963.

"I'd say it was something we weren't ready for," concludes Garda Sergeant Bill Herlihy. "Harry Lush and ourselves were in contact and we knew it was going to be a big event. One of the things that got to the crowd was the fact that the Beatles didn't appear. But they were the first celebrities of that nature to come to Ireland and, looking back, I'd say we weren't really prepared for it."

Perhaps understandably, the Gardaí at the time struggled to find appropriate words to express their frustration with the events of the night. As so often happens, it took the acute eye of a cartoonist to cut to the chase. The artist in question, who worked for the *Evening Herald* and who was appropriately called 'RIP', drew a wonderful cartoon for the edition of the following day. The drawing featured an exasperated Garda, surrounded by mop-topped Beatles' fans, exclaiming, "Give me traffic control to pest control any day." The Gardaí were certainly happy to see the backs of the Beatles!

NIGHT OWLS

Back in the safety of their hotel bedrooms, the Beatles set about planning the remainder of the night ahead. Although departing the following morning for Belfast, they were pumped up after the concerts and ready to go. First, they gave an interview to Liam Kelly from the *Evening Herald* as recompense for their escape from the Adelphi. Next, George Harrison had a commitment to join his mother and relatives in Drumcondra for a family gathering. Last, all four wanted to go somewhere away from the fans for a drink.

Following the *Evening Herald* interview, George departed for the family get-together, travelling by taxi the distance from the Gresham to Drumcondra of little more than a mile. Back in the hotel the others set about calling room service. All four planned to meet up in an hour. Down on O'Connell Street, stragglers shouted for the Beatles. The sound rose upwards to their suites. A few hundred yards down the street, at Nelson's Pillar, the last of the buses set out for the suburbs.

The late-night city noise was soon interrupted by the sound of knocking on the Beatles' door. Paul Russell, of Starlite Artistes, entered with a request for an interview on behalf of future concert promoter Hugh Hardy, who was home on holidays from New York. At the time, Hardy wrote for the *Irish Echo* and presented an Irish radio programme called *A Ramble*

In Érin. The programme was broadcast on WJRZ and was transmitted from the city of Newark to listeners across the Hudson River. Broadcasting the music of artistes like Bridie Gallagher, the Clancy Brothers and the Gallowglass Céilí Band, the show was a valuable outlet for the Irish music industry.

Among those whose songs featured on *A Ramble In Érin* was the songwriter Mai O'Higgins, whose compositions included 'Dungarvan My Hometown', 'My Dublin Bay', 'Sweet Youghal Bay' and 'Beautiful Bundoran'. Hardy suggested to Mai that the two should meet for a meal on his return to Dublin. The venue they chose was the Gresham. As it happened, Mai knew of Paul Russell from the time his father was stationed with the Guards in her hometown of Dungarvan. That connection would prove fruitful to Hardy at the Gresham Hotel.

Hardy was also fortunate that on 5 November, just two days prior to his dinner date, Brian Epstein had flown to New York to negotiate appearances by the Beatles on *The Ed Sullivan Show*. Breaking into America, where so far the group were unknown, was top of the band's agenda. From his base in New York's Regency Hotel, Epstein not only brokered three prime-time appearances for the Beatles on the coast-to-coast show but he also set about arranging publicity and accommodation for the visit. In the context of events unfolding in America, the fact that a New York radio personality was also in the Gresham must have seemed to the Beatles like manna from heaven.

"Mai O'Higgins and I agreed to meet at the Gresham Hotel for dinner at about seven o'clock, by chance on the night the Beatles were there," Hugh Hardy explains. "Mai had brought along a couple of friends. Before we went down to dinner, at about quarter past seven or half-seven Mai said, 'Let's take a walk up to Abbey Street to see the *craic* up there in relation to the Beatles.' That was the first time I had ever heard of the Beatles. We went up and there were thousands and thousands of fans in Abbey Street, around the Adelphi cinema. They were in front of the cinema, all aged about 15, 16 or 17. We were a couple of hundred yards away. That was as close as we could get. They were all girls screaming for the Beatles. We stayed there for a while and then walked casually back to the Gresham.

"We had our meal and were breaking up to go home our separate ways. The dining-room we were in was downstairs in the Gresham, but when we got up to the lobby we couldn't get out because the place was totally surrounded by a cordon of Gardaí. We thought, 'No problem, we'll sit down in the lounge, watch the movers and shakers going up and down, and wait.' There were lots of people passing up and down the lobby that Mai O'Higgins knew. One of the few people I recognised was Maisie McDaniel. I recognised her from her photograph on an EP which I played on my radio programme. She was walking up and down the lobby with her manager at the time, George O'Reilly.

"Another person I recognised was Paul Russell. He knew Mai O'Higgins and she called him over. She said, 'This is Hugh Hardy. He is a disc jockey in New York. Maybe the Beatles would like to meet him.' Mai, of course, was widely stretching the truth about my job as a 'disc jockey'. Paul said, 'I'm sorry, Mai, but they are not seeing anybody.' Paul went about his business and Mai said, 'Oh God, Hugh, it would be great if you could meet the Beatles.' To which I retorted with the immortal words, 'Actually, I'd rather meet Maisie McDaniel.'

"About 15 minutes later, Paul came back over to us and he said, 'Mai, the Beatles will meet your friend.' Paul took me up to their room. I had never seen or even heard of the Beatles before. I hadn't seen a photograph and didn't know anything about them. The door to the room opened and there was this big double bed with John and Paul lounging on it and Ringo over on the other side. I think they had collarless jackets on or something like that. But what really struck me was that they had these mops of hair, which wasn't the style at the time. I was familiar with some of the showbands and, the year before, I had been good friends with Butch Moore and the Capitol, who had come to America to play in the Irish ballrooms. They had 'short back and sides' and were clean-cut. Suddenly, here were these guys who had long hair and were what you might call scruffy.

"Paul Russell said, 'This is Hugh Hardy.' They all nodded and said, 'Hello.' Paul then uttered the words, which were a total lie, 'Hugh is a disc jockey in New York.' To describe me as a New York disc jockey was stretching the imagination to the absolute limit. Being a disc jockey was a far cry from playing the Clancy Brothers' 'Brennan On The Moor' or 'Fine Girl You Are', or Bridie Gallagher's 'The Boys From The County Armagh'. All of a sudden, John and Paul jumped up from lying on the bed, went on their knees and in mock pleading said to me, 'Oh, will you play our record?' 'Play a record,' 'Will you please play a record?' I thought they were nutcases. Here were these guys with long hair pleading with me to play a record. I said, 'Yeah.'

"I was there five, six or seven minutes. We chatted about America, the music and New York for a while. They clearly wanted to break into the American market. They were very mannerly. We shook hands with the promise that I would play their records. And off I went down with Paul Russell. Ten days later I headed back to New York. I remember when wrapping up my trip to Ireland on the radio I played 'Love Me Do', which I had bought and brought back with me. I said, 'If you do go home to Ireland you won't hear Irish music on the radio any more. What you will hear is a group from Liverpool called the Beatles, and they sound like this.....'. I played about a minute or so of 'Love Me Do'. It was months later before the Beatles exploded in America."

Meanwhile, out in Drumcondra, George Harrison linked up with his relations and his mother. The meeting took place at the home of John and Doris ffrench, 55 Clonturk Park, who were first cousins of George's mother Louise. Both families were close. "John ffrench was an accountant," says Tony ffrench, second cousin of George. "He and his wife Doris lived in the very last house in Clonturk Park, on the right-hand side of the road, near Tolka Park. George's mum had been over to visit before and had stayed in the house. George had also stayed in Clonturk Park when he was young. Indeed, there was a photo taken of him in O'Connell Street when he was over as a boy."

The ffrench family ancestors had originally migrated from Normandy to Wexford. In time, the clan split up, with one wing remaining in Ireland, primarily in Dublin, and the other wing moving to Liverpool. In Liverpool, Louise's father dropped the double 'f' in the family name reducing it to the simpler 'French'. He became the uniformed commissionaire at the New Brighton Tower. His daughter Louise eventually fell in love with and married Englishman Harold Harrison, a ship's steward who in time found work as a bus driver. However, Louise never lost interest in her relatives in Ireland. She frequently visited from Liverpool, staying with cousins in Drimnagh, Dun Laoghaire and Drumcondra. Her cousins John and Doris ffrench from Drumcondra travelled in the opposite direction to stay with the Harrisons.

Louise also brought George to stay with the relatives living in Dun Laoghaire. There were nine children in the family, likewise called ffrench. "Aunt Lou was a cousin of my father, who was an accountant also," explains Colm ffrench, from the Dun Laoghaire wing of the family. "I remember her well. She was a heavy smoker. She used to come over to Ireland quite a lot. When George was a young boy of somewhere between seven and ten, he came to visit us as well. I can remember him staying in our house. We lived in a place called Crofton Road. I was older so I didn't spend much time with him. But we have photographs taken with him in our back garden. Aunt Lou was a close cousin of my father's. For instance, I have a brother who lives in Manchester and she would have helped make the arrangements for the catering for my brother's wedding over there. I remember on one occasion she was coming to stay and my father did up the house, which he wasn't good at. He ended up falling and having a stroke and he died. She came over for his funeral."

Colm ffrench's sister, Doreen, also recalls the visit of George and Louise to Dun Laoghaire. "I remember him coming when he was very young, about eight," she says. "He was a small, skinny, dark-haired fellow. He was a good-looking lad. They came over by boat. They stayed in our home for about two days and then went on and stayed with other relations after that, including with Uncle John and Aunt Doris in Drumcondra. We had other cousins in Wexford but I don't know if they went there.

"Lou was a very jolly person. She was lovely, very nice. She was real bubbly and very likeable. She was a very tall, blonde woman and very pleasant. George was very close to her. Her sister sometimes came too. They might come over every couple of years. I was about 12 or 14 at the time so I only vaguely remember George. I was that bit older."

Once Beatlemania took off in 1963, Louise Harrison was in her element. She rode the roller-coaster of her son's success, turning up in all sorts of places, appearing backstage at concerts, sitting with screaming fans in auditoriums and talking to excited girls outside stage doors. Lou also turned up for shows at the Cavern, where she was known to the regulars. She even travelled to Wembley to attend poll-winners' concerts. Not surprisingly, Beatles' biographer Hunter Davies described her as "one of nature's ravers."

Immensely proud of her son's achievements, she welcomed interaction with the fans. They came from literally everywhere to the Harrison family home. There, Lou served them tea and answered questions about George's early years and his rise to fame. The fans adored her. They arrived from all parts of Britain and Ireland, and from as far away as the USA, just to say hello. Many established lifelong friendships. She even attended one enthusiast's wedding. It wasn't long before she attained celebrity status, signing autographs and soaking up acclaim on her son's behalf.

Lou answered tens of thousands of letters. At the time of the tour, some 400 – 500 letters were arriving at her house each day. A record 30,000 cards were delivered for George's twenty-first birthday, which he celebrated just over three months after the Irish visit. A special post office van usually delivered the mail. Patiently, she sat down each day and wrote beautiful, detailed, personal, handwritten replies to fans. She estimated she was writing about 200 letters a week. Once a month she dropped into the Beatles' fan club to pick up another stack of 2,000 or so photo-cards. She spent a fortune on postage. The fans spent a fortune writing back.

George's success transformed her life. A jolly, outgoing woman, she loved the buzz, the travel, meeting people and keeping in touch with family and friends. She and Harold opened fêtes, especially Catholic Church fêtes, reflecting her own religious beliefs. She judged beauty contests. She never felt shy delivering public talks about the Beatles. It was all such a turnaround for this former greengrocer's assistant and mother to four children. Nothing had ever been like this before. Even Harold, a Corporation bus driver, enjoyed the excitement. He sometimes accompanied her in her public activities. He welcomed the fans when he was home from work.

Lou also took an interest in her son's financial well-being, occasionally discussing his monetary affairs with her cousin John, the accountant in Drumcondra. "There was talk that my Uncle John used to go over and advise my aunt because, at certain stages, they weren't too pleased about the financial recompense that was due to George," remarks cousin Colm ffrench. Geoffrey Ellis, who later became Chief Executive of NEMS Enterprises, confirmed that George was the Beatle most concerned with the financial side of their activities, "enquiring about earnings, percentages, commissions and so forth. That he felt keenly about his perceived inequities in the tax system was borne out by the words of his song 'Taxman'." Brian Epstein also recognised George's fascination with finance. "George is the business Beatle," he once wrote. "He is curious about money and wants to know how much is coming in and how and what best to do with it to make it work."

There was good reason for George's interest in the Beatles' financial affairs. Unlike Lennon and McCartney, who had 20 per cent shares in their publishing company Northern Songs, George and Ringo had no stake at the time in songwriting revenues. From record sales, George and the other three Beatles received one old penny between them from each single sold, amounting – after 25 per cent was deducted by NEMS – to less than one-fifth of a penny each. Regarding tours, each Beatle held an equal share in Beatles Limited, which acted as a conduit for the group's concert revenue, hence the band's fascination with touring.

Despite their growing fame, George and the other three Beatles were far from flush. During the first weeks of summer 1963 each of the Beatles reputedly received a wage of £50 a week. The payments were made in envelopes, not unlike pay packets handed out to industrial workers or office clerks. In part, the poor remuneration resulted from contracts signed up to six months in advance, when the group had much less popular appeal. Epstein's gentlemanly business style, along with his commercial naïvety, didn't help either. As he once put it, "The main thing is to fulfil contracts and exchange good will with good people." Even the Roy Orbison tour, which ran from May into June 1963, secured only £100 a night for the Beatles while Orbison received $5,000 a week plus air travel.

By the time of the autumn tour in 1963, Epstein claimed that all four Beatles between them were earning a wage of some-where in the region of £1,000 – £1,500 a week. But with most of their income taxed at 70 per cent, and some soon being taxed at rates as high as 98 per cent, ready cash was scarce. It was bewildering to Lou and George, who discussed the issue with their cousin the accountant. The information they gleaned later formed the basis of George's questioning of Brian Epstein as to where the money was going.

Given her Irish connections, Lou inevitably joined the Beatles for their visit to Dublin in November 1963. She proved a massive hit. At the airport she spoke to fans, signed autographs and hung out with the Beatles as they waited for transportation into Dublin. Newspaper reports noted her presence. She also attended the Adelphi shows, creating a *frisson* of excitement as word got out that she was there. Fans sought her out to have a chat. Subsequent legend had her dancing in the aisles of the Adelphi, although that's unlikely. Following the concert, she made her way to Drumcondra.

"I was there the night George and Lou came to my uncle's house in Clonturk Park," says Doreen Broderick (née ffrench), one of the cousins from Dun Laoghaire. "We were asked if we all wanted to go up. My brother-in-law drove the whole lot of us up there in his car. It was terrible weather, very cold. There were nine of us in the family and five or six of us went. We all had young families at the time and we were mostly living in Dun Laoghaire.

"We got there about eight o'clock that night. We were sitting there for hours before George finally arrived. There was all of us plus my uncle's family of three children, along with my uncle and aunt. There might have been others as well. The house seemed full to us. They had a lovely house. You walked into a narrow hallway. The front room was the sitting-room and it was open to the back dining-room. If you went straight down the hall there was a little kitchen. We sat in the dining-room and sitting-room and they had the folding doors open. There wouldn't have been enough space for us in one room.

"Aunt Doris was very fussy about her house. She'd have everything just perfect. Uncle John was a gentleman. You'd just love him. He was my godfather. He was laughing and thrilled at the idea of having a celebrity come to the house. I think he thought that all the Beatles would turn up but they didn't. Aunt Doris was thrilled too and she was buzzing around the place. They had supper for us all and drinks if you wanted them. They had sandwiches and cakes and other little bits, with tea and coffee. The food was already laid out on the table when we arrived. We were all sitting there and chatting. We were all in awe at the thought of meeting George, the way he had turned out.

"He arrived after the shows. It was very late. He came by taxi, I think. I remember him coming into the house. We were all thrilled to bits meeting him. I think he was wearing what he wore onstage. We were all remarking about how he was dressed. He sat down with us and he was deluged with questions. We were all on top of him, asking him things. We were asking about the Beatles, where he was going, what he was doing, how he was getting on and all that. He must have been sick of us all. He was very nice and very normal. He was so natural, a very ordinary type of guy. We couldn't understand that because he was so famous.

"I had young children and they had said to me, 'Get his autograph, Mum.' So I got his autograph for two of them. I only had two at that stage. He wrote, 'To Geraldine, Love, George Harrison' and 'To Monica, Love, George Harrison.' When my daughters went into school the next morning they brought in the autographs with them. There was pandemonium. They were stars, having someone related to them like that. Unfortunately, I later lost one of the autographs but I still have the other.

"He had asked the taxi-man to wait for him. He probably stayed an hour or even more. We all waited until he left, in case we'd miss anything, and then we left too. We all came home, back down to Dun Laoghaire. That was the last time I saw George. I never saw him or heard from him after that. He lost touch altogether. But the night in Drumcondra was a night to remember."

Another relative promised a fan that she would ask George for his autograph at the get-together in Drumcondra. She was as good as her word. "My friend and I were going into the second show at the Adelphi," explains the fan Sandra Grant, who was then aged 16. "We got up the stairs and we were standing around waiting to get into the theatre. They were probably trying to clear up the rubbish from the first show. We were in what was like a holding bay. There was this tall, elderly woman there, an elegant person who was very well-dressed. She was standing on the semi-circular balcony at the top of the stairs. We started talking to her for no reason other than we were all on the one spot.

"She happened to say that her nephew was on the show. I said, 'Who would that be?' She said, 'George Harrison.' I said, 'George Harrison! He's my favourite.' He always seemed to me to be the underdog of the group. He was the quiet, gentle one. I always had a sneaking sympathy for him. He was overwhelmed by the notoriety of John and Paul for their songwriting ability and Ringo for his personality and his looks. She actually took out of her bag a Polaroid photograph of George doing the washing-up in the council house in Liverpool. She took out another photograph of him in the back garden with his parents. They were little, coloured Polaroid photos, like you got in those days. I begged her if possible would she get an autograph for me. She couldn't understand how anybody could be looking for an autograph of somebody. But she said the family were meeting up later and that if she got an opportunity she would.

"She told me she worked at the hat counter in a shop in George's Street. The next morning, instead of going to work I went straight to the shop to see if she had the autograph. I whizzed off on the bus into town and ran all the way from Eden Quay up to George's Street. I was there at nine o'clock on the dot. I went in and recognised her immediately. I asked her if she had got the autograph. She said she had. There were counters there with very deep drawers where the hats would have been stored. She opened the drawer and she took out the autograph. She gave it to me. I practically kissed her with gratitude and thanked her so very much for remembering me. That's how I got George Harrison's autograph."

Not all of the relatives travelled to the get-together in Clonturk Park. One cousin, Tony ffrench, was into traditional music and wasn't a fan of the Beatles. Another cousin, Colm ffrench, was into jazz. Interestingly, both, just like their cousin George, shared a passion for music. But rock 'n roll was a step too far. "I never went to meet him," Tony ffrench recalls. "I was invited but I didn't accept. I was 24 at the time and I didn't like the music. At the time the Beatles became famous I was into the revival of traditional Irish music, like the Clancy Brothers. That's what I opted for, not pop. The rest of the family went for the Beatles' stuff. They were all very proud of him and had watched his progress. I also admired him for doing his thing. Had it been one of the Clancy Brothers I would have gone."

Colm ffrench didn't travel either: "I knew it was happening but I didn't feel like going. I was a very big jazz follower and couldn't stand the Beatles. I didn't like their music. At the time George came to visit in 1963, a strange thing happened. On the day of the visit, the phone rang in Dun Laoghaire and I picked it up. All I could hear was, 'Hello! Is George there?' I was wondering what sort of a prankster it was. It happened over and over again. After a while I rang the Posts and Telegraphs and I told them I was being besieged and badgered. I was wondering how someone got my name and number. A few days later this friend of mine, who was called Harrison and who lived in Drumcondra, said to me, 'I hope you got plenty of phone-calls because I got fed up and I kept on putting the callers through to you.' He was getting them because he was a Harrison from Drumcondra."

It was well after midnight when George Harrison departed Clonturk Park and returned to the Gresham. Dublin, that dark November night, was deserted. Cold gusts of wind swept through O'Connell Street. Sporadic rain showers left a veneer of wet on the pavements and roads. Only hardy souls braved the elements as they headed home from dances or made their way to and from work. Late-night drinking was available in dockers' pubs down the quays or in a handful of labourers' bars speckled throughout the city. Hotel guests could order drinks from night porters. Otherwise, nightlife was restricted to two 'clubs'. One, which was called the Arts Club, was located on the south side of the city. The other, in Groome's Hotel, was close to the Gresham. It was to Groome's that the four Beatles headed.

"They asked me where they could get a 'gargle' late at night," Paul Russell remembers. "They didn't want to go to bed in case they'd miss something. They were all wired up. So we got a laundry van and smuggled them out to Groome's. We knew it was open all night. We came out the laundry exit of the hotel and we brought them to the side of Groome's, down the lane. I knocked three knocks on the door and the girl let us in."

Already in Groome's were 40 – 50 actors and actresses together with Wesley Burrowes, author, playwright and subsequent scriptwriter for Telefís Éireann's ratings-topping soap opera *The Riordans*. "The Beatles were playing the Adelphi, we were playing the Olympia," says Burrowes, who was celebrating one of his first stage triumphs, the musical *Carrie*, which followed the twists and turns of a maid in a large Dublin hotel. It was receiving rave reviews since being presented at the Dublin Theatre Festival. "We were having a big party, after midnight, thinking the world of ourselves. *Carrie* had been quite a success. We were packing them in. It did terrifically for us. We had never known it so good, so we thought we were the greatest ever.

"Groome's, which was just opposite the Gate, was the big place everybody went. It had a front room where the politicians came in. The back room was where the arty people and the actors went. We were in the back room. It was pure drink and everybody trying to impress each other. We saw these four guys standing around. We really didn't know a lot about the Beatles. Not an awful lot of attention was being paid to them. The Beatles' long hair wasn't in style then, so we looked down our noses at these young hooligans. They had suits on but it didn't help. I suppose they were brought there as Groome's was the only answer to the nightclub phenomenon. There was either that or the Arts Club.

"One thing I remember very well was that we had a wee girl with us in *Carrie* who used to be in *The Riordans* as well. George Harrison came over to her and asked her would she like to dance. This was unheard of in the back room of Groome's although there was music playing. She told him to 'shag off.' Afterwards, when she realised who it was and what she had just turned down, she was very mortified. They may have chatted to a few other people. And they had a few drinks. The fact that they just had a big hit down in the Adelphi didn't register at all. They weren't members of the Dublin scene and that was it. We were revolting people. We felt we were the stars and who were these fellows coming in off the street? It was as simple as that."

From Groome's, Paul Russell brought the Beatles to a late-night party. "It was somewhere around Ballsbridge," he recalls. "There was a piano-player who was working in a club there. He had played with one of the showbands for a while. It was kind of a shebeen in the basement of a small hotel. We went to hear him playing. My brother-in-law – Grace's brother – was a doctor in Trinity at the time. He came with us. The Beatles all sang 'Underneath The Lamplight' and all the old British drinking songs. We all sang our little pieces. I think I sang 'The Moon Behind The Hill' or 'The Green Glens Of Antrim', which was my forte then. We had a tremendous party until five o'clock in the morning. And we were banjaxed."

That night, the Beatles never went to bed, although they did return to the Gresham in the early hours of the morning. "I think I slept in a chair in the Gresham for a while, I'm not sure. But the Beatles certainly never made it to bed," Russell remembers. "I didn't have any sleep for a few days, there was so much going on. There was giddiness and everyone was on a high. It was the 'Swinging Sixties' and what tomorrow would bring didn't matter. But the following morning, Paul McCartney came to me. 'This is personal, Paul,' he said. 'I need a big favour, mate. We need to get driving licenses. We can't go into a driving licence office in England.' They couldn't go into one in England because they'd be mobbed and killed. The hysteria was at 110 per cent over there but not here. They didn't have licenses but they were good in England with Irish driving licenses.

"It was seven o'clock in the morning. I think they were still hung-over from the night before. I had the car hidden in the back, behind the laundry exit. So we went up to Kildare Street and we went into the office. I had arranged it through my contacts to open the office early. I was parked outside. I got a couple of policemen that knew my father and they kept an eye on things. One was in plain clothes at the time. He was helping me to keep an eye in case anyone copped the fact that I was there with the motley crew. The driving license people gave Richard Starkey, Paul McCartney, John Lennon and George Harrison Irish driving licenses, to all four of them."

Surprisingly, the story of the Beatles' late-night and early-morning revelries was never unearthed by the national press in the wake of the group's departure. Quaintly, in the context of subsequent media developments, journalists at the time either missed out on the potential scoops or respected the fine line between private and public lives. The events were buried or ignored. Likewise, details of the ffrench family get-together never made it into the papers. That George established some sort of contact with his cousins was alluded to but never comprehensively reported. The cousins, themselves, kept a low profile.

Among the actors at Groome's their visit was barely remarked upon either, even in subsequent months when their fame reached stratospheric proportions. By then, the writing career of Wesley Burrowes had blossomed. "*Carrie* was meant to go to England," Burrowes says. "Jack Hilton was very taken with it. He wanted to take it to Sadler's Wells after *My Fair Lady*, which was running at the time. He wanted Maureen Potter to come and play in it. He told us that he would need to have us free for the pre-London run. I had no choice but to leave my job. I did, and he was paying us a small retainer. Everything was all set. Then he died. I was left with nothing.

"The interesting thing for me was that Peter Collinson, who was the director of *Carrie*, was working out in Telefís Éireann. He eventually did the original *Italian Job*. He felt a little bit responsible for it all. He said, 'Listen, would you come out to work in Telefís Éireann? They are looking for somebody in the script department.' I didn't even have a television set. I took him up on it and the rest was history."

In years to come, vague mentions were made of George's Irish ties and his links with Drumcondra. Passing references were also made to his mother Louise and her Irish roots. Sadly, for the most unfortunate reasons, news of the family's cross-channel connections resurfaced in 1969. In that year, just six years after the Irish tour, Louise became seriously ill. A brain tumour was diagnosed and a long medical battle ensued. George spent a lot of time at his mother's side. Things became complicated when his father Harold developed ulcers, also requiring hospitalisation.

The smell, the atmosphere of hospitals and the scent of death engraved themselves on George's brain. He was inspired to write 'Deep Blue', a song forever redolent of his mother's final days. She died in 1970, with George by her side. With her death, contact between the ffrench clan in Dublin and the Harrisons in Liverpool largely died too. The vital link no longer existed. As a consequence, memories faded of that dark, wintry night in November 1963 when one of the Beatles visited his cousin's house in Drumcondra at the height of the group's fame.

"I remember hearing about Lou's death," Doreen Broderick

144

(née ffrench), cousin of George Harrison, concludes. "It saddened us all. I remember saying how awful it was. None of us went over for the funeral because we all had young families and we were starting off married life. We couldn't even afford it at the time. But we continued to follow George's career. My girls would say, 'There's our cousin,' 'Do you hear our cousin?' They would tell everybody he was their cousin. Then, George passed away too. But without Lou's letters and visits, something was missing. She was the only link we had, at that stage, with Liverpool and with George. So her death was sad in more ways than one. It was the end of an era."

BELFAST

Early on Friday morning, 8 November, the daily newspapers were delivered to the Beatles' suites at the Gresham Hotel. The headlines were depressing. Splashed across the front pages were stories of madness and mayhem. "Many Arrested As City Crowds Riot," led *The Irish Times*. Reporter Cathal O'Shannon and his colleague Tony Kelly produced a vivid description of the arrests, broken bones, smashed windows, damaged cars, injured Gardaí, scuffles and screaming girls that had characterised the chaos in Middle Abbey Street and elsewhere.

"Many Injured As 'Beatle' Crowds Run Riot In City," proclaimed the *Irish Press*. "Last night was the wildest night in Dublin for many years. At least 100 people were injured or fainted, windows were smashed, traffic bollards damaged, a number of cars overturned, and several were arrested," the newspaper reported. "Dublin Gardaí Battle With Beatles Fans," featured on the front page of the *Irish Independent*. Beside it was the headline, "Death Penalty Bill: Dáil Division Is Likely." Thankfully, parliamentary debate on the issue of abolishing hanging was unrelated to the previous night's events!

As the Beatles scanned the national dailies, early editions of the evening papers were being prepared in nearby Middle Abbey Street and Burgh Quay. "'Battle' Scenes For The Beatles," screamed the *Evening Herald*. "The Beatlemania that gripped

Dublin last night and shook Middle Abbey Street and O'Connell Street subsided completely today," wrote reporter Michael Ryan. "Morning After The B-Storm," headlined the *Evening Press*. "It was 'B'-Day plus one in Dublin today as the city got around to clearing up the debris – the aftermath of the 'Beatle' invasion which struck last night with all the frenzy that has followed the Liverpool 'beat' singers' group wherever their tour has taken them," read the front page report.

Inside the papers, reviews were mixed. "We couldn't hear a word the boys sang or a note they played," declared columnist Tom Hennigan of the *Evening Herald*. "Everything was drowned in that sea of screams. Not that we cared. When one has heard some of the greatest voices in Europe sing Ponchielli's 'La Gioconda' one has nothing but pity and contempt for such as the purveyors of the 'Mersey Sound.' What happened in Dublin last night just wasn't funny. If this is the sort of mass hysteria aroused by the Beatles wherever they go – and recent newspaper headlines and photographs are no credit to them and their followers – then they and people like them should be banned from this city in future."

The Irish Times adopted a mostly positive tone. "If you want to hear the Beatles, buy their records," advised one of its reporters. "When the Liverpool beat sounded in the Adelphi Cinema, Dublin, last night, it could hardly be heard for the screams – ecstatic, joyful, hysteric, demented – from Dublin teenagers. A pity this, because the Beatles, in spite of their theatrical gimmicks, their long locks and 'with-it' suits, have a great act. It is sheer showmanship and real ability which has brought them in less than two years from a small, pub-singing group to the top of the 'pop parade'."

Writing in the *Evening Press*, Ken Stewart was equally encouraged. "It's a pity some enterprising disc company didn't arrange to make a 'live' recording of last night's memorable beat show at Dublin's Adelphi," he remarked. "An exciting, colourful package that would be extremely difficult to surpass for sheer entertainment value, it was an all-stops-out affair, with an audience to match the mood. If audience reaction is any criterion, the artists involved in this spectacular presentation are assured of greatly increased record sales and a wonderful reception whenever they choose to return to Dublin."

Locked in their bedrooms, the Beatles refused to do interviews. Acting as spokesman, Beatles' roadie Mal Evans said in the early morning: "It was a wonderful reception, but the boys feel bad about the people who got hurt. Although it was a hectic night outside the theatre, the boys had a much quieter time. It was only when they left by the rear door in a van and reached O'Connell Street that they really got a look at what had been happening while the show went on. This was our first show in Ireland and naturally we were a bit worried about what sort of a reception we would get. The boys were extremely pleased with it – they enjoy the enthusiasm and all that."

Shortly before midday, the Beatles left the Gresham Hotel for Belfast. Prior to departing, they said their goodbyes to Paul Russell. "It was very sad," Russell reflects. "They had been very gracious to me. It was a big coup for me personally. I was very impressed by the fact that they came, did the job and left. They had a tremendous interest in me, which was very nice. I got to their wavelength. I was like an extension of Arthur Howes. I had tears in my eyes. To me it was the greatest time in my life."

Approximately 100 fans watched as the Beatles walked to their car. There was no commotion. "One found it hard to credit that 12 hours previously the Beatles had been the cause of so much trouble, involving at times thousands of people," *The Irish Times* commented. They travelled with window blinds drawn and were cheered by onlookers at various points on the trip. "Although we came to Belfast in closed cars, people seemed to know who we were," Ringo later recalled. "We could hear them shouting in the towns and villages we passed through, but we weren't allowed to look out of the windows."

Irish and British Customs officers stopped them, but only for autographs. At a press conference that afternoon Paul McCartney referred to the event: "The Customs officers asked us had we anything to declare, but we had none." Amused at being asked by a Customs official for his signature, McCartney said jokingly, "Your fame spreads, you know." Customs formalities weren't quite as routine for the support acts, who travelled by coach. Working off a different time schedule and travelling separately from the Beatles, they were given a thorough going-over.

"I can remember we got stopped at the border," says Jeff Williams of the Kestrels. "We had crossed the border, straight through, on an earlier trip to Ireland. But on this occasion they seemed to not like us very much. We had to get out of the coach and go through Customs. That was quite unusual. They searched the coach. I don't know what they were looking for, maybe drugs. When the Kestrels split up I went into the police force. I eventually got promoted to the rank of sergeant and got put in the drugs squad. They said to me when I took over, 'With your experience in show business you should be the ideal person to deal with drugs and things like that.' So maybe that's what they were thinking at the border!"

By prior agreement, Ulster Television met the Beatles at a prearranged spot just into Northern Ireland, where they conducted an interview. Typical of the Beatles, it was more like a deranged conversation than an incisive report. The package was broadcast later that day on the evening edition of *Ulster News*. Under RUC escort, the Beatles then headed for Belfast. There they taped an interview for BBC Northern Ireland's teatime news. Although the Beatles had agreed to mime a song for the broadcast, time pressures precluded it and the group moved on.

Excitement was already growing in the city-centre by the time the Beatles arrived. All eyes were focused on the ABC Ritz cinema in Fisherwick Place, which was the venue for the evening concerts. Opened in 1936 and with an Art Deco design, it was often described as 'Ireland's Wonder Theatre'. Only that year, 1963, its name had been formally changed from the Ritz to the ABC. With 2,200 seats, there had been a mad scramble for the 4,400 tickets available for the Beatles' back-to-back shows. The black market was thriving. Tickets bought for 6/6, 8/6 and 10/6 were selling for up to £10 each, which was a small fortune at the time. It was believed that close to 20,000 fans were looking for tickets. Luckiest of them all were the two fans who headed the queue on the day they went on sale – they got free tickets.

"Tickets had gone on sale less than a month before the shows," recalls Chris Hill, who was aged 16. "I got up at two o'clock in the morning the day they became available. I cycled down Malone Road on my bicycle in order to queue up for them. I wanted to become a photographer and I wanted to take photographs so I needed good seats. I was one of the first 20 people in the queue. I needed front row seats but I only got second row seats, near the middle. I bought six 10/6 tickets for myself and my friends. I remember when I was queuing up that morning this girl with bright-red hair came walking past. She was quite strikingly different. Someone pointed out that she was Cilla Black. She had played the previous night in Belfast and she was just walking past the venue in the early morning. This was before she became a big star."

Valerie McCleary, who was also aged 16, slept on the pavement around the corner from the ABC to get tickets: "About three of us went – two of my chums and myself. I think we took old army sleeping-bags with us. We also took a flask of tea and a sandwich. It was about ten o'clock at night when we got there. A whole lot of other kids were there too. We got tickets up in the balcony, in the middle price range."

Fans lucky enough to buy tickets were soon under pressure to sell, remarks yet another 16-year-old, Teddy Copeland: "Between the time when the tickets went on sale and the time of the concert, the Beatles became a lot more popular. Me and the mate had queued outside the cinema to get tickets. We had gone down about half-seven in the morning. We got half-decent seats downstairs. My mate had one ticket and I had the other right beside him. Some other fellow got to hear about us. He approached my mate and offered him £3, which was a big sum of money. He sold it. The fellow then came up to my house and coaxed me up and down to sell mine.

"He must have coaxed me for an hour and a half. He was about four years older than me. He was saying, 'You're going to be sitting beside me.' So eventually I gave in. I sold it for the same amount, £3. They had cost 6/6 each. However, my uncle, who was only five years older than me, had a wife who was pregnant. She couldn't go. I got her ticket and I got in for free. My mate also got in. He bunked in. He got in through the side door. So we were both there. My ticket was front row on the balcony, just looking down on the Beatles. They were class seats."

The ABC cinema was a scene of expectancy by the time the Beatles arrived, which was shortly before four o'clock. Hysterical teenagers were congregated on the street outside. Many of them were walking up and down, hoping to spot the Beatles arriving or to figure out which entryway they would use. Some had spent days badgering cinema management for a job cleaning the Beatles' dressing-rooms or sweeping the floors. Others had asked staff to pocket the Beatles' cigarette butts and to pass them on. Three young boys had enquired if they could bake a cake and bring it to the cinema, just in case the Beatles got hungry!

To the sound of cheering, the Beatles were ushered into the ABC. There to greet them was Ann McGowan, area secretary of the Northern Ireland branch of the Beatles' fan club, who presented the boys with shillelaghs. Photographed with the Beatles for the papers the following day, she was the envy of every girl in town. "I was only 17 at the time," says McGowan, looking back. "I had applied to run the fan clubs of Gerry and the Pacemakers and the Beatles. I was turned down for Gerry and the Pacemakers. But I got the Beatles. This was before they became famous.

"I can remember sitting with the Beatles and getting my photographs taken with the four of them. I was made to kiss Paul McCartney on the cheek for one shot. I had my hair permed for the day and I had my mother with me. She met them as well. I was scared witless. But they were fabulous with me. I was working at the time. I worked for an accountant and I had to get out of work to do it. I was on the front of the *News Letter* the next day. My boss wasn't impressed. He laughed but you know what accountants were like in the '60s! It was a chance of a lifetime. They were very humorous. They were very nice boys."

Following the presentation, the Beatles held a routine press conference for the local media. "The press conference was held in the cinema auditorium," recalls Stanley Matchett, who worked as a photographer with the *Belfast Telegraph*. "There was no liaison officer, no press room, nothing organised like it would be today. There were very few people there. There were no tables and no mikes like there would be now. It was very off the cuff. The Beatles were climbing about in the empty theatre and sitting in the seats.

"They posed for a few pictures. One of them had a movie camera, a Super 8, and he was shooting a bit of film. I got a shot of him with the camera up to the eye as he photographed the other three. They were great. They were a joke a minute. It was all a bit of banter. You couldn't get anything serious out of them. Somebody would ask them a question and they would give a corny answer to it. It was like the Marx Brothers. I got their autographs at the time. I got them in an ordinary little blue autograph book that you could find anywhere. I brought it around in my camera case. People always co-operated with me. I had a whole string of people in it, like the Rolling Stones, Cliff

Richard, Tina Turner, Tom Jones and the Beatles. Eventually, I gave it away to my relation."

At the press conference John Lennon claimed to be "tired," saying the touring was "hard work." He was reported to be in quiet mood. Paul spoke of his experience with Customs when crossing the border. Ringo said he was enjoying the Irish leg of the tour. George, who was carrying his shillelagh, once again explained his Irish connections. "The Beatles were in irrepressible form and soon convinced the dozen or so newspaper men and women present that far from being the popular conception of beatniks, they were normal young men full of the joys of life," the *News Letter* reported.

Once the press conference was finished, the Beatles retreated to their dressing-rooms to prepare for the shows. "The dressing-rooms were two floors up above the stage level," recalls Hugh Brown, who was a trainee assistant manager at the ABC cinema in Derry and who came up to view proceedings in Belfast. "There were a couple of large dressing-rooms and several small ones. They were tailor-made for stage shows. They were put in when the ABC was built in the 1930s. They weren't as luxurious as dressing-rooms today. But you had mirrors, lights, dressing-tables which were basically benches, and the rooms were purpose-built. That's where the Beatles were put."

Trapped in the cinema, the Beatles were starving. "Kay Kennedy was a journalist with the *News Letter* and she gave them Kit Kats," says Terri Hooley, the Belfast music authority and record shop owner. "She met them backstage after they had just arrived. She was there to interview them. They were sitting around a one-bar fire, cold and hungry. She always said how sorry she felt for them. She had some Kit Kats with her and she gave them to the Beatles."

Outside the cinema a massive police security operation was in place. Codenamed 'Operation Beatle' and orchestrated from the City Commissioner's office, it was designed to avoid a repeat of the mayhem in Dublin. The core of the strategy was two-fold. First, learning from the experience of Dublin, crush barriers were erected to control the crowd. Ticket holders would be funnelled into the cinema through a line of parallel barriers. Ticketless bystanders would be corralled alongside. Every effort would be made to stop fans crashing into each other, which had happened in Dublin.

Second, it was identified as essential that the crowd could see the Beatles depart. The frustration and disappointment of fans might, in this way, be minimised. Confusion as to whether the Beatles had left would be avoided. Once the Beatles were seen to be gone, the mob would clear quickly. "We decided to bring the Beatles out the front way," a senior police officer explained. "That has been done in few other cities, but we think this is best because it enables the crowd to see exactly what is happening. Otherwise, you can have sudden rushes started by rumours."

It was further questioned – facetiously, no doubt – by Nationalist MP Patrick Gormley at Stormont whether the B Specials would be mobilised for the event. Harry Diamond, Republican Labour, commented that the Minister's reply would be appreciated as most people would prefer to shave the Beatles rather than shoot them. Desmond Boal, Unionist, wasn't amused: "Does the Minister agree that the form and content of these questions, couched in frivolous terms and marked by nothing but an inadequate and uncultivated sense of humour, does nothing to enhance the dignity of this House?" To cries of "Order, Order," the issue was settled as to whether the B Specials would be putting in an appearance when Minister of Home Affairs, William Craig, replied curtly, "No, sir."

Back at the ABC Ritz, crowd numbers grew in the lead-up to the first concert, which was scheduled for half past six. The barrier of steel and the wall of police proved effective. Ticketholders entered the cinema in an orderly fashion. Among them was 62-year-old grandmother Mrs Simpson, from Malone Heights, who was accompanied by her nine-year-old grandson.

Fans without tickets were held in check in the street outside. Teenagers at the stage door were enthusiastic but restrained.

"It's funny how things stick in your mind but I can remember walking into the ABC," John Toner, aged 20, remarks. "You know the way you get wee flashes in your life? There were about four steps up to the old ABC, on the old corner entrance. I still have the picture in my mind of the long sign saying 'ABC' and me walking in that night. There was great anticipation going in. There was fun and joy and everybody was on top of the world. We felt we were so lucky to have got the tickets. We were privileged people."

Onstage, the opening acts – the Vernons Girls, the Brook Brothers, Peter Jay and the Jaywalkers and the Kestrels – went through their well-practised routines. The format was identical to Dublin the previous night, Northampton the night before that, Slough the night before that again and all the autumn tour shows from 1 November right through to 13 December. "The only support act I remember was the Kestrels," Teddy Copeland recalls. "They covered the Beatles' song 'There's A Place', which was on their first LP *Please Please Me*. Everybody had bought it. The lights went down and they played the music. All the kids went crazy because, when they heard the first few bars, they thought it was going to be the Beatles. Obviously it wasn't. But that got a great response."

Following the Kestrels, Frank Berry went through his regular pre-Beatles warm-up routine. He stalled and delayed as the backstage set-up was changed. He teased and taunted, badgered and baited while testing the audience's capacity to withstand stress and strain. The screaming got louder and louder. Girls cried and shook with nervous tension. There was agitation, excitement and fretful unease. Eventually, with the auditorium rippling as if charged with live electricity, it was time for the Beatles.

"I was speaking to the Beatles as they waited to go onstage," Dolores Graham, aged 16, remembers. "I was an ice-cream girl in the cinema and I was selling them that night. I went about with a tray in the circle and the front stalls. We sold the ice-creams during the intermission. The Beatles had to pass me to go down to the stage. They were stalled upstairs by the rooms where we stored the ice-creams in the fridge-freezers. There were about seven of us ice-cream sellers there, four in the 'A' room and three in the 'B' room. They were talking to us while they were waiting for the signal to go on.

"The Beatles were good fun even though they were about to perform. Nothing seemed to annoy them. They had their Beatle suits on them. They had the make-up on and the Beatle boots. Paul McCartney was going down first. John Lennon was the last. He was lovely, a total gentleman. Ringo was a bit of *craic*. George was alright but Paul was a bit distant. I didn't like him at all. They were saying how lovely it was to be in Ireland, how we were very nice people. I spoke to them again, later on, when they came back up the stairs to the changing-rooms. They were joking and laughing. They were very pleasant and very happy. They loved a bit of *craic*, so they did.

"I got the Beatles' autographs, every one of them. I had met Roy Orbison also. I had to bring his silver tray up to him. He gave me a £10 note. I wanted to frame it but I spent it before I could. I got the Rolling Stones as well. I had a book with pink pages and blue pages. I had all their autographs but I gave them to my children to play with. They are all gone now, including the ones from the Beatles."

Hysterical screaming greeted the Beatles as they arrived onstage. A shower of jelly babies, identified by George as his favourite sweet, flew through the air. Girls hyperventilated and fainted. Just as in Dublin, teenagers pulled at their hair and shook their heads in bewilderment. They cried uncontrollably. Struggling to find suitable superlatives, one newspaper described the fans as being "deliriously excited."

"Everybody was waiting for them," says Valerie McCleary. "Suddenly you saw these four guys on the stage. I remember thinking, 'I'm not going to scream.' As soon as they came onstage a rain of jelly babies came down on them. I just started screaming and pulling my hair. I screamed my head off. It was like a fever. They would call it crowd hysteria today. There were no stage decorations whatsoever. It was just these four guys singing although we couldn't hear them at all. The sound systems were pretty poor at the time and you couldn't hear a thing. You would nearly get trampled on. People were losing it completely."

The atmosphere was frenzied, agrees Laurence Brush, aged 14: "The girls went crazy as soon as the curtains opened. Their arms were going. They had their hands up to their faces. They were squealing. People were jiving and twisting. I remember a few of the girls fainting at the front and being carried away. It was mayhem. We had all bought the magazines and the records, but the fact that the Beatles were there took your breath away."

Even ice-cream seller Dolores Graham, who was in the front circle, was completely caught up in the excitement: "The crowd just went mad. Girls were collapsing all over the place. The St John Ambulance men were carrying them out. It was very exciting. The atmosphere was electric. It was marvellous. I was jumping up and down myself. I had a sore throat the next day from the screaming. I nearly gave away my ice-creams, I was so happy."

Teddy Copeland was fortunate that the sound of the Beatles rose upwards to his seat in the front row of the balcony: "The volume coming up from the stage was clear and clean. The sound was raw but that's what the Beatles were about in those days. There was nothing sophisticated about it. They were a very good live band. They came across well. Obviously, you didn't have the same acoustics that you'd have in a recording studio. But it was very similar to the music they were putting on vinyl."

Higher up at the back of the house, ABC projectionist Danny Devlin could also hear the music while working the spots along with two of his colleagues. "We hadn't done rehearsals," he remembers. "We just had a plan outlining what they were going to sing and what colours were needed for each song. That was given to us by London, who would have been dictating what way it was going to work. The Beatles would have been elsewhere doing the same thing. There was always a set-list where stage shows were concerned. It would outline what the stage was to be like, what colour the spot had to be, different sounds or whatever. The sound was excellent where we were. It was probably bad down below because everybody was shouting. But because I was up on a height the sound was coming up to me very clearly. I was also getting the sound on a sort of a monitor or an amplifier into the box."

Just in front of the stage and seated in the second row, budding photographer Chris Hill was also occupied, snapping away with his camera. "I was concentrating on using up my half roll of film," he recalls. "Because of where I was, pretty close to the front, I could hear fairly well. The Vox amps weren't very far away from me and were pointed in my direction. But there was a huge amount of screaming and shrieking behind me. I had a Werra camera, which had a Zeiss lens. The camera was an East German model. It had one lens. It wasn't like I had a zoom lens. My father had bought it for me the previous Christmas as a present. I missed most of the concert because I was concentrating so much on getting my angles. I didn't have time to enjoy the moments."

The Beatles ran through what had already become a well-refined, note-perfect autumn tour routine. From 'I Saw Her Standing There' through to 'Twist And Shout', they reproduced the same set-list of ten songs performed the previous night in Dublin and replicated each night of the tour. Choreographed identically, with the same stage movements, song introductions, ad libs and end-of-show bows, it is easy to see how the group soon tired of the repetitive formula. That mattered little, however, to the fans at the ABC Ritz in Belfast.

"On the night it was bedlam," remarks projectionist Danny Devlin. "It was very exciting. I remember at the time saying they were the greatest group I ever heard. There was nothing like them. They were absolutely brilliant. Gerry and the Pacemakers were excellent too. I had seen Cilla Black, the Bachelors, Heinz, Cliff Richard and all those. But I thought, at that time, that the Beatles were the best. It was really a powerful night."

Valerie McCleary, who hardly stopped screaming, was wrecked by the end of the show. "At that time we had our hair up in bouffant hairstyles, with all these pins," she remembers. "I think I was wearing black slacks and a sweater, which was the cool thing to wear. I wore flat black shoes because I was too young and not yet into high-heels. The boys were starting to wear their hair like the Beatles and a lot of them were wearing these round-necked jackets. A lot of them wore suits with shirts and ties. But the big thing was my hairstyle. I came out, as my mother said, looking like I had been dragged through a hedge backwards."

For John Toner the whole event was a blur: "I don't remember any of the songs or the singing because it was all just a big mass of sound. The sound that they made was unique in that it was loud for the equipment they had. But it was one of those experiences in life where you say, 'I'll remember this, the sense of occasion.' The music was incidental. It was a profound sense of occasion. It was great to be able to say you had been there."

Teddy Copeland was also in bits. "The atmosphere was terrific," he concludes. "It was complete and utter hysteria. It was incredible. But when they finished off with 'Twist And Shout' it was something else. The magic of it was electric. It put the icing on the cake. I had seen the likes of Lonnie Donegan but he was nothing compared to this. The Beatles knew their job. They were very young men but they had been around the corners a few times. They'd already done Hamburg a few years before that. Some of the groups coming in had only been at it 12 months or so but not the Beatles. I never saw anything like it in my life."

Just 25 minutes after the Beatles had started, the closing notes of 'Twist And Shout' signalled that the concert was over. The Beatles bowed and the group were gone. It was short and, for most, it was sweet. "It was a show the young people will want to remember and the older generation will try to forget," was one newspaper's concluding assessment.

Although the first show was regarded as "orderly," the second performance degenerated into chaos. Fuelled by the excitement of fans emerging from the half past six show and pumped up by the sounds coming from inside, the second house went wild. Several young girls stormed the stage. At least one was carried bodily away. Two 15-year-old girls tried to take off their clothes but were restrained by police. Girls stood on seats. Empty drink cartons, concert programmes and papers were thrown onto the stage. Ushers struggled to keep the crowds in check. The heat was unbearable. Adults, overcome by the noise and the sweltering atmosphere, left the theatre. St John Ambulance volunteers worked overtime reviving those who had fainted.

Once the second show concluded, some 2,200 energised, demented Beatles' fans poured from the cinema out into Fisherwick Place. They joined an estimated 1,000 other fans waiting outside. As the *News Letter* reported, they congregated there "like a massed choir of starlings at feeding time." Contained behind crush barriers, they were patrolled by a wall of police. Fans sought the best vantage point. Some scaled lamp poles. More pressed against crush barriers, pushing the police back. At one point the barriers were breached and injuries were sustained. Six girls fainted as the crowd pushed their way towards the cinema doors.

"I can remember coming out into a sea of people," says Valerie McCleary. "I sort of panicked at being so pushed and jostled. I can remember being frightened by the crowd, by this mass of bodies. There was a lot of jostling at the front and I didn't like being in the middle. So we stood on the edge of the crowd. The cinema was on a corner and people were right out into the middle of the street. They were all screaming, yelling and jumping up and down. People were asking, 'Are they coming?' I don't recall seeing them coming out. I'm not very tall. It was just too much really."

Chris Hill also witnessed the pandemonium on the streets: "The chaos outside the cinema was something else. The whole centre of town was bedlam. There were thousands of people there. Belfast hadn't experienced this number of people and screaming girls before. There were crowds down the back alley looking up where they thought the Beatles were. There were girls screaming and shouting up at the windows. This I had seen on TV but never live in the street. The atmosphere of the night was exceptional."

Inside the cinema, plans were hatched to ensure the safe departure of the Beatles. Roadie Neil Aspinall proposed a stealthy escape but the RUC had different ideas. "After the show, we were going to smuggle them out in a furniture van," Aspinall recalled. "The police saw the theatre manager and said the boys should be seen by the fans, to avoid confusion." With the police winning the argument, staff first went about emptying the auditorium and toilets of people. Only a handful of St John Ambulance volunteers were allowed to remain in the foyer. There they attended to the last of the injured from the concert and those who became distressed from the mêlée outside. A small group of cinema managers and police stood near the cinema doors. A limousine waited outside the entrance. It was almost half an hour since the show had concluded and it was time for the grand departure.

"The decision was made to take the Beatles out through the foyer, through the front doors and away through the crowd," says Hugh Brown, ABC trainee assistant manager who was observing proceedings in Belfast. "The plan was to wait until the theatre was empty and then bring them out so that the public could see them depart. They didn't want people hanging around. They didn't want a repeat of the Dublin fiasco.

"There was the usual crush to get them out to the car. People outside didn't know if they were going to come out through the stage door, which was at the back of the theatre, or through the front door. The whole of Fisherwick Place was chokka and people were up the side waiting at the stage door. There was tremendous excitement among the crowds outside trying to get a glimpse of them. There were many people there who weren't members of the audience and a lot of the audience hung around as well. But a tunnel was carved out for the Beatles.

"The one thing I clearly remember was that when they were going out through the foyer there were a number of people there who had passed out. They were being treated by the St John Ambulance. There was one young girl out for the count. But as the Beatles passed through the foyer, she sat up and shouted 'Ringo.' She collapsed right back down again. The Beatles then got into the car and the car slowly made its way away from the theatre."

Immediately, fans rushed the half mile to the Grand Central Hotel, where the Beatles were booked for the night. "The crowd came hurtling towards me like a stampede of white elephants," wrote a *News Letter* reporter. "For a moment a child of ten was poised in front of this mob, and then she was hauled aside by an adult. I dodged between two ambulances, having a keen desire to live, and they raced screaming past." The fans joined another mass of teenagers who were already awaiting the group's arrival at the hotel. Crowds thronged the street. Boys stood on car roofs or climbed trolleybus poles hoping for a good view. Traffic in the city was delayed for up to half an hour.

In business since 1893, the Grand Central was *the* hotel in town. The gala dinner celebrating the launch of the Titanic was held there. Winston Churchill, Al Jolson, Mario Lanza and Bob Hope were distinguished previous guests. Clayton Moore, who played the Lone Ranger, visited and insisted on wearing his mask even in the dining-room. Gene Autry had wooed fans by singing from the hotel balcony back in 1939. The Rolling Stones stayed there as well. "The Grand Central Hotel was the posh hotel in town then," remarks Ritchie McLardy, who attended one of the concerts. "It was literally a 'grand' hotel and very nice. The pop stars would stay there. It was at a time when the centre of the city was thriving. It was the best place to stay."

Minutes after leaving the ABC, the Beatles arrived at the Grand Central Hotel. "They rushed straight to their rooms," recalls John Toner, who was a 20-year-old trainee hotel manager. "They stayed in our studio-suite rooms, which were on the first floor. There were six studio-suites in the whole hotel. They were a new idea in the 1960s. They were large rooms with a foldaway bed and had everything in them. The bed went up into the wall and you could have a boardroom meeting there. They could become an office.

"Food was already in their rooms at the time they arrived. It was arranged to be there and they never went anywhere else in the hotel. Outside was total mayhem. The crowds were into endless screaming. It didn't go down or up. It was all the time. The traffic was stopped. There was a sense of fear because of the crowd and we were hoping nothing would happen. In the whole of my hotel career, there never has been an occasion like it with VIPs. I never came across anything like it again."

At its peak, the crowd outside the hotel numbered a couple of thousand, including the last stragglers who were making their way home from the second show. "I remember going past the Grand Central Hotel afterwards to see if we could catch a glimpse of the Beatles looking out a window," says concert-goer Valerie McCleary. "We kind of hung around but we realised it was pretty hopeless. There were lots of kids there. I wasn't into waiting to see pop stars. So we just stood around for ten or fifteen minutes and then we took off."

By midnight, calm had returned to the city-centre in Belfast.

Although a Friday night, all was quiet. Local hospitals were relieved that no more than a handful of casualties had resulted from the hysteria at the cinema and hotel. Estimates varied on the numbers who had fainted, with figures ranging from 12 – 100. There were no arrests, although a few unruly teenagers had been taken into custody and given a "stern telling-off."

On the morning of Saturday 9 November, the city of Belfast picked up the pieces from the commotion the night before. Corporation workers cleaned up the debris that stretched in a line from Fisherwick Place to the Grand Central Hotel. The ABC Ritz cinema also swept up a massive accumulation of rubbish. "When they were cleaning the stage it was all jelly babies," ABC projectionist Danny Devlin remembers. "That's what they were all throwing at them. There were millions of them on the stage. If they hadn't been dirty I would have eaten them myself. The rest of the place was OK. At least they couldn't move the seats or anything."

An estimated 100 fans were present when the Beatles left the Grand Central Hotel and headed for Aldergrove Airport. "I remember them checking out," John Toner, trainee hotel manager who was on duty that day, recollects. "I didn't check the Beatles out myself. They never came near me at all, although I later checked out Rolf Harris when he stayed with us. As a young trainee manager I was scared of someone going out without paying their bills. I remember I handed Rolf Harris the bill and said, 'Could you please pay.' He took it and I thought he was signing it. Instead, he drew a duck on it and handed it back to me. He just flicked with the pen and in a flash he had the duck drawn. The beautiful duck was laughing at me. I was naïve to think that he paid his own bills. But I never had that sort of experience with the Beatles. They just came out of the passenger lift and they were away."

Remarkably, less than 48 hours had passed since the group's arrival in Dublin. In that time, hundreds of autographs were signed, press conferences were held, photo-calls attended, interviews granted and four concerts performed by the Beatles. Some 9,000 fans had seen them, if not heard them, live onstage. It was as if some sort of tropical cyclone had struck Dublin and 48 hours later, after leaving a trail of destruction in its wake, dissipated as it departed from Belfast.

"I can remember the flight from Belfast," says Jeff Williams of the Kestrels, recalling the return trip to London. "It was a terrible flight because it was a terrible day. I can always remember landing down into London. You couldn't see your hand in front of your face because of the rainy clouds. It was very bumpy. Looking out the window there was nothing to see except clouds."

Back in Belfast the clouds cleared and the wintry sun shone in the wake of the Beatles' departure. A strange calm returned to the city. The stress seemed to ebb away. Girls returned to their work in mills, bakeries and behind shop counters. Young men returned to their jobs building ships or working in offices or factories. Others went back to their colleges and schools. Yet they all knew they had seen something special at the ABC Ritz. Even the lukewarm recognised that things would never again be the same.

"I remember seeing *A Hard Day's Night* about eight months later," recalls journalist Colin McClelland, who missed the Beatles' concerts in Belfast and who was a late convert to the new music scene. "My girlfriend brought me to the film. I was only a moderate fan of the Beatles at the time. I still had that Elvis Presley-style haircut, probably with the Brylcreem. I remember coming out of the film. It must have been a Wednesday afternoon because I remember the blinds in the shops were down. I just caught a glance of myself in a window and saw my hair. I tried to push it down. That era was gone. Everything had changed forever."

AFTERMATH

Poor old Patrick Kavanagh! Poet, columnist, critic and controversialist, he certainly took a hammering in the wake of the Beatles' visit in November 1963. Aged 59, he unashamedly flew the flag for the anti-poppers. This was the same Patrick Kavanagh who, in his column in the *RTV Guide*, lashed out at the newfangled weather forecast on television, arguing that he preferred "our old country custom of looking at the butt of the wind." He reserved much more pointed vitriol for the Beatles.

"'Have you got over the Beatles yet?' is a question often asked of me," Kavanagh wrote defiantly in the *RTV Guide* shortly after the Beatles' departure. It was an appropriate conundrum to tax this cudgel-bearing representative of all those old fogies opposed to the Beatles. He was far from contrite. "A more untalented outfit was never inflicted on us," he concluded. The Beatles were nothing more than "a super-organised business designed to make the quick buck and then go on to something else....of course these Liverpool lads are only tools which will be discarded when the time comes to run 'The Buddhist Song Group'. Shops will be full of saffron robes. Showbiz is surely a queer biz these days."

Kavanagh was also less than sympathetic to the girls who had fainted at the shows, referring to the practise as this "swooning female stuff." He added: "I do remember reading in eighteenth-century novels of the smelling salts being put under the slumped female's nose. But it hadn't to be bought by the barrel as I read that several barrels of sal volatile had been on tap to keep the teeming screenagers in the perpendicular at a beetling session."

Patrick Kavanagh wasn't the only one at the centre of the storm. Irate county councillors, newspaper columnists, music critics, broadcasters, judges, youth leaders, ratepayers and especially the fans all had something to say in the controversy that ensued, both north and south of the border, following the Beatles' departure. GAA fans, soccer fans, teddy boys, corner boys, the concert promoters, the Government, the Gardaí and especially adults were all dragged into the war of words.

A councillor laid the blame at the feet of Telefís Éireann. "What the young people did outside the Adelphi and inside is being inculcated every week by the Telefís Éireann showband shows," he said. "Young people are actually being instructed by television in their hysteria." The Coiste Gnotha, or governing body, of the Gaelic League demanded that the Government ban "exhibitions" similar to those of the Beatles.

Dublin's Lord Mayor, Alderman Seán Moore, also went on the rampage. Speaking at a Fianna Fáil function in Jurys Hotel, with Taoiseach Seán Lemass in attendance, he expressed his "sadness" over what he referred to as the "moronic barbarity" of Thursday night. Dublin's Ratepayers Association wasn't happy either. Moves to saddle ratepayers with the anticipated bill of "thousands of pounds" would be resisted, declared Councillor James Kelly, leader of the ratepayers' party in the City Council. "It seems appalling to us that the ratepayers should have to pay for damages committed by vandals and hooligans," he added.

Schools took a grim view of events. "I was in boarding-school in Mullingar," says Eamon Carr, who was a Beatles' fan and later a member of Horslips. "News came in through a couple of the day-boys that there had been riots in Dublin. I had developed a sort of embryonic mop top. I was also a member of the Beatles' fan club. So when the news of the riots was reported, they were all looking at me as if to say, 'You're part of this conspiracy.'

"The next thing was that the head appeared during religious instruction or whatever it was. He muttered to the priest that was teaching us. I was called out and frogmarched to a little room under the stairs. They had brought in this army barber from the local barracks in Mullingar. He took out his clippers and cut my hair. It was a pretty crude job. They sent me back in disgrace into class saying, 'Let that be a lesson for you. We'll have none of that Beatles *craic* around here.' All they were short of doing was branding my forehead with the letter 'B' for Beatle. It was a bit like wartime France. It was great. It gave me a sort of 'badge' at school."

John Olohan, who had attended one of the concerts, likewise found himself in trouble with teachers. "I got the works the next day in school," he recalls. "'Were you responsible for all this mayhem?' I was asked. One teacher took me out and said, 'I believe you were at the Beatles' concert and you were involved in all this craziness in Dublin. I have a good mind to just throw you out of this school for being involved in that.' I specifically remember he used that phrase, 'I have a good mind ....'. I said, 'I wasn't involved in it. I was just at the thing.' He kind of passed it off then. But there were a couple of hoors in the school who were delighted I got into trouble. I was one of a small group interested in the Beatles. The rest of the fellows would have been into the *Farmers Journal*. The idea of pop music of any description would be strange to them."

Also in hot water was Lena McDevitt, who had travelled to Dublin Airport with her friend Kaye Ryan to see the Beatles: "My mother was dead by that stage and, when I went home, I had to own up to my father. I didn't have any choice because some reporter talked to us afterwards and we were in the paper that evening. The paper had our names in it. My friend was quoted as saying that the Beatles were 'the mostest.' My father saw it. He was quite pedantic about the English language and went on about how there was no such word. I was denying that she ever said it but she did. We did use that word at the time. He wasn't happy at all."

To be fair, newspaper reports in the wake of the Beatles' visit must have shaken anyone of a nervous disposition or anybody calling themselves adults. Acres of newsprint were devoted to the debate. The press went to town. 'Quidnunc', writing in the Saturday edition of *The Irish Times*, put it bluntly: "'Why don't they turn the hoses on?' 'Why don't they turn the grapeshot on?' Fair comment, and both, in my opinion, perfectly reasonable reactions to the display of moronic barbarity put on by the youthful (and not-so-youthful) citizens of Dublin, in O'Connell Street and Abbey Street, Dublin, on Thursday night."

Continuing his diatribe, 'Quidnunc' took what can only be termed a 'sniffy' view of the night's proceedings: "In the Adelphi auditorium, I waited for the second appearance of the phenomena with as little embarrassment as is possible for a Methuselah in the presence of infants (average estimated age of audience: 18 years). At last, four hairy youngsters appeared onstage, to be greeted with shrieks and whistles. Three of them walloped electric guitars which appeared to be amplified to the decibel limit; the fourth walloped a set of drums.

"They all opened their mouths and made noises that sounded to me like: 'Mew; Me-ooh; me-ooh; me-ooh-ooh!' The words were unintelligible, but it didn't matter all that much anyway since the noises from the stage were pretty well swamped by the animal squeals, shrieks and whistles from the audience. The only impact that I got was one of juvenile, but not particularly talented, high spirits. I was, of course, sent – sent away."

'Quidnunc' also described the scene outside the Adelphi as fans hoped for a glimpse of the Beatles: "Any head that appeared at any upstairs front window of the Adelphi was greeted from the street with a noise that could only be compared with the baying of jackals. It didn't matter that the head had no relation to the Beatles, and it is certain that the noise had no relation to any sound that is normally heard from rational human beings."

Some pop journalists were equally unimpressed and, no doubt, somewhat alarmed. 'Paul Jones' wrote in the *Evening Press*: "Personally I might be termed a 'square' since I must admit that the Beatles failed to arise in the Paul Jones breast little more than ordinary enthusiasm, and were I to choose between them and any of our own modern showbands, I would definitely vote with the home product. Given the same hairdos and the same advance publicity, I don't doubt that any of the Irish showbands could perform with as much success as our friends from the Merseyside, whose goofy gooning would remind one of the 'Stooges', supposing that the latter had been issued with modern musical impediments."

Across the border, in Belfast, Judge Topping was also less than supportive of the Beatles. "I do not know whether the progress of the Beatles through Belfast can be likened to a plague of locusts or not," he remarked, "but I hope that we never have to deal with this type of group again." He was speaking during hearings where £70 was awarded to a gentleman whose £2,000 Lancia car was damaged while parked outside the Grand Central Hotel. A similar sum was awarded against Belfast Corporation in respect of a broken plate-glass window.

On appeal, the verdict in the Lancia car case was upheld by Lord Justice Curran, who was told that six teenage boys had climbed onto the car to get a better view of proceedings at the hotel after the Beatles' arrival. The car's driver, George Leckie, who was having dinner on the premises, was informed on the night by the police about the extent of the damage. "From what I have heard of the Beatles' crowds they are a pretty lively lot," Lord Justice Curran said. "We have evidence that they broke past a line of police and got to the door of the hotel. They could not have cared less about the damage they knew perfectly well they would cause."

In the pro-Beatles camp, Telefís Éireann's Gay Byrne and newspaper 'agony aunt' Angela McNamara defended the group and their fans. "I don't see anything terribly wrong in it, I must say," Byrne wrote regarding the hysteria. "Those who are saying it is a disgrace seem to me to be very good at conveniently forgetting guys like Valentino, who received just as much hero-worship from fans as the Beatles have ever done. We did not hear so much about it in those days simply because there was no TV and radio and newspaper coverage was not as wide as nowadays." Siding with him, Angela McNamara said, "Banning the Beatles would not get at the root of the problem. Certainly I would ban them if they are immoral, but they are not. The root of the trouble lies in the homes."

The *News of the World* also investigated the root of the malaise, using expert analysis to probe the psychological depths of the fans' fevered brains. Surreptitious purchasers of what at the time was regarded as a 'scandal sheet' received a lesson in the psychology of hysterical behaviour. "This is one way of flinging off childhood restrictions and letting themselves go," a psychologist was reported as saying. "The fact that tens of thousands of others are shrieking along with her at the same time makes a girl feel she is living life to the full with people of her own age. This emotional outlook is very necessary at her age. It is also innocent and harmless. It is a safety valve. They are also subconsciously preparing for motherhood. Their frenzied screams are a rehearsal for that moment. Even the jelly babies are symbolic."

Outraged postbag contributors, for and against, wrote to newspapers under various pseudonyms to express their views. Their letters were signed 'Beatles Abu', 'Ratepayer', 'Ban The Beat', 'Not Bitten', 'No Square', 'Non-Screaming Beatle Fan', 'No Hypocrite', 'Termite Fan', 'Country Cockroach', 'Pop Fan' and, of course, 'Beatle Fan', to name but a few. The debate raged for weeks. "Clean up our country of thugs, teddy boys and so on, and make it a place for decent people to live in," one contributor wrote. Another slammed the "rabble which had lost (if it ever had) the most primitive conception of civilised conduct." 'Pro-Beatles' explained that she liked to "twist and jive and try to extract some fun from life." A distressed 'Anti-Pop' warned that "far worse than the damage to property might be the damage to public morality, health and order likely to be caused by the artificial stimulation of hysteria in adolescent girls and violence in adolescent boys."

Are the teenagers to blame? 'Proud To Be Teenager' asked *Evening Press* readers. "No, it is the adults and the parents of those teenagers who are to blame," the writer of the letter declared. "The teenagers were looking to the Beatles to give them what was lacking in their own homes. The present-day adults should buck-up and help the teenagers instead of criticising them. Try to realise you are living in 1963. Part of the art of becoming an adult is to make allowances for and to tolerate others. So grow up!"

Whatever the perceived validity of their grievances, adults back in 1963 were clearly squandering their words and wasting their time. The kids wouldn't listen. Within days, Beatles' fans on the east coast were glued to their television sets, watching ITV's broadcast of the previous week's Royal Command Performance. Transmitted on Sunday 10 November, it contained four numbers sung by the Beatles – 'From Me To You', 'She Loves You', 'Till There Was You' and 'Twist And Shout'. "On that show they were wearing two-tone tops whereas in the Adelphi they wore grey Beatle suits," says John Olohan. "Otherwise, it was basically the same show. Watching it you got a flavour of what the concerts were like. It was amazing to see it on television. You had to watch it on transmission. At that time there was no such thing as a video recorder. Video recorders were like science fiction back then."

The following week, Telefís Éireann's *The Showband Show* broadcast the short insert recorded in the ballroom of the Gresham Hotel. The comedy sketch went down well, although it wasn't accompanied by a sung or a mimed number. "They have come; been heard and seen (by some) but not all of us have been conquered," one music critic commented after the television broadcast. "It will be interesting to see whether or not some of our own modern showbands can now get into the act with some entirely different sounds."

By that week also, the Gael Linn recording of the Adelphi performances had been processed, edited and dubbed and was available for public viewing. Although ominously titled 'The Beatles Pay Unwelcome Visit', the newsreel showed the enthusiastic crowds along with the Beatles in full musical flight. "The Gael Linn newsreel came out every Friday," explains Morgan O'Sullivan. "It was like *Pathé News*. What would happen is it would go away to London on, say, the Thursday night in this instance. We'd get the rushes back on the Sunday night. We'd cut them on Monday and on Tuesday evening we'd put the commentary on. It would be in the cinemas on the following Friday. This happened with the Beatles' concert we filmed in the Adelphi."

Another cinematic treat hit the screens in the lead-up to Christmas. From 22 December an eight-minute feature on the autumn tour was presented in selected venues. Filmed at the ABC cinema in Ardwick, Manchester on 20 November, the special edition mini-feature contained shots of the Beatles performing 'She Loves You' and 'Twist And Shout'. It also featured backstage shots of the Beatles along with footage of hysteria and mayhem.

"The *Pathé News*, which was called *The Beatles Come To Town*, was a big hit," says Tony Foran, the trainee projectionist who had worked in the Adelphi on the night of the Beatles' concerts. "It was in colour and Techniscope. The *Pathé News* was usually only about seven or eight minutes long. But the cinemas booked out because people wanted to see the one on the Beatles. The main feature film didn't matter. It didn't mean anything to anyone. All people wanted to know was when the *Pathé News* was on. They could have run the *Pathé News* on the Beatles 12 times a day and had full houses."

Irish record sales of the Beatles boomed in the run-up to Christmas, fulfilling one of the goals of the tour. At a time when the ownership of TV sets was tiny, one purpose of tours was to showcase the stars and help sell their records. Not only would those at the concerts tend to buy singles, EPs and LPs, but the press coverage would generate wider publicity as well. 'I Want To Hold Your Hand' became one of *the* presents that festive season. So great was demand that the single shot into the Irish charts less than a week before Christmas Day. However, not for the first time, a Beatles' new single was restricted to second spot by Brendan Bowyer, whose rendition of 'No More' occupied top position over Christmas. Yet it sold well. So too did the LPs *Please Please Me* and *With The Beatles,* not to mention the EPs *The Beatles (No. 1), The Beatles' Hits* and *Twist And Shout.*

Suppliers to showbands and beat groups also cashed in on the boom. "Get with it showbands....get Commer," read an advertisement from Buckley's Motors of Whitehall in Dublin. The ad referred to a minibus – ideal for bands – with "panoramic windscreen," "full-forward control" and "quieter running." It cost £975 for an eight-seater, ex works; £995 for a twelve-seater. Additional features, costing extra, included a built-in record player to help bands pass the time and keep in touch – and rehearse cover versions of Beatles' hits – while on the road.

Instrument suppliers made a killing as well, charging up to £600 for full sets of gear for six-piece bands. Guitars cost from £30 – £160, amps and speakers from £20 – £145, drums from £70 – £160, with the most common method of payment being through hire purchase. "Once a kid puts a guitar strap on his shoulder, he transforms himself into a Beatle," was how one salesman put it. "To complete the Beatle picture there are the suits (we'll leave the haircuts out of it). One group pays up to £50 a suit and renews them every six months. But many of the lesser bands don't have suits. They get by with jackets over their normal wear."

Chris Hill, the 16-year-old schoolboy from Belfast who brought his camera to the ABC Ritz, also made a small fortune. "I must have taken about 15 or 16 shots of the Beatles onstage," he recalls. "I got a lovely one of Paul McCartney against a black background, mouth open. It was a classic pose. The quality in those days was hit-and-miss but the quality of these ones was exceptional, especially considering how and when they were taken. After the concert I sold maybe 1,000 prints of the Beatles onstage. In today's money it amounted to probably about £3,000, which is a lot for a 16-year-old schoolboy. I had girls in three schools selling shots for me, for no commission. They just wanted the glory of selling these Beatles' photographs. They begged me to let them sell them. I made a fortune but, according to my diary, I spent it very quickly as well."

Remarkably, even Aer Lingus tried to cash in on the Beatles. Writing in the *RTV Guide* on 13 December, Gay Byrne reported how the airline was attempting to woo the group on board for their forthcoming trip to America. Also in the bidding war were BOAC, Sabena and Pan Am. "Aer Lingus are trying to figure a way to get them swiftly from Liverpool to Dublin to get on the Boeing or alternatively from London to Shannon to pick it up there," Byrne wrote. "The boys would love to travel Shamrock, but it means a double journey. I can tell all concerned, however, that the decision has not yet been taken and we'll see who'll win in the end. Place your bets now, and in the meantime, there are more strings being pulled behind the scenes than there are in the entire Beatles forty-minute stage act!"

For the tour organisers, the jaunt around Britain and Ireland was a big money-spinner. Jeff Williams of the Kestrels took a stab at the sums. "I don't expect the whole package cost more than about £5,000 a week," he concluded. "That's the figure I used to work on. I think we in the Kestrels made about £200 a week. Including the Beatles, I don't think it would have been costing much more than about £5,000 a week to put out and it went on for six weeks. You can imagine the sort of money that was made."

Taking Jeff Williams' estimate, total outlay for artistes amounted to in the region of £30,000 for the full six weeks of the tour. With tickets selling for 6/6, 8/6 and 10/6 in venues holding from 2,000 – 2,500, gross revenue for the 34 venues, at two concerts a night, would have been in the ballpark of £65,000. Discounting transport, hotels and publicity, gross profits of well in excess of £30,000 – representing margins of more than 50 per cent – were made by the tour organisers. Better still, the transactions were in cash.

"It was all cash," Jeff Williams remarks. "It was all cash going through the box office. We got paid in cash. It was like a job; you got paid in cash in those days. All the programmes were cash. If we were short of cash, we always used to go and see the driver and he'd sub you a few quid out of the takings from the programmes. I would have thought they must have made a fortune on those. That, I think, is where the money was made. It was all cash and nobody really knew how many programmes were sold."

For the Beatles themselves, the hysteria intensified in the weeks after Dublin and Belfast. The remainder of the autumn tour was manic, with teenagers going wild in cities like Manchester, Wolverhampton and Newcastle and in smaller centres like Exeter, Cambridge and York. The tour was relentless, continuing for a further 35 days. Even on the evening of their departure from Belfast back to England they appeared at the Granada cinema, East Ham, London. At least on that day, their tiredness was tempered by news that their forthcoming single 'I Want To Hold Your Hand', due for release at the end of

November, was being tipped to achieve one million advance-order sales.

Not surprisingly, worn down by the hectic schedule, Paul McCartney succumbed to gastric flu a few days after the Irish tour, causing the cancellation of the Beatles' concerts in Portsmouth on 12 November. They were rearranged for 3 December, which was one of the few days the group were supposed to have off. The tour also coincided with the death of President John F Kennedy, who was assassinated in Dallas on 22 November. That Friday night – exactly two weeks after their Irish visit – the Beatles were appearing at the Globe cinema in Stockton-on-Tees, Durham. The news came as a shock. "I remember coming offstage and John Lennon said to me, 'John Kennedy has been assassinated,'" Roger Greenaway of the Kestrels recalls. "Everyone remembers where they were when John Kennedy died. Lennon was a great practical joker, always up to tricks. I said, 'Yeah, yeah, it's not a very funny joke.' But, of course, President Kennedy had been assassinated."

The lives of John, Paul, George and Ringo, throughout November and December, were a blur of cars, planes, trains, press conferences, hotel rooms, concert venues and radio and TV appearances. They were harried and harassed, pestered and pursued. They signed thousands of autographs. Add in a TV appearance on the BBC's *Juke Box Jury* along with numerous other media engagements, and the tour, which stretched up to 13 December, became the maddest in pop music history. By the time of their Christmas shows, which ate into time off over the festive season, the Beatles had been labouring like workhorses. Not only that, but the hysteria was multiplying exponentially.

"I was compère of *The Beatles Christmas Shows* at Finsbury Park," says Rolf Harris. "I did my own spot with all my own songs and then I'd say, 'Now, listen, kids. These guys are amazing. Last night nobody heard a word because everybody screamed. For goodness sake, listen to them. They are just fantastic. Here they are....the Beatles!' From that moment on, the screams just drowned them out. They could have been miming, for all that you could hear. You couldn't hear a thing they did for the whole of their spot."

American networks came to film the phenomenon. Fan club members were entertained at a special concert in Liverpool. Describing the frenetic pace to filmmaker Richard Lester one day, Lennon explained how their lives had become "a room and a car and a car and a room and a room and a car." That image would underpin the Beatles' forthcoming film – a masterpiece of pop cinematography, *A Hard Day's Night*, described in time as "the *Citizen Kane* of jukebox musicals."

The film had evolved in the immediate aftermath of playwright Alun Owen's Irish visit. Producer Walter Shenson explained what happened: "He came back and was astute. He said the Beatles get off the plane to go to the hotel; they go to the concert hall; they get back on the plane. They don't know whether they're in Dublin or San Francisco. They were literally prisoners of their success. And they would travel in a cocoon of Liverpool. There would be the manager, the road manager, the publicity man, the guy who carries the equipment – all chums from home. The Beatles didn't know where they were half the time. That was the essence of Owen's screenplay."

Having returned to England, Owen had set about writing his film script in the lead-up to Christmas. It wasn't to be any old script. Rejecting the boy-meets-girl, happy-go-lucky, fantasy pop film format of the late 1950s and early '60s, Owen opted for a grittier yet light-hearted approach. "We're not going to have a story that ends at the London Palladium with the vicar smiling and giving the boys the thumbs-up sign from the stalls," Owen said. "Instead, I want to capture the sharpness and humour of their fantastic personalities. There must be plenty of movement so that everyone can see the Beatles as they really are offstage."

Drawing from events in Ireland, Owen presented a documentary-style storyline depicting the frantic lives of the Fab

Four. It was an action-packed comedy, with the Beatles eluding rampaging fans, killing time in hotels and on trains, attending a press conference, performing in front of hysterical girls and dealing with the madness of Beatlemania. "The plot of our film covers 36 hours of life as a Beatle – or rather Alun Owen's impressions of what it is like – and we use our own names," is how George Harrison described it. It was premièred at the London Pavilion on 6 July 1964, to enormous acclaim.

The Liverpool mannerisms of the Beatles were exactly as witnessed by Owen during the Irish leg of the autumn tour. "Alun Owen came and hung out with us for a few days," Paul McCartney reflected, "which was great because he picked up all the little things, little jokes, the sarcasm, the Beatle way of humour, John's wit, Ringo's comedy; he picked up our characters, which was good." Mersey slang words such as 'grotty', a derivative of 'grotesque', received their first general airing. The film was littered with other strange words like 'potty', 'posh' and 'swine'. Even the title of the film came from a casual remark by Ringo who, after an exhausting day, coined the phrase 'A Hard Day's Night'.

The Beatles were depicted as victims of fame, trapped by success, which reflected their experiences in Ireland. "One of the nicest things about their characters is the way they remain agreeable and good-tempered under often very trying conditions. They emerge as four very different people," Owen remarked. John was creative and cynical. Paul was adorable and cute. Ringo was sad and under-appreciated. George was serious and intense. In time, one wondered whether Owen had ingeniously captured or invented the characters of all four Beatles. Either way, Owen's scripting defined the Beatles for the decades ahead.

Events unfolding during the making of the film resulted in the return to Ireland of two of the Beatles. On the set of the movie George fell for Pattie Boyd, a 19-year-old blonde, blue-eyed model and film extra. In the run-up to Easter 1964, with the couple's relationship deepening, Brian Epstein suggested they take a short private holiday. Epstein was paranoid about publicity involving girlfriends and the impact it might have on the band. Even the smooth transition of John from single to married hadn't softened Brian's view. He therefore proposed that George and Pattie visit Ireland over Easter, suggesting as a venue the quiet Dromoland Castle Hotel in County Clare. John and Cynthia accompanied them on the top-secret visit.

The Irish media got wind of the venture. "They arrived by private plane at Shannon Airport on Thursday night and were whisked away across the tarmac out the back way from the airport in a car driven by a member of the Dromoland Castle staff," the *Evening Herald* disclosed in forensic detail. The paper informed readers that not only were John and Cynthia occupying the hotel's presidential suite at the rate of £140 per week but that the party would be checking out the following Tuesday.

"A member of the staff said today: 'Never have we seen girls in jeans in the hotel before, but they are nice quiet people – and they keep to themselves,'" the report continued. "Pattie Boyd was the girl in the sky blue jeans and sweater, and wearing navy blue jeans was Mrs Cynthia Lennon. Last night they dressed for dinner and formed a gay group in one corner of the great diningroom which was once the library of the castle. The Beatles have requested that there should be no publicity about their visit and have directed the staff to deny that they are in the hotel. However, John and Cynthia, hand in hand, took a stroll down by the lake in the grounds but hurriedly retreated back into the hotel at the sight of a few cross-Channel photographers."

Hot on their scent, the English tabloids were soon camped at the hotel, asking questions about who was with George and if John was accompanied by Cynthia. "This was my first experience of that sort of thing," Pattie later recalled. "The manager tapped their phones and we could hear them sending back the most awful things to Fleet Street. It was impossible to get out."

Confident of putting the press off the scent, John and George checked out at reception, where they were quizzed by reporters about who they were with. Insisting they were alone, they emerged into the rain and left by car for Shannon Airport. As they sped away, John and George glanced out the rear window hoping to see the press in hot pursuit. The press, who were not to be fooled, stayed put, convinced that the two Beatles were lying.

With the connivance of the hotel, Pattie and Cynthia dressed up as maids, wearing white caps and aprons, and pushed a wicker basket down to the laundry room located away from the front of the building. Although observed by reporters, no one twigged what was happening. Jumping in the basket, they were eventually hoisted into the back of a laundry van and transported to Shannon Airport. Although pleased with their ingenious escape, on their return to London the airport was packed with reporters. The following day, George's relationship was splashed all over the British press.

By that stage – just five months after their Irish visit – the Beatles had ratcheted up the last few gears to mega-stardom. They 'owned' the pop charts. Pre-orders for Beatles' singles smashed all sales records. Over three million advance orders, spanning Britain and the USA, were received for 'Can't Buy Me Love'. Seventy-three million Americans watched their first appearance on *The Ed Sullivan Show*, broadcast on 9 February, which was organised by Brian Epstein during the group's Irish visit. Their concerts at Carnegie Hall and in Washington DC were mind-blowing affairs. By the beginning of April the Beatles occupied the top five positions in the *Billboard* charts. If there was ever total domination by a pop group, this was it.

"It was all Beatles, Beatles, Beatles," says Tony Jackson, original lead singer with the Searchers. "Don't get me wrong because I think the Beatles were the best band ever. They were the best band that ever walked the earth. They were great guys and we had some smashing times with them. In '64 we were voted second to the Beatles in the NME poll. But there was such a gap. Although we were second, we were second by a mile or 20 miles."

Despite their meteoric rise, hopes were high that the Beatles would undertake an extended Irish tour, including Limerick and Cork, in 1964. The music press made all sorts of predictions, speculating on visits in January, February or later. Optimism was fuelled by the huge number of international stars who had arrived in 1963, even after the Beatles' departure. Adam Faith had put in an appearance the week following the Beatles, while Bobby Rydell and Helen Shapiro also performed two weeks after that.

"Will the Beatles visit Limerick?" the 'Limerick Roundup' column in *Spotlight* speculated in the wake of the Beatles' visit. "For weeks now the city has been buzzing with rumours. The position at present is that Paul Russell, promoter of the Beatles Irish tour, is negotiating with Irish cinemas for two concerts at the Savoy Limerick and the Savoy Cork. If the talks are successful the Beatles will visit both these venues late in January."

Paul Russell had reason to be hopeful. "It was on McCartney's mind," Russell recalls. "He's the one who said to me that they were going to do Limerick and Cork. He loved the Irish countryside. He wanted to go fishing with me and go down and see Dromoland Castle. He always said to me, 'I'd love to go down the Shannon.' He wrote on many occasions and he was always on about how much Ireland meant to him. It wasn't so much about the Adelphi or anything. There was a camaraderie at that time because I had helped them to get to Ireland. And everyone in England loves Dublin because of the few jars. They were going to come back but events overtook them. America was the big thing and that was when they disappeared."

Fintan Russell – Paul's brother – also remembers the letters from McCartney: "I know that Paul McCartney wrote to him in beautiful longhand writing. He had them in the house. One of the letters he wrote mentioned, 'We'll see you next June.' McCartney also invited him over to one or two functions but, at the time, he was so busy he couldn't go. I remember him showing the letters to my mother. She was there saying, 'Who is Paul McCartney? Is he a pal of John McCormack's?' I remember those letters lying around the house. But he used to say to me, 'I don't know if we'll be able to do it because by that stage they will be huge.'"

Both Limerick and Cork were humming with excitement at the prospect of what was in store. The Savoy in Cork, with 2,262 seats, was a demonstrably suitable venue, staging contemporaries of the Beatles such as the Rolling Stones, Tom Jones, Engelbert Humperdinck, the Yardbirds and, later, the Bee Gees. "In the very first issue of *Spotlight* in 1963, we featured Brenda Lee on the cover. I had interviewed her backstage after her appearance at the Savoy," says Corkman John Coughlan, editor of *Spotlight* who promoted many shows at the venue. "A huge number of the big pop acts appeared there, with the Rolling Stones being the highlight. The manager was very enthusiastic about the extra revenue he could earn from these concerts.

"The Savoy was a good venue. It had a good backstage area. There were good lines of view. From the ground floor you were looking up at the act and the upper balcony was quite steeply pitched so everyone could see. The acoustics were good. It was a seated venue as well, unlike the City Hall in Cork where it was all foldaway chairs. It was one of the few cinemas in Ireland that doubled as a big concert venue. The Savoy in Cork, and the Adelphi and Carlton in Dublin, were as big as any of the venues the Beatles would have played in Britain in those early days. I could have envisaged the Beatles playing there. There's no reason why it couldn't have happened."

The Savoy in Limerick was somewhat smaller, holding 1,500,

although it too hosted some major international stars. "Roy Orbison, the Tremeloes and also Tom Jones played there," recalls Paddy Brennan, who later promoted many English acts in Limerick through the local Rock 'n Roll Club. "It was like one of the old English Victorian theatres. The ornate work was wonderful. The acoustics were especially good because of the way the ceiling was curved. That was Richard Harris's local cinema as a young fellow. He would have hung around in the café. The première of his film *Bloomfield* was held there as well. The Beatles certainly would have filled the place. The 3,000 tickets for the two shows would have been snapped up immediately if dates in the Savoy had been set up for the Beatles."

Unfortunately, the proposed 1964 tour, including visits to Dublin, Belfast, Cork and Limerick, was not to be. The Beatles outgrew the aspiration long before it could be realised. Instead, the group made just one last appearance in Ireland and that was a somewhat unexpected and controversial visit on 2 November 1964. The venue was the King's Hall, Belfast.

KING'S HALL

Towards the end of September 1964 the telephone rang in the office of Belfast impresario Trevor Kane. On the line was promoter Arthur Howes, calling from London with a most attractive proposition. The Beatles, who were only weeks away from starting their autumn tour, had a free Monday on 2 November. "Is there any chance," Howes asked, "that the King's Hall might be available on that date?" Although coming very late in the day, especially considering that the tour had been organised the previous April, it was a challenge that no businessman in his right mind could turn down.

At the time of the phone-call, Trevor Kane was in his early 30s and established as one of Ireland's leading promoters. With an office in High Street, Belfast, his company Trevor Kane Promotions had built a name for itself as an importer of international stars. Often linking up with Arthur Howes Promotions, Kane had brought in acts like Adam Faith, Marty Wilde, Tom Jones, Gerry and the Pacemakers and Billy J Kramer and the Dakotas. He managed the College Boys and Witnesses showbands. He also co-ran the Boom Boom Room in Belfast.

"It wasn't a surprise that Arthur telephoned because I was bringing in a lot of artistes from England through him," Trevor Kane recalls. "The surprise was that he was offering me the

Beatles, who were at their peak at the time. I already had the lease of the King's Hall because I was running ice-skating, boxing and wrestling there. It was the old King's Hall ice-rink, run by boxing promoter George Connell and myself. That was the only place big enough to take the Beatles and we were the only ones who could get the venue. We could only get the Beatles for one night so we decided to run six o'clock and quarter to nine concerts. Nothing like it had ever been done before."

The economics of the venture were impressive. To begin with, the capacity of the King's Hall was in excess of 8,000. With two back-to-back shows, a total of more than 16,000 paying fans would not only quadruple what Belfast's ABC cinema could hold but it would set a record for a Beatles' one-night stand in Britain. With seats selling for 15/- and 20/-, the take on the night would be unprecedented for Ireland. Audience size was also more in line with house capacities the Beatles had become accustomed to on their recent tour of America.

Additionally, the concerts on the preceding night, Sunday 1 November, were at the Astoria cinema in Finsbury Park, London. The day after the King's Hall, Tuesday 3 November, there was a free day to allow for a return to London. The shows scheduled for the next day again, Wednesday 4 November, were in Luton, just north of the English capital. With the surrounding events so close to London Airport, the logistics of the venture couldn't have been better.

With the bones of the deal agreed, Howes sent one of his advance road managers to Belfast to assess the technical details. "They used to put the stage at the top of the King's Hall, looking down the venue," says Kane. "We decided not to do that because it wasn't giving out good enough sound. We became the first people to put the stage halfway up the side of the hall. The people in the balcony were overlooking the stage. It also fitted more punters in."

Negotiations were the toughest he had ever known, Kane

was reported as saying at the time. "Before I could even get a chance of having them," he commented, "their management wanted to see everything from the seating plan of the hall to a detailed list of exits and entrances and full details of acoustics." In short time, however, the technicalities were dealt with and the contracts between Kane, Howes and Epstein were signed. Everything was ready for a 1 October announcement, leaving the standard lead-in time of approximately one month for ticket sales for the shows.

Once announced, the date of the visit generated enormous controversy as it clashed with the forthcoming Royal Command Performance. The press went to town. At the previous year's performance, John Lennon had remarked when introducing 'Twist And Shout': "For our last number I'd like to ask your help. Would the people in the cheaper seats clap your hands and the rest of you just rattle your jewellery," an obvious reference to those in the royal box. A year later, the press speculated that the royals had been insulted and the group snubbed as a result.

"It certainly was controversial," Trevor Kane remembers. "The Beatles had been keeping the date of the Royal Command Performance free and they ended up playing at the King's Hall. There were two theories. One was that they hadn't been asked to appear at the Royal Command and therefore they got in touch with Belfast to use that as an excuse. The other theory was that they were saying that their booking in Belfast was agreed already, that they had done the contract with me and couldn't let me down, so they got out of the Royal Command in that way. The papers made a big meal of the controversy. It went on for weeks." Lennon later clarified the issue, pointing out that following the group's appearance in 1963 they always rejected further offers: "Every year after they asked us, but we always turned it down. Brian went through hell telling Lew Grade that we wouldn't do it. Brian was on his knees pleading to us, 'Please do the Royal Variety,' and we always replied, 'No, we've done the Royal Variety.'"

As far as Beatles' manager Brian Epstein was concerned, the purpose of the 1964 autumn tour was simple – to cash in on the group's massive fame and to rake in the money while keeping the 'home' fans happy. In truth, the whole of 1964 had been an extraordinary financial success. Concerts in France had been followed by appearances on *The Ed Sullivan Show* and sell-out shows in America. Hysteria had greeted the Beatles during a three-week tour of Australia and New Zealand and short visits to Sweden, Holland and Denmark. A further gargantuan tour of America had been undertaken from August into September.

The Beatles' first film, *A Hard Day's Night*, had opened to rave reviews. Records were broken all over the globe. 'Can't Buy Me Love' and 'A Hard Day's Night' became international chart-toppers. Crowds of 300,000 and 250,000 turned out to see the Beatles in Adelaide and Melbourne respectively. A crowd of 200,000 lined the streets of Liverpool to welcome them home for a civic reception. Beatlemania had, itself, gone mad – and it was no longer just in Britain but throughout the world.

Despite the exhausting year behind them, Epstein set in place a late autumn tour of back-to-back nightly shows in 27 different venues throughout Britain, amounting to a total of 54 performances. Not coincidentally, the tour led up to the Beatles' Christmas single release 'I Feel Fine' and the LP release *Beatles For Sale*. The concerts were spread over 33 days, from 9 October – 10 November, with barely a break in-between. One of the few scheduled respites, on 2 and 3 November, was swallowed up by the engagement eventually arranged for Belfast.

Brian Epstein co-promoted the tour in conjunction with his long-standing ally Arthur Howes. The bulk of the venues available to them were cinemas, which the Beatles had completely outgrown. In sharp contrast to the large auditoriums available during the late summer tour of America, these venues could hold only 2,000 – 3,000. With box office revenue so tightly curtailed, the plan was to cut costs to the bone. Financial leakage was reduced by minimising the number of middlemen and associates. Even the support acts were chosen to keep costs on the floor, with Epstein looking no further than to his own 'stable of stars' to pad out the bill. Only one of the performers, Mary Wells, involved any real cash outlay.

With the exception of Wells, the support acts were all signed to Epstein's North End Music Stores (NEMS) Enterprises which was, by then, based in Argyll Street, London. One of the best-known of the acts was Cavern Club favourites the Remo Four. Contemporaries of the Fab Four, they were a polished band and had, at an earlier stage, rivalled the Beatles in popularity. Michael Haslam was another Epstein discovery, who specialised in big-voiced ballads. From Bolton, he had genuine talent but, like other minor NEMS acts, was submerged by his manager's involvement with the company's big stars, especially the Beatles.

The story was no different for the Rustiks, who Epstein had signed earlier in 1964 after spotting them while judging a TV talent competition. Their record 'What A Memory Can Do' went nowhere. Perhaps the most surprising slow-burner was Tommy Quickly – a Merseyside rock 'n roller who had flopped with the Lennon-McCartney composition 'Tip Of My Tongue'. Writing in his autobiography *A Cellarful Of Noise* in 1964, Epstein waxed eloquent about Quickly and declared emphatically, "He is going to be a star." It was a brave prediction, especially as Epstein went on to describe how another of Quickly's recordings, ominously titled 'You Might As Well Forget Him', had bombed in the charts.

Of the five NEMS acts, only Sounds Incorporated would achieve a modicum of national and international acclaim. Boasting a big saxophone sound, they were consummate musicians and in 1964 had released a moderately-successful single 'William Tell'. They were renowned for their live performances and would later open for the Beatles at Shea Stadium. Not even they, however, could come close to the stature of Mary Wells, who was one of the first big stars of

Motown. She had a string of hits including 'My Guy'. That she was one of the Beatles' favourite American singers helped explain her presence on the tour.

"It was basically Brian Epstein's stable along with Mary Wells," the Rustiks' drummer Bill Covington agrees. "It was a big break for me. I was a kid of 17. I must have been the youngest person in the whole Epstein set-up. The others were 23 or 24. That was my first flight when I went to Belfast. It was my first time in another country. My head was spinning with the excitement of it all.

"One day I was in Plymouth looking at the Beatles on TV and buying their records in a shop. The next thing I was in London, signed up with Brian Epstein and part of a Beatles' tour. Coming from the south-west of England, there I was in London where people were still walking around at nine o'clock at night. The lights were still on, whereas in Plymouth everybody was in bed by six o'clock. I would walk into Epstein's office at any time and one of the Beatles would be there discussing what they were doing. It was an amazing experience.

"We were paid £30 a week at the time of the tour, which was a lot of money back in 1964. Expenses used to come out of the wages, like hotels and stuff like that. Sometimes you'd come away with very little money. But I never begrudged Brian that because he gave us everything. He gave us a van and we didn't have to maintain it. He bought us lots of quality clothes. We'd get suits designed in Soho. So I have no complaints about the treatment.

"Unfortunately, all the bands on before the Beatles were cannon-fodder. There's no other word for it. The Rustiks were just an average band. We played four songs on the tour, I think. We understood what was going to happen. We were just part of the build-up to the climax, which was the Beatles. We knew exactly what our role was. The moment of supreme pleasure had to be delayed and delayed and delayed for as long as possible. We were there just as a lead-up to the final moment, which was the Beatles. The audience weren't interested in us whatsoever."

On the afternoon of Monday 2 November, the Beatles touched down at Aldergrove Airport and were taken directly to the King's Hall in Balmoral. Unlike the previous year, when they had travelled in a leisurely fashion from Dublin and stayed in the heart of the city, this time the centre of Belfast was ruled out of bounds. Under strict instructions from the police, the car transporting the Beatles was banned from approaching Royal Avenue or its surrounds. Instead, the entourage, which was escorted by police, headed for Donegall Road where cars were switched to put fans off the scent. From there the cavalcade made its way to the King's Hall where the Beatles were shut away until the concerts were over.

"I picked them up at the airport, around lunchtime," says promoter Trevor Kane. "They came in my car, which was a big Mark 10 Jaguar. We had a police escort, which amounted to a couple of cars at least. They guided us to the King's Hall and stayed with the Beatles later when they went to their hotel. But we didn't stop at the hotel first. We went straight to the venue and from the moment they arrived they were locked inside."

One of the minders at the venue was John McCabe, who was working at the time for George Connell, co-promoter of the visit. "I was asked to come in on the night and help out," McCabe recalls. "My job was to stay with the Beatles in their room and look after them, to see that they got all they wanted. Security was very strict. They were very big at that stage. There was a terrible crowd around. Everybody wanted to see them or talk to them but nobody was allowed in. We were told strictly to keep people away. It was a struggle to keep them out. The Beatles just sat there and chatted away to one another, killing time."

Trevor Kane adds: "The conditions they had in the King's Hall weren't very comfortable. There was no luxury about the place. The room we converted into a band-room for them was a place which we previously used for hiring ice-skates. It was a big room off the King's Hall. They had very few visitors. A few journalists got to meet them although they didn't hold a press conference. There were very few people who met them face to face. They just flew into Belfast and flew out as quickly as they could.

"The one thing I remember was that there were about 1,000 autograph books sitting in the corner of the band-room for them to sign. All the punters had left them in. The Beatles sat there and signed them. They hadn't an awful lot to do. They had brought pre-printed, signed pictures with them and gave them out as well. The Royal Ulster Agricultural Society had also left in a very prized possession, which was their visitors' book. They asked if the Beatles would sign it. This book had kings and queens in it, people like Mario Lanza and everybody who had visited the King's Hall. It was a big book and very precious. Halfway through the night I found it among the heap of about 1,000 autograph books. They had signed it and just flung it into the corner. I managed to rescue it. It could just as easily have gone out the door.

"We had to bring in outside caterers to provide a meal for them. It was a firm called Isabeals. They had a restaurant in the centre of Belfast and they were a well-known catering firm. I believe they had a contract for all the catering at the King's Hall, when there would be the Spring Show or whatever. It's very funny because the Beatles all ordered pork steaks. Strange to think that Paul McCartney and his wife later became avid vegetarians! I also brought in a trolley of drinks to them. Immediately, Ringo asked, 'Where's the coke?' It was Coca-Cola he was asking for, not the other stuff. That's what they wanted."

By late 1964 the buzz from touring was disappearing for the Beatles. The novelty of being locked into dressing-rooms or being chased by fans was fading. The excitement of performing to manic, hyperactive young kids had worn thin. The concerts were no longer about music; they had become an 'event'. Not only could few people hear the Beatles but, in bigger halls, many couldn't see them onstage. Only a tiny fraction of potential concert-goers were able to secure tickets, resulting in disillusionment and resentment among fans.

As their fame grew, so too did their isolation. "The Beatles were in a different league by then, they were megastars," remarks Bill Covington of the Rustiks. "They were treated completely differently, with different hotels and with no access to them whatsoever. It was understandable because the likes of the centre of Belfast would come to a standstill if kids found out where they were. It was mad. You cannot believe how mad it was. The kids were out on the street and they'd tear you apart. The kids were frenzied. When people get involved with anything, whether it is politics, music or religion, a cult thing can develop and people can get whipped up into a frenzy. People went crazy. The kids would do anything.

"Some kids would always find out where the Beatles were staying because they were very clever at sussing situations out. They would say, 'My dad owns this hotel' or 'My dad is the chief of police. If you don't believe me, here's his number.' The guy at the door was left thinking, 'Shit, what if it's true?' It was a massive power that was unleashed. It was very scary because you were at the mercy of people. There was no control over the situation at all. As a result, they planned their entrances and exits like a military operation. They had to come up with some sort of strategy to keep them away from the fans. They came off the plane, gave a bit of a wave to the fans, got straight into a car and they were gone.

"It was very different from 1963. They never shared the same plane or coach as us. They seldom mixed with us. Airports would bend over backwards to get rid of them quickly. They couldn't have an airport held up by the Beatles. They wanted them in and out as quickly as possible. They'd block off routes and everything. It was the same in the city as well. In Belfast the chief of police said, 'For God's sake, get these roads closed down and get them in and out as fast as you can.'"

Wherever they visited, the Beatles were confined to hotel bedrooms at secret locations, with their food delivered by room service. They seldom appeared in public and couldn't visit bars or clubs, as they had done in 1963. George hated flying and resented intrusions to his privacy. John was also nervous of air travel. Paul still loved the fame, while John had tired of it. All four were struggling to cope with life on the road.

"John Lennon wouldn't speak to anybody," Bill Covington observes. "I've been in the same room with him and, while he knew I was there, his head was somewhere else. He was always distant, unless you had something really exceptional to offer. Otherwise, he had no interest whatsoever. He wasn't easily impressed. The others you could engage in a conversation but not Lennon.

"Paul McCartney was fine. I remember he was coming out of one of the shows in London and he was talking to Rob, our guitarist. The press were swarming all over McCartney. They pushed Rob out of the way because they had no interest in him. McCartney said, 'Hey, hey, hey. This is my mate, Rob. We're talking. If you want an interview with me, then wait until I've finished talking to my pal or you do it with us together. But don't be treating him like that.'

"Ringo Starr was a superb guy. He was very easygoing. There was no 'big time' about him. I loved George Harrison's guitar work. In fact, he borrowed the Fender Stratocaster belonging to Rob, our guitarist, a couple of times on the tour to play on the show. But we didn't see them much. They'd be off doing their own thing. They had their own interests and lives. John was married to Cynthia. Paul was with Jane Asher. George had Pattie Boyd. And Ringo was with Maureen Cox, the hairdresser from Liverpool. They had their own lives at the time."

The Remo Four, with their Liverpool roots and Cavern Club pedigree, remained close to John, Paul, George and Ringo during the 1964 tour. Ranked number three group in a 1961 *Mersey Beat* poll, they were admired by the Beatles. "I went to school with Paul and George, so I knew them all well," says bass guitarist Don Andrew. "Before the national tour started we saw a lot of each other. In the Cavern there would be three groups on most nights. Usually we were on immediately before the Beatles. We played with them more than any other band and must have done more than 100 shows like that, as well as the tours. They were just one of the other groups, and the lucky ones.

"We never went out with them socially during the tour because we were locked in from when we got there to when the show finished. You couldn't get out because the whole place was surrounded by girls. We used to sit talking in the dressing-room. Our lead guitarist, Colin, was probably technically the best lead guitarist to come out of Liverpool. George used to really look up to him. Colin was also a year or two older. George would come and ask Colin, 'What do you think of this?' He'd play a solo he had rehearsed for an album they were doing. He'd ask, 'What do you think I should do here?' He'd get his advice. Other than that, we had the same chat with them as with all the other bands.

"The only Beatle who was a little distant, because he was so much his own man, was John. He'd have a laugh with you but he kept to himself a lot and he had his own view of the world. He used to hate all the handicapped kids being brought in to meet the Beatles before the show. Everywhere we went they used to line them up backstage before the show began. There would be the Lord Mayor and all his cronies plus this group of unfortunate kids who were going to meet the Beatles. John used to hate it. He'd be pulling faces behind them and doing mimics. Other than that, he was just one of the Mersey gang."

Shortly after six o'clock the Rustiks kicked off the first

concert at the King's Hall, Belfast. Comedian Bob Bain, who was acting as MC, introduced the various acts: the Rustiks followed by Michael Haslam, Sounds Incorporated and Mary Wells up to the interval, with the Remo Four and Tommy Quickly preceding the main act of the night – the Beatles!

"Pandemonium broke loose in the King's Hall," was how one of the following day's papers described the scene. "Belfast capitulated to the Merseyside as Beatlemania swept the hall. Frenzied fans screamed, waved and stamped their way through two sittings of the Beatle Show. Thousands of fans packed the well of the hall for the first show, and the excitement built up as the star-studded bill, which included American coloured singer Mary Wells, played to a tensed up crowd. An hour after the start the atmosphere was electric. Then came the Beatles."

The newspaper report was, by all accounts, an accurate summary of the now-guaranteed maelstrom of screaming and crying that, like a high-pitched whine, accompanied the Beatles on tour. Girls looked at each other and screamed. They screeched at the Beatles. They wept violently, their bodies in spasm. Some of them, overcome by emotion, curled up on their seats in foetal positions, looking bewildered and addled. Others collapsed in a faint on the floor.

They flung purses, pennies, programmes and pieces of paper at the Beatles onstage. They tore their coats off, abandoned their seats and surged forward towards the front of the hall. Police and stewards manned a barricade of crush barriers to keep them away. "It was chaos," one newspaper reported the next day, as the fans "rocked the stadium to its foundations." It was like some sort of primeval ritual or bizarre rite. A year before, the madness was a novel, unusual, bemusing feature of a Beatles' performance. But things had moved on – it was now no longer part of the act; it *was* the act.

The Beatles launched through their set. John Lennon performed old favourites 'Twist And Shout' and 'Money (That's What I Want)', which by late '64 were two of the group's trademark numbers. Ringo Starr showcased his talents with the Lennon-McCartney composition 'I Wanna Be Your Man'. Paul McCartney belted his way through the old Little Richard classic 'Long Tall Sally'.

The remainder of the tracks came from the LP and movie *A Hard Day's Night*, including the title track which was written by Lennon but sung by both Lennon and McCartney. George performed 'I'm Happy Just To Dance With You'. McCartney blasted out 'Can't Buy Me Love' and crooned his way through 'Things We Said Today'. Lennon sang 'I Should Have Known Better'. Both Lennon and McCartney performed 'If I Fell'.

"My friend Barbara Anne McCabe and I were probably the youngest people there," recalls Gerri Gilliland, who was aged 12. "She came over to my house one day and said, 'Would you like to go to the Beatles' concert with me or should I ask Laura Fusco?' I nearly died. Barbara Anne wasn't even a Beatles' fan. In those days you were either Beatles or Rolling Stones. She wouldn't play a Beatles' record on her record-player and I wouldn't play the Rolling Stones on mine. But her dad helped with the special events at the King's Hall and he had got tickets. So Laura Fusco got bumped and I got the ticket.

"We went in our little mini-skirts, two little schoolgirls looking like little rock 'n rollers. We had front-row seats, right in front of Paul McCartney. We could hear them because we were right in front of them. They were brilliant. We were screaming and standing up on the chairs and pulling our hair. I was pulling my hair because everybody was pulling their hair. I was so excited. I thought I was going to faint. There were all these photographers from the *Belfast Telegraph* and I was thinking to myself, 'Oh, God, my mother is going to see this in the morning.' I thought I was going to get in trouble the next day.

"Mr McCabe brought us backstage. It was pandemonium. We were ushered quickly through. I don't even remember it because I think I was in shock. I had this little autograph book that my uncle had bought me in Hamburg. It had a little lock on it, like a diary. So I got all the Beatles' autographs. I got Neil Aspinall on the same page. I also got Bob Bain, who was the host. I got Mary Wells and the Remo Four. Later on I saw the Kinks, the Beach Boys, Dave Dee Dozy Beaky Mick and Tich, Sandie Shaw, Millie, the Troggs. But they were never as good as the Beatles."

It was a shambles trying to get people out of the first show and into the next, says promoter Trevor Kane: "There was very little time between the six o'clock and quarter to nine shows. We had to clear everybody out of the first show. There were old wooden chairs there which were moveable and just had numbers stuck on the backs of them. They had to be lined up properly again. Between the wee girls standing up on these chairs and literally wetting themselves, there was a bit of furniture rearranging to be done. We had a big clean-up job to do as well.

"In the meantime, the crowd were queuing around the block to get into the second show. We were worried that we wouldn't get the second show started on time. But we had a great staff there and we got everything cleared. We had people there who worked for us in our dance business, unlike today where they'd have bus-loads of staff. It was a great concert, a wonderful event. It was mayhem but it all worked well in the end."

Valerie McCleary, aged 17, attended the second show but as a special guest. "I had met the guitar player of Sounds Incorporated, John St John, when I was 16 and I was madly in love with him," Valerie explains. "I was star-struck. I had met him at the Plaza ballroom the previous year, when Sounds Incorporated played there. I met him after the show, when my brother went over to chat to them. I was very shy but I sat down beside them. John came back with us to our home and came in for a cup of tea. After that he would send me postcards from wherever he'd been.

"John came to Belfast three or four times and we would meet

up. It was a nice brush with stardom. He would walk me home and he'd sit in our tiny little kitchen with a cup of tea balanced on his lap and a biscuit. He'd be talking to my father, who would not go to bed. When you think back on it, it was so innocent. We couldn't believe it at the time that there were girls actually trying to get into the Beatles' room to do nasty things with them. That was totally beyond my ken at the time.

"The night of the Beatles' show, I met John at the King's Hall. He brought me in behind this sort of barrier around the stage. It was a protected area, to the side of the stage. Some of the guys from Sounds Incorporated were there. I met Mary Wells' guitarist. They were all standing around, looking at the rest of the show. I was so close to the Beatles on the stage that I could have touched them. I was standing there, looking up at them.

"There was this incredible noise of screaming when the Beatles came on. It was like a train. The crowd were going mad and there were people falling over. There was this incredible volume of people and these poor guys were trying to sing. You couldn't speak because no one could hear you. I could hear the Beatles singing because I was standing so close. I think it would have been difficult to hear them out in the crowd. The mikes were tiny so they couldn't have been throwing the sound that much. But I was overwhelmed to be within just a few feet of them.

"It was a very different show to the one in 1963. There were lots more people there, for a start. I think the whole thing was more professional and less provincial. The music-hall thing that was there before had gone. It was a lot more like the concerts we see now. It was geared more to younger people. We thought they were filling big halls because there were so many fans but I suppose they were filling big halls to rake in the money. They wanted to get us all in there. After that, it got bigger and bigger and bigger until the fiasco at Shea Stadium. That put the lid on it.

"We all went back to the hotel bar afterwards. John St John took me there on the bus, a red double-decker bus. I remember people looking at him and going, 'I know that guy.' They were all staying in some big hotel in the centre of town. We sat in the bar. I kept hoping Paul McCartney or somebody would walk in. I thought, 'Any minute now George Harrison is going to come down for a pint.' I think the support acts even thought the Beatles were in the hotel. I don't even think they knew where they were staying. They would say, 'The guys are tired. They're not going to come down now.' So I didn't get to meet the Beatles."

Unknown to virtually everyone in Belfast including the support acts, immediately after the last show the Beatles had been spirited from the King's Hall to the Culloden Hotel on the outskirts of the city. The Culloden was a nineteenth century mansion located on the Holywood hills, about five miles from the centre of Belfast. A former palace for the Bishops of Down, it had only been opened as a hotel in 1963. It was the perfect location for the Beatles – far away from the city-centre and difficult to access. It was quiet, secluded and plush. Only a close inner circle knew that the Beatles were booked there.

"The Culloden Hotel was the top hotel in 1964 and it was out of the way," according to promoter Trevor Kane. "Rutledge White, of White's Home Bakery, owned it at the time. Somehow, word got out. He was hounded by the fans. They were down there asking the chambermaids if they could have the cigarette-butts out of their ashtrays so that they could have something the Beatles had touched. He told me that young girls were up there with tears in their eyes asking could they have the soap out of their bedrooms. This was at seven the next morning. He said to me, 'God, Trevor, I'm having trouble with all these people coming down here.' It was a bit of a problem at the time. But the next morning the Beatles were up and gone, and they flew back to London."

Arriving back in London on Tuesday 3 November, the

Beatles prepared for another hard grind in the run-up to Christmas. The following day they attended the final mixing of their new LP, which was due for release at the beginning of December, just in time for the Christmas market. That night they performed at the Ritz cinema in Luton and continued to tour until 10 November. The group then got ready for the release of their forthcoming single 'I Feel Fine' and their new LP *Beatles For Sale,* not to mention their *Beatles Christmas Shows* at the Odeon cinema, Hammersmith, London, scheduled to run from 24 – 31 December.

It had been an exhausting year for the Beatles. They were shattered from the flights, the touring, the concerts, the film-making, the interviews and press conferences, the TV and radio appearances, the composing and recording, the promoting and the fans. The infectious disease that was Beatlemania had run rampant throughout so many countries, races and creeds that hardly any part of the globe was untouched by their presence. If 1963 was the year when the Beatles conquered England and Ireland, then 1964 was the year when they conquered the world.

Unfortunately, the struggle for world domination had come at a price. All semblance of privacy was gone. They were stalked by overzealous fans. Promoters, concert hall managers, celebrities, politicians, beauty queens, charities and just plain ordinary folk all wanted their photographs taken with the Beatles. Journalists begged for interviews because newspapers, magazines or even comics sold out if the group appeared on their front covers. Everyone demanded a slice of their time.

The turmoil was reflected in their lyrics. For the first time, the Beatles filled an album, *A Hard Day's Night,* with entirely self-penned work and the results were disturbing. There were tears, cries for help, sadness and words of loss, especially in tracks like 'Tell Me Why', 'I'll Cry Instead' and 'Any Time At All'. Lennon, who had composed most of the songs, wrote of "working like a dog." Soon, songs appeared with ominous titles like 'Help!'. No one got the message, perhaps because the melodies were so appealing, the rhythms so infectious and the lyrics so catchy. No one analysed the concerts either. At the shows the strains were all too apparent, with an audience that wouldn't listen and a band that wondered, 'Why bother?'

"By late 1964 the Beatles couldn't care less," says Bill Covington, drummer with the Rustiks. "They could be singing in Russian or Arabic, or swearing, and who would know? The Vox amps couldn't be heard past the front of the stage. It was just bog-standard equipment they were going around with. Unless everybody was dead quiet and everybody was listening as in a proper concert, you could hear nothing. They had just become something to scream at. In a theatre with everybody screaming and with the place feeling like it was going to collapse with the noise, nothing could be heard. You couldn't believe the volume of the noise. You couldn't hear anything past the front row. They'd come out and there would be five million decibels all the way for 20 minutes. It was pointless. It was a complete waste of time.

"They had come to the conclusion that they were just going to have to go out and do the same thing every night. There was no creativity. All the creativity was being distilled into a 20-minute repetitive slot. It was repetition, repetition, repetition. Some people would love that and do it for the rest of their lives. But they didn't. They were so creative they always wanted to be moving on. The deal was that they would do the touring because that's how you built up this massive following. That's how record sales were made. That's what they wanted the most. The problem was the thing that they wanted the most they hated doing. They were just doing it because it was part of the deal.

"The Beatles were still wearing suits and bowing at the end of performances, which wasn't them. There was no swearing and no smoking onstage. The hair had to be cut in a certain way. They had to do certain songs. Their whole persona had been gradually altered and squeezed into a stage presentation where there was no spontaneity, no electricity. It was just repetition, note for note, beat for beat, word for word. All the enjoyment had been completely eradicated. They were just manufacturing the goods. It was like being in a factory.

"Epstein had turned them into a predictable product that everybody felt safe with. The image they presented onstage and on TV was perfectly acceptable to mums and dads, who would let the kids go to these concerts. Epstein came from a selling environment and looked on them in the same way as a washing-machine or a television. He was only copying people like Larry Parnes, who had done it before with Billy Fury and others. It wasn't rock 'n roll, which is spontaneous, loud and unpredictable. For presentation and saleability you have to alter things. And he altered them.

"So, what was the point? At the end of the night the place would be in uproar, they'd take a bow and the curtains would close. They'd trundle off. Another one done! You could tell they were completely fed up. They hated it. You could see that in their faces, especially in John Lennon who could be the most vitriolic, aggressive and obnoxious bugger around. I think they had decided, by that stage, that they weren't going to be touring anymore. It was pointless. They were going to be a recording band only. That was the feeling I got."

When John, Paul, George and Ringo flew out of Aldergrove Airport on 3 November 1964, it was obvious to everyone that they would never be back. Ireland no longer featured on their map. Even England was too insignificant. But it really didn't matter. From then on, their onstage musicianship disintegrated and, most places they went to, they looked intensely unhappy.

There were a few more money-spinning ventures, like the tour of America in August 1965 and, in particular, the hair-raising concert at Shea Stadium before 56,000 fans. There were other chaotic tours to Japan, the Philippines, West Germany and America in 1966. But by then it was all about big stadiums, fat paychecks, bad sound and the Beatles couldn't be bothered. For them, rock 'n roll had lost its heart and soul. The show had become like a circus, and the Beatles knew it.

"A year later about a couple of hundred girls went out to Aldergrove Airport to stand where they had first got sight of the Beatles," promoter Trevor Kane concludes. "They wanted to say, 'This is where we first saw them.' It was a big commemoration event. The nostalgia was that great. It made me realise how lucky we were to get the Beatles when they were at their peak. They were the big ones and we were very lucky to have them. There have been many other big artistes here since then but people still talk about their visits. It was the end of a bit of history. After that, we never saw the Beatles in Ireland again."

POSTSCRIPT

Three Beatles' fans who attended the concerts in Dublin and who were interviewed for this book went on to establish celebrated careers as actors. One of them, Frank Grimes, within seven years of bluffing his way into the Adelphi without a ticket, was nominated for a Tony Award in New York for his performance in Brendan Behan's *Borstal Boy* and was voted 'Most Promising Actor On Broadway'. Grimes eventually settled in England. There he appeared in numerous stage, screen and TV shows, including *Casualty*, *Heartbeat*, *Kavanagh QC* and *Holby City*.

Another actor, John Olohan, might be remembered for his role as the sergeant in two episodes of the comedy series *Father Ted*. He also appeared in *Ballykissangel* and *Glenroe*. His stage credits include plays by Hugh Leonard, Frank McGuinness, Bernard Farrell, Tom MacIntyre, Jim Sheridan, Neil Donnelly, among many others. He also featured over the years in a number of films.

"In the 1970s we did a production of *John, Paul, George, Ringo.... And Bert*," Olohan recalls. "I played Bert in it. Barry McGovern played John Lennon. The end of the first act was the Beatles singing 'She Loves You'. It was mimed and overlaid with screaming. Because I was the one who remembered the concert, I re-created the set-up. I used to come down in the audience and

I used to stand at the back of the theatre, looking up. It was just incredible to watch the re-creation. It was as if I was at the concert all over again."

A third budding actor, who was sitting downstairs in the Adelphi, eventually became Ireland's most identifiable commercial voiceover artist. Since recording his first commercial in 1980, there is hardly an accent or a dialect that Jonathan Ryan hasn't attempted. He also forged a successful stage and screen career, appearing in the movies *Patriot Games*, *In The Name Of The Father*, *Kidnapped* and *Omagh*, to name but a few.

Stage and screen star of the future Donal McCann also attended the Dublin concerts although he was there in a work capacity and is now deceased. Donal, who was the copyboy elevated to *Evening Press* feature writer for the night of the shows, in time became one of Ireland's greatest theatrical stars. He delivered titanic performances in a variety of Dublin productions. He also became well-known for his role in the television serialisation of *Strumpet City* and his film roles in *Miss Julie* and *The Dead*. Described by *Newsweek* as "a world-class star," McCann died in 1999, aged 56, after a battle with cancer.

Yet another theatrical figure, Wesley Burrowes, who was celebrating the beginnings of his career down in Groome's the night the Beatles walked in, became one of the country's most successful screenwriters, authors and playwrights. He is best known for his scripting of *The Riordans*, *Bracken* and *Glenroe*. Less known is that he wrote the lyrics of 'If I Could Choose', which was Seán Dunphy's entry in the 1967 *Eurovision Song Contest* in Vienna.

Perhaps unsurprisingly, a relatively sizeable number of teenagers and musicians who attended the concerts on both sides of the border went on to establish distinguished careers in the music business. One of them was future rock star Bob Geldof, who was brought along to the Beatles' press conference by his sister as a 12-year-old. He later became famous as lead

206

singer of the Boomtown Rats and for his role in *Live Aid*. He was also knighted. Another concert-goer, Brush Shiels, who was downstairs at the Adelphi, was already mad into music in 1963 – and still is. Founder of Skid Row, he played in the band along with both Gary Moore and Phil Lynott. Eventually he went solo.

Within nine months of the Beatles' Dublin appearance, John Keogh's band had changed their name from the Caravelles to the Greenbeats and had appeared at Liverpool's Cavern Club, the 'home' of the Beatles. They were also hired as resident band on Telefís Éireann's *The Showband Show*, which was later presented by Keogh. Following three years on the road full-time with the Greenbeats, he eventually settled down to a job as producer/director with RTÉ.

"It was a fantastic night, memorable because the Beatles were so big at the time and a night never to forget," Keogh remarks. "I had seen Marty Wilde in the old Theatre Royal, who was very good. I had seen other bands. But I had never seen anything as big as the Beatles. I'm glad I went because, soon after, I would have to have gone to America, Australia or Japan or somewhere to see them. Six months later, there was no way they would ever have taken a gig in the Adelphi. It was patently clear that they would never come back to Ireland. I was very lucky to see them when I did."

Brian Lynch had a parallel career to John Keogh's, joining both the Caravelles and the Greenbeats where he played bass guitar. He also found employment in RTÉ. Similarly attracted to the media was Eamon Carr, who became a well-known journalist. Before that – no doubt in response to having his Beatle haircut pruned by his teachers – he took his anger out on his drum kit in Horslips.

The son of Catherine Cahill – the young girl who climbed into the Beatles' dressing-room at the Adelphi – won an Oscar with co-composer Markéta Irglová for 'Best Original Song' in 2008. Named Glen Hansard, and known for his work with the

Frames, the song was 'Falling Slowly' from the movie *Once*. His mother attended the Oscars ceremony and, over 44 years later, finally met Ringo Starr.

"I told Ringo what happened at the Adelphi," Cahill recalls. "He broke his heart laughing. At the end of the night, when he was leaving, he came over and he gave me a big hug and he put this thing in my hand. He said, 'Here, that's for you for not getting into the concert.' When I looked, it was a little badge saying 'Ringo for President.' I'll treasure that for the rest of my life."

Among those moving into music management was Ted Carroll, the bank official and part-time promoter who sat in the 10/6 seats at the Adelphi. He later handled Skid Row and Thin Lizzy. Hugh Hardy likewise succumbed to the management bug although he concentrated on the showband and nostalgia sides of the business. After managing Larry Cunningham and the Mighty Avons, he made his name as promoter of a large number of tours.

The career of showband star Eileen Reid, who met the Beatles at the Gresham, took off after the group's visit. In 1964, while fronting the Cadets, her recording of 'Fallen Star' shot to number one in the Irish charts. She also recorded the classic 'I Gave My Wedding Dress Away'. After a long career as a singer and many more hit records, she eventually won fame for her roles in pantomime.

"It's great to have the photo now," Reid says regarding the publicity shot taken with the Beatles in the Gresham. "It's only now you say, 'Oh, my God!' They were so mega afterwards. It was lovely to meet them. And the boys in the Cadets were really delighted with themselves because, don't forget, they were musicians too."

A few of the support acts had notable careers in the decades ahead, particularly some of the Kestrels. Not long after their appearance in Dublin, Roger Cook joined the group. After the collapse of the Kestrels in 1965, he and Roger Greenaway formed one of the most successful songwriting partnerships of the late 1960s. Among their compositions was 'You've Got Your Troubles', which was a smash hit for the Fortunes. Also, for a time, Greenaway and Cook performed under the pseudonym 'David and Jonathan', achieving success with, of all things, the Lennon-McCartney composition 'Michelle'.

"It got to the stage where the Kestrels had a lot of records, had some success on TV but never really cracked it," Greenaway observes. "A couple of the guys wanted to try solo careers. The last guy who joined our group before we split was Roger Cook. And the rest is history. We had a big hit as David and Jonathan in America with 'Michelle'. We toured America doing radio shows and people were ringing in saying, 'OK, John, own up' and 'OK, Paul, own up.' They thought that, because of the English accents, that's who we were. Everybody thought it was the Beatles."

The Kestrels' Tony Burrows joined the Ivy League, followed by the Flowerpot Men and White Plains. He had an amazing number of hits, including 'Let's Go To San Francisco' with the Flowerpot Men, 'Love Grows (Where My Rosemary Goes)' with Edison Lighthouse, 'My Baby Loves Lovin'' with White Plains, 'United We Stand' with Brotherhood of Man and 'Gimme Dat Ding' with the Pipkins.

The 'memory man' of the Kestrels, Jeff Williams, took a completely different career path after the demise of the group. He joined the police force where, no doubt, his remarkable ability to recall dates, facts and all sorts of information proved invaluable. He was eventually awarded an MBE. "That tour was just unbelievable," Williams says today. "People would never, ever credit the reaction from the crowds. It was fun. It wasn't like a job where you had to go to work every day. I have wonderful memories. People are quite shocked when I tell them 'I toured with the Beatles.'"

Like the Kestrels, the Vernons Girls were drowned in the wash that followed the arrival of the Beatles. They effectively disbanded in 1964. Two of the earlier group members married stars – Joyce Baker wedded Marty Wilde and Vicki Haseman wedded Joe Brown. Another early member Maggie Stredder, whom I interviewed, achieved success with the Ladybirds.

Unfortunately, of the three Vernons Girls who appeared in Ireland, one – Maureen Kennedy – was killed in a tragic car accident. Of the other two, Jean Owen, who I also interviewed, changed her name to Samantha Jones and went solo in 1964. She released numerous singles and albums and achieved chart success on the Continent. She remained in the music business into the 1980s.

The Brook Brothers left the business within a few years of the Beatles' tour. "I just got an ordinary job and went back to school part-time, in the evenings," says Geoff Brook. "I got my 'O' levels and my 'A' levels. Eventually I got a first-class degree through the Royal Institute of Chemistry. It took me eight years from the time I stopped playing to find something to fall back on. Ricky did a similar sort of thing. He was in the electronics and physics side. He eventually moved to Canada."

Peter Jay and the Jaywalkers continued to tour and perform after the Irish visit and went on to become a hugely popular and innovative live band. Some say that their emphasis on live performing interfered with their chances of achieving chart success. Eventually, Peter Jay called it a day and moved into the circus business in Great Yarmouth. Before that happened, however, the band toured Ireland.

"We came back and did a tour in Ireland in 1964, on the back of the Beatles' tour," Peter Jay remembers. "We did a lot of the ballrooms. We went to places that literally hadn't a piano. They would borrow a piano from somebody's house and wheel it down the road. The showbands were an inspiration to us. We were playing different instruments, including the saxophone, and doing a little bit of comedy. We were in that vein and they were fantastic to us.

"I also can remember we went to see a picture in Ireland

once, in a little tiny picture-house, and at the end they played this thing which we didn't know the hell what it was. We just sat there. When we turned around, the whole place was standing up, looking at us. Gingerly, we stood up. It was the national anthem! We had a fab time there, incredible."

The fates weren't kind to any of the support acts at the King's Hall concerts in 1964. In 1992 the great Motown star Mary Wells died of cancer at the age of 49. Sounds Incorporated struggled on until the early 1970s, when they finally disintegrated. The Remo Four continued in business in various guises, backing Tommy Quickly and Billy J Kramer and recording with George Harrison until eventually disbanding in 1970. The outcome was equally depressing for the Rustiks, Michael Haslam and Tommy Quickly.

"Epstein had a massive clearout around March 1966," Bill Covington of the Rustiks recollects. "He wanted to concentrate on the Beatles. He got rid of us, Michael Haslam and Tommy Quickly. I remember we got a phone-call saying that Brian wanted to see us in the Saville Theatre. I thought, 'Here we go.' We went over there. He said, 'It's not working out.' There were a lot of harsh words from Rob, our guitarist. Angry things were spoken at the time. I could see Brian's face getting redder and redder and redder.

"We were accusing each other of not fulfilling expectations. For example, Brian Epstein produced our records. He was absolute crap. He didn't know what he was doing. He was saying to the guitarist, 'What's that strange sound you keep getting on the strings? You know that sound where your finger slides up?' The guitarist said, 'It's my fingers.' He said, 'Can you put some baby oil on it to stop it?' I thought, 'Well, that's going to work alright, playing the guitar with your hands covered in baby oil!'

"He was saying we were not writing songs. We were saying his expectations were unrealistic. How did he expect us to be like Lennon and McCartney? We were saying, 'This is the first time we've seen you for months.' The place was swarming with press and photographers. They were climbing all over us. He was livid. Our contracts were up and he said, 'That's the end of it.'

"How can you live in the same camp as the Beatles? You just cannot do it. As soon as someone said 'There's the Rustiks, they're the next Beatles' it was the kiss of death. There was no comparison between the Beatles and any other band. It was an impossible position. Epstein was expecting us to come up with material which would equal the Beatles. And we couldn't."

Emigration took its toll on some of those who attended the concerts. Lena McDevitt, who was aged 15 when she travelled to Dublin Airport for the Beatles' arrival, left for Australia in 1969 and has lived there ever since. Her friend Kaye Ryan eventually departed for Spain. Josephine Tyrrell, who was 15 when she met the Beatles backstage at the Adelphi, soon emigrated to Holland and has remained there in the intervening years. She did, however, have a brief moment of fame following her introduction to the Beatles.

"We knew there were photographs taken by one of the daily newspapers," Tyrrell says. "Friends of ours, where we lived, told us that a huge photograph of us was in the newspaper's window. We went down to see it. When we got there, there was a big crowd gathered and they all started screaming, 'That's them. That's them.' It was a bit scary. We were proud, of course, that we got to see the Beatles but we were young and we didn't expect that such a big deal would be made of it. We didn't think that other people would be looking up to us because we got in to see them and meet them."

Valerie McCleary, who saw both concerts in Belfast, eventually emigrated to Germany. Before that, she moved to England where, unfortunately, her 'fling' with John St John of Sounds Incorporated came to an end. "The affair with John St John ended after I went to live in London when I was 18 or 19,"

McCleary explains. "We met up once in London and it fizzled out after that."

Gerri Gilliland, who attended the King's Hall concert, relocated to the USA, partly to escape the Troubles. "There were bombs going off, the IRA was there. That was a big part of it. I was frightened actually ... that and the mould growing on the walls in my apartment," she later said. "My first two years were hell here. My first bed was a mattress. I couldn't sleep on the floor anymore, so I grabbed it off the street. I had no winter coat, so I got one at the Salvation Army, which I still donate to today. They were good to me." Today, Gilliland runs a highly-successful collection of bars and restaurants in California, located not far from her 40-acre Malibu ranch.

Of those who remained in Ireland, a surprising number went on to develop high-profile media careers. Jimmy Magee, who was at the Adelphi, became one of Ireland's best-known sports broadcasters, working with Radio Telefís Éireann. Éanna Brophy, who also attended at Dublin, ended up as a respected newspaper journalist and columnist, notably with the *Sunday Press*. Ken Stewart and Morgan O'Sullivan, who were both present at the Adelphi, achieved fame as golden-voiced presenters on radio and television. In time, Morgan O'Sullivan also became a leading figure in the Irish film industry, producing many well-known films and heading up Ardmore Studios.

Liam Kelly, the reporter who travelled with the Beatles in the back of the *Evening Herald* van, was appointed by the *Daily Mirror* as one of their men in Ireland. Another newsman, Derek Ball, gave up on his agency at Dublin Airport in the mid-1970s but remained in the media business. Yet another journalist, Cathal O'Shannon, who was just starting with *The Irish Times*, developed an esteemed career as an RTÉ presenter. Tommy Nolan, who worked the lighting at the Adelphi and who had a spat with John Lennon, likewise worked with RTÉ.

Photography also attracted a number of those who attended

the shows. Chris Hill, who spent his time shooting the Beatles at the first Belfast concert, eventually moved into the business and compiled a number of successful books. Pat Maxwell, who chanced his arm to get the Beatles in a classic pose at Dublin's Adelphi, developed his photographic agency into one of the finest in the country. Roy Bedell, who snapped the Beatles at the Gresham, remained with RTÉ as a stills photographer. Stanley Matchett, from the *Belfast Telegraph*, went on to receive an MBE for services to photography. "That was a nice touch," he remarks. "I'd like to be able to say that one of my Beatles' pictures helped me get it but I don't think so."

Many of those in the cinema business also developed successful careers in the years ahead. Harry Lush, manager of the Adelphi, remained in the job until 1981 and continued to be respected around Dublin. He died, aged 88, in 2005. Noel Rennick, who was Assistant Secretary of Adelphi-Carlton Ltd and who turned up for one of the shows, became Managing Director of the company in the late 1960s. Hugh Brown, who as a trainee assistant manager observed proceedings in Belfast in '63, also progressed in the business.

It was amazing the number of autographs signed by the Beatles on their Irish tours. Samples can be found hidden away all over the country. Some of them, unfortunately, have been ruined with the passage of time. Others have remained in mint or near-mint condition. More disappeared for a variety of reasons, among them Lynn Geldof's LP which she got signed at the Adelphi press conference. "My father gave it to someone when I was away some years later," Geldof recollects. "He lent it to the mother of some other people and I never got it back. I was boiling with rage. It's gone."

Ken Ronan, who bumped into the group in the Gresham, still has his set of signatures. "They are in bad condition at this stage because I made the mistake of putting Sellotape on the paper to try and preserve it," he remarks. "I thought it was going off a bit and I thought Sellotape would help. I think that just hastened its demise. Years later I got George Best's and Matt Busby's autographs. But the Beatles topped them all."

Hugh Hardy was astute enough to ask for the Beatles' signatures before he said his goodbyes at the Gresham Hotel. "Before I left I asked them for their autographs, which they duly gave to me," Hardy recalls. "I was staying with my sister and at breakfast the next morning her two teenage daughters were at the table. I just happened to say, 'I met the Beatles last night.' Talk about screaming! I said, 'Let me see, somewhere here I have an autograph.' I pulled out the piece of paper and I gave it to one of my nieces. They headed into school, surprised that their uncle had met the Beatles the previous night. After school they brought their friends back home to meet the guy who shook hands with the Beatles.

"Not long ago my wife and I were on a cruise and we stopped in Honolulu. We were walking up the main street and there was this shop that specialised in memorabilia. I went in. They had Elvis and Babe Ruth, all that type of stuff. I said, 'How much would an autograph from the Beatles be worth?' They said, 'It's hard to put a figure on it until we would see it, but we would be talking about $8,000 to $10,000.' When I came back to Ireland I called my niece and asked her, 'By the way, do you still have the autographs of the Beatles I gave you?' She said, 'No, I gave them to my best friend and next-door neighbour and she is now in Wexford. Why do you ask?' I said, 'It's OK, I was just wondering.'"

Other mementoes disappeared too. "I collected, in chronological order, two books of newspaper clippings regarding the Beatles," says Sandra Grant, who was aged 16 when she went to the concert in Dublin. "I had every photograph. I charted their progress. My ticket to the Adelphi was in it as well. They were brilliant scrapbooks. I married five years after the concert and my mother cleared them out. She threw the whole thing in the bin. Nobody realised the significance at the time, although my mother did in her latter years."

Occasionally, bits and pieces of memorabilia from the Beatles' visits turn up. "I was looking at *Record Collector* one day, many years ago, and this guy was selling a signed copy of the *Twist And Shout* EP," Northern Ireland Beatles' fan Trevor Halliday remarks. "It turned out that he owned a shop and lived close to me. It was signed by all four Beatles for a policeman who was minding them at the Grand Central Hotel. He was one of their bodyguards on the visit. I dashed over to him the following morning hoping to be able to buy it on the spot. I actually took enough money with me to buy it. The guy was a bit hesitant about even showing it to me. He had it under the counter but he wouldn't let me see it. I wondered why.

"Eventually, he told me he thought I might have been the dad of the young lad who brought the record to him. He was worried that maybe he brought it to him without the father's approval. I convinced him that I was a genuine Beatles' fan and I wanted to buy it. So he let me see it. It transpired that the guy had an offer for around £300. I said, 'I'll give you £300 now, on the spot. I have it here with me.' He said, 'I want to hang on for a few weeks. I might get a few offers from America or Japan or somewhere.' He apparently got an offer for another £20 from Japan and he sent it to the guy in Japan. He didn't even ring me to tell me. If he had told me he had an offer for £320 I would have said to him, 'I'll give you £350 for it.' But it was gone and that was it."

Sadly, of the four venues central to the Beatles' 1963 visit – the Adelphi, the Gresham Hotel, the ABC Ritz and the Grand Central Hotel – only one is still functioning. The Adelphi cinema in Dublin was closed in late 1995. Although a portion of its façade is still evident, the cinema was demolished and the site is currently used as a car park. Cars drive in through what was the entrance on that famous night in 1963 when the Beatles came to town.

The ABC Ritz cinema in Belfast was demolished and replaced by a hotel. The Grand Central Hotel in Belfast became an army barracks during the Troubles and was eventually pulled down. It now forms part of a shopping centre. Only the Gresham in Dublin remains operational as a 'living' monument to the Beatles' first visit. Both the King's Hall and the Culloden Hotel are still in business and reminders of the concerts in '64.

Fortunately, the Adelphi stage that the Beatles stood on is still in use as part of the flooring in the old John M Keating's bar-cum-restaurant in the former St Mary's Church, Mary Street, Dublin. "I bought the whole stage when the place was being pulled down," explains John Keating. "It must have been somewhere between 2,000 and 3,000 square feet. I bought it for nostalgic reasons and because I thought the boards should be kept for posterity. We had to go in and take the boards up, store them for a number of years and then put them down again.

"Why did I do it? I love the Beatles. Who doesn't? But a lot more people performed on that stage as well – Cliff Richard, the Troggs, Roy Orbison, Louis Armstrong, Maureen O'Hara, Ella Fitzgerald, Johnny Cash, the Clancy Brothers, the Bachelors, the Dubliners, the Beach Boys, Russ Conway, the Bee Gees, Victor Borge, Cilla Black, the Rolling Stones, Marlene Dietrich, Ronald Reagan, the Walker Brothers, Helen Shapiro and Max Bygraves, to name but a few."

Mortality, too, caught up with a number of those connected with the tours. Brian Epstein, who couldn't make it to Ireland in '63 because of commitments in the USA, died tragically in 1967 from an overdose of sleeping-pills. He was aged 32. Beatles' roadie and personal assistant Neil Aspinall passed away in 2008, aged 66, from lung cancer while receiving treatment in New York. The other Beatles' roadie Mal Evans, who helped out in Dublin and Belfast, was gunned down by police in Los Angeles in 1976.

Frank Hall, who went on to front the popular *Hall's Pictorial Weekly* on Telefís Éireann and who became the Irish film censor, died in 1995. Playwright Alun Owen, who wrote the script for *A Hard Day's Night* based on the '63 visit, continued to write for the stage and TV up until his death in 1994, at the age of 69. Arthur Howes, the great concert promoter, passed on too.

Unfortunately, some of the central figures in the Irish tours vanished almost without trace in the intervening years. It took the best part of a year to locate Paul Russell, from Starlite Artistes, who helped promote the '63 visit and who knew the Beatles well. "Paul Russell eventually left Ireland and went to work as an artiste in Germany," broadcaster Ken Stewart informed me. "I corresponded with him after he left Ireland. We exchanged several letters and I sent him stuff out which was related to music and what was going on around Ireland. I haven't met him in years. He disappeared after that."

As I discovered, Paul Russell headed to America in 1978. Before that, he had not only worked in Germany but had also toured Africa and Italy as a singer and drummer. "When the Beatles thing was over, I had a kind of a down period where I didn't do too much," Russell recalls. "I got kind of burnt-out with the show business thing and I opened a shop. Grace, my wife, opened a shop too. It wasn't a good time. It was getting to the 1970s."

Among Russell's final, and finest, achievements was bringing the Stylistics to play in Dublin. More recently, he has continued in the entertainment business across the Atlantic and today works in PR and consults in theatre in the USA. Yet, all these years later, he has never forgotten the Beatles' visit in 1963. "I have a picture autographed by them on my desk, in their little outfits, the ones with the cufflinks and the mohair suits and the no-collar jackets. It says, 'To Paul, with love.' It's signed by all four of them. I still have it," he says today.

The long-suffering Frank Berry, who laboured at introducing the Beatles night after night back in 1963, has vanished. "He has disappeared," Mal Cook, formerly of Arthur Howes Promotions, remarks. "He went on to play one of the crew of the B-52 in the film *Dr Strangelove*. I think he eventually went into the antiques business." Despite a long search, he couldn't be located.

Sadly, two of the Beatles are missing too. John Lennon was coldly gunned down in New York in December 1980, at the age of 40. George Harrison passed away after a long battle with cancer in November 2001, aged 58. Both, at one stage or another, became highly disillusioned with the touring, mania and sheer claustrophobia of being a Beatle. Perhaps George put it best: "There was more good than evil in being a Beatle but it was awful being on the front page of everyone's life, every day. The Beatles were doomed. Your own space, man, it's so important. That's why we were doomed because we didn't have any."

Eventually, all those 15-year-olds and 16-year-olds who attended the concerts grew up and tackled the challenges of life. Many of those I spoke to are now grannies and granddads and no longer the screamers or jelly baby throwers of 1963 and '64. "It was seven grandchildren ago," concludes Teddy Copeland, who was aged 16 when he went to the first concert in Belfast. "That's how long ago it was. The Beatles came along and seemed to lift everything. It was a simpler time. It was great to live through it. It really was. I wish I was so lucky to be able to do it again."

ACKNOWLEDGEMENTS

There are many people to be thanked for their help with this book, including pop stars Brian Poole, Rolf Harris, Jeff Williams and Roger Greenaway of the Kestrels, Peter Jay of Peter Jay and the Jaywalkers, Jean Owen and Maggie Stredder of the Vernons Girls, Bill Covington of the Rustiks, Geoff Brook of the Brook Brothers, Don Andrew of the Remo Four, Eileen Reid of the Cadets, John Keogh and Brian Lynch of the Greenbeats, Brian Tuite of the Stellas, Brush Shiels, Adam Faith, and Tony Jackson of the Searchers – the latter two who were interviewed by me shortly before their unexpected and tragic deaths.

My special appreciation to former staff of the Adelphi and ABC Ritz cinemas, the Gresham and Grand Central hotels, Aer Rianta, Aer Lingus, Radio Telefís Éireann, the Garda Síochána, NEMS Enterprises (especially Geoffrey Ellis) and Arthur Howes Promotions (notably Mal Cook). Broadcasters Larry Gogan, Jimmy Magee, Ken Stewart, Arthur Murphy, Ronan Collins, Jimmy Greeley, Val Joyce and Bunny Carr were most helpful. My gratitude also to promoters Pat Egan, Derek Nally and Ted Carroll, Bill O'Donovan formerly of RTÉ, photographer Bobby Hanvey, lecturer Joe Erraught, actor Bryan Murray, Larry Behan formerly of the Adelphi, Gerard Lovett of the Garda

Síochána Retired Members Association, Bill Maxwell, Bart Cronin and Brian O'Hagan.

Seán Reynolds was particularly generous with old magazines, books and photos of the era. Also helpful were Judy Hamilton from Belfast, Jim Hempenstall, Tom Fennelly, Brigid Murphy of the Irish Air Line Pilots Association, David Lowe, John Holman, Pete Nash of the British Beatles Fan Club and Pete Brennan of Beatles Ireland. The *Andersonstown News* and the *Hampshire Chronicle* helped locate interviewees, as did Richard Reed of the *Henley Standard* and journalist Eamon Carr. Thanks also to Martin Mulholland of Belfast's Europa Hotel, showband manager TJ Byrne, former Aer Lingus pilot Michael O'Callaghan, Paul Charles of the Asgard Agency in London and Peter Foot of *Encore* magazine.

Linda Monahan of Typeform deserves special praise for her design of the cover. Typeform's Roy Thewlis and Pat Conneely were also a pleasure to work with, as were all at ColourBooks especially David O'Neill. Others providing help include Kasandra O'Connell, Sunniva O'Flynn and Karen Wall of the Irish Film Institute, Irene Stevenson of *The Irish Times* and Máire Harris of Gael Linn. Henry Horsewell assisted with the near-impossible task of locating Geoff Brook. Weeshie Fogarty, Ned Keane, Tom Keith, Mai O'Higgins, Pat Higgins and Fintan Russell were all instrumental in finding Paul Russell after such a long lapse of time. My appreciation also extends to the man himself, Paul Russell, who was informed, perceptive and a pleasure to deal with.

Many publications and newspapers were helpful, among them old editions of *New Musical Express*, *Record Mirror*, *Pop Weekly*, *Teenbeat*, *Mersey Beat*, *RTV Guide*, *Spotlight*, *Irish Press*, *Irish Independent*, *The Irish Times*, *Sunday Press*, *Sunday Independent*, *Evening Press*, *Evening Herald*, *News Letter* and *Belfast Telegraph*. Other invaluable sources include Mark Lewisohn's *The Complete Beatles Chronicle* and *The Beatles*

Live!, Ray Coleman's *Lennon* and *Brian Epstein: The Man Who Made The Beatles*, Hunter Davies' *The Beatles*, Geoffrey Ellis's *I Should Have Known Better*, Michael Braun's *Love Me Do*, Keith Badman's *The Beatles Off The Record*, Billy Shepherd's *The True Story Of The Beatles* and Andy Babiuk's *Beatles Gear*.

Additional books include Brian Epstein's *A Cellarful Of Noise*, Peter Brown and Steven Gaines' *The Love You Make*, Brian Southall's *Northern Songs*, Ian MacDonald's *Revolution In The Head*, Steve Turner's *A Hard Day's Write*, Alan Clayson's comprehensive biographies of all four Beatles, Johnny Rogan's *Starmakers And Svengalis*, Christopher Sands' *The Gresham For Style*, Vincent Power's *Send 'Em Home Sweatin'*, Fergal Tobin's *The Best Of Decades: Ireland In The 1960s*, George Harrison's *I Me Mine* and the official United Artists' souvenir book *The Beatles Starring In 'A Hard Day's Night'*.

Pat Maxwell gave permission to use his excellent photo of the Beatles drinking tea at the Adelphi. Mirrorpix provided shots of the Vernons Girls, Alun Owen and the Beatles backstage at the King's Hall. The RTÉ Stills Library authorised the use of the photo of Paul Russell with the Beatles at the Gresham Hotel, while the National Library of Ireland furnished the image of the Beatles emerging from the ABC Ritz. My thanks also to Gael Linn and the Irish Film Archive of the Irish Film Institute for the still showing the Beatles playing at the Adelphi, to Chris Hill for his photo of the group onstage at the ABC Ritz and to *The Irish Times* for supplying the group-shot of the Fab Four. On a broader note, Úna O'Hagan provided direction and encouragement throughout all the stages of this project, which stretched over 18 months. Her help was invaluable.

Finally, I want to thank my son Seán Keane, who read some of the early chapters and advised me on issues of style and content. As always, Seán was a guiding light who encouraged, inspired and brought joy to everyone's lives. Among Seán's friends, who helped in more ways than they could imagine, were

ACKNOWLEDGEMENTS

Shane Morris, Paddy Rhatigan, Joe Ryan, Eoin Mullany, Gavin Moran, Paddy O'Sullivan, Michael McSweeney, Michael Birdno and Garry Sullivan. Others include Kay and Brendan Healy and their daughters Rachel, Rebecca, Rowena, Ruth and Róisín, not forgetting Rhiannon. Seán's passing away during the writing of the book was a cause of immense sadness but memories of him – just like those of the Beatles' visits in 1963 and '64 – will live on forever.